LEARNING TIME

LEARNING TIME

IN PURSUIT
OF EDUCATIONAL
EQUITY

EDITED BY

**MARISA SAUNDERS
JORGE RUIZ DE VELASCO
JEANNIE OAKES**

HARVARD EDUCATION PRESS
CAMBRIDGE, MASSACHUSETTS

Paperback ISBN 978-1-68253-106-8
Library Edition ISBN 978-1-68253-107-5

Library of Congress Cataloging-in-Publication Data

Names: Saunders, Marisa, editor. | Ruiz-de-Velasco, Jorge, editor. | Oakes, Jeannie, editor.
Title: Learning time : in pursuit of educational equity / edited by Marisa Saunders, Jorge Ruiz de Velasco, Jeannie Oakes.
Description: Cambridge, Massachusetts : Harvard Education Press, [2017] | Includes bibliographical references and index.
Identifiers: LCCN 2017028932| ISBN 9781682531068 (pbk.) | ISBN 9781682531075 (library edition)
Subjects: LCSH: Schedules, School—United States. | School day—United States. | School year—United States. | Academic achievement—United States. | Students with social disabilities—United States. | Educational equalization—United States. | Educational change—United States.
Classification: LCC LB3032 .L42 2017 | DDC 371.2/42—dc23
LC record available at https://lccn.loc.gov/2017028932

Published by Harvard Education Press,
an imprint of the Harvard Education Publishing Group

Harvard Education Press
8 Story Street
Cambridge, MA 02138

Cover Design: Endpaper Studio
Cover Photo: Hero Images/Getty Images

The typefaces used in this book are Adoble Garamond Pro, ITC Legacy Sans, HeronSans, and Tungsten Rounded

CONTENTS

PREFACE

THIS COLLECTED VOLUME of papers and essays looks beyond traditional notions of "schooling" to embrace more and better learning time for youth in neighborhoods of concentrated poverty. As we document in the pages that follow, expanded and well-designed learning time can have real benefits for student achievement and growth, offers teachers more time to collaborate and to personalize instruction, and gives working families a better match between their busy lives and their children's school schedules. This expanded time also provides community organizations, employers, and other youth-serving agencies more opportunities to participate in positive youth development.

This book was inspired by initiatives at the Ford Foundation and the James Irvine Foundation in California, both of which have made substantial investments in a broad array of local, regional, and national efforts to rethink how time is used in schools and communities. The ultimate goal of their efforts was to advance universal college and career readiness and lifelong learning for all youth. At the Ford Foundation, the More and Better Learning Time initiative focused on innovative projects that demonstrate how time can be expanded and reorganized to provide better learning opportunities and improved outcomes in schools serving the nation's most vulnerable young people. More broadly, Ford's strategy included advancing compelling ideas and evidence about the more effective use of expanded time, generating public support for these reforms, and promoting changes in federal, state, and local education policy that might enable these reforms to become normal practice.

In California, the James Irvine Foundation tackled what is arguably the most change-resistant sector of the K–12 education system: the American high school. This foundation has initiated projects aimed at dramatically increasing the proportion of low-income and minority youth who complete high school prepared for college, career, civic participation, and lifelong learning. At the heart of this effort is a major investment in developing and promoting academically challenging career and technical education pathways that reach beyond the school to engage regional employers and community-based partners across a reconceived day and year. Students gain the opportunity to learn outside of the classroom, work alongside professionals, encounter unexpected challenges, and integrate their knowledge and skills from multiple content areas to solve real-world problems.

The impetus for these philanthropic efforts was a growing body of evidence that wealth and social inequalities are pervading every aspect of American life and that, since the mid-1970s, education has come to play an alarmingly diminished role in moderating that basic trend. In December 2015, and again in June 2016, the editors brought together a highly respected group of educators, system leaders, and scholars to address what public education might need in order to become an equity driver in America. Following those meetings, many in our study group agreed to contribute to this edited volume. The contributors aim to interrogate emerging models of expanded learning time and to help build our knowledge base about practices and public policies that can accelerate the sustainable scale-up of equity-centered reforms. The editors hope that these chapters will contribute to what we expect to be a vigorous national debate over the future direction of school reform, including the feasibility and value of expanded learning time.

Before closing, we would like to acknowledge the unremitting efforts and contributions of many who made this book possible. We are especially grateful to Anne Stanton, whose generosity of thought inspired us from beginning to end. We would not have gotten very far without the diligent and passionate work of our impressive chapter authors and colleagues at the Annenberg Institute for School Reform at Brown University and the John W. Gardner Center for Youth and Their Communities at Stanford University. In particular, Vianna Alcantara and Jeremy Nha Nguyen provided consistently excellent day-to-day research assistance and attention to details that make good work better. Meredith Kunz lent her sterling copyediting skills and attention to style and language to this endeavor. Nancy Mancini was always ready to offer professional insights and suggestions that kept us moving along on schedule. We owe a debt of gratitude to our editor at the Harvard Education Press, Doug Clayton, who saw value in this project from the very beginning and encouraged our efforts. And, not least, to our friends and colleagues at the Ford and James Irvine foundations: thank you for the privilege you afforded us to make this contribution to the field.

INTRODUCTION

JORGE RUIZ DE VELASCO, JEANNIE OAKES,
AND MARISA SAUNDERS

WE LIVE TODAY in an ecology of growing inequality, where economic, political, and social disparities increasingly constrain the education and, therefore,
the life chances of children who grow up on the wrong side of the divide. A
recent study by the Organisation for Economic Co-operation and Development (OECD) found that the United States has among the lowest levels of
intergenerational social mobility—and one of the tightest relationships between parental socioeconomic status and students' achievement and subsequent earnings.[1] Indeed, recent research has highlighted the consequences of
growing income inequality in the United States.[2] Researchers confirm that,
more than ever, family wealth is tightly associated with markedly better educational outcomes for children and youth living in wealthy families.[3] These
outcomes hold true along a continuum of measures, including grades and
standardized test scores, rates of participation in extracurricular activities,
graduation rates, and rates of college enrollment and completion.[4]

The chapters collected in this volume make up a sustained exploration
into what public education needs to be a forceful driver of social equity in
America. Specifically, the authors address the proposition that, for schools to
disrupt the strong link between family background and educational success,
we must continue to rethink what counts as "education." And, in doing so,
we must reach beyond the constraining concept of "schooling" to embrace a
youth-sector approach that brings the time and resources of all youth-serving
public agencies, community-based nonprofits, and family-engaged organizations to the task of creating sustained expanded learning opportunities in
communities of concentrated poverty. We recognize that education is one
of many drivers of social equity, but our commitment to universal public

1

education remains the single largest collective investment—in dollars and human capital—to that end.

THE CURRENT STATE OF ECONOMIC AND SOCIAL INEQUALITY IN AMERICA
Economic and Spatial Dimensions

Huge and increasing numbers of American children live in poverty today. Sixteen million children live below the poverty line, and 22 million children live in households where no parent has full-time employment.[5] Additionally, these children and their families are increasingly living in economically segregated communities. From 2000 to 2007, family income segregation grew in almost all metropolitan areas, extending a trend since 1970. Indeed, in 1970, 15 percent of families were in neighborhoods that were classified as either affluent (with median incomes greater than 150 percent of the median income for the metropolitan area) or poor (median incomes less than 67 percent of metropolitan median income). By 2007, this percentage more than doubled—31 percent of families lived in neighborhoods that were either affluent or poor.[6]

Racial Segregation

American families are also increasingly living in racially segregated neighborhoods. Black children are three times more likely to be poor than white or Asian children, and they are six times more likely to live in areas of concentrated poverty (i.e., within census tracts with poverty rates of 30 percent or more). Latino and Native American children are similarly vulnerable. Native American children are six times more likely to live in areas of concentrated poverty, while Latino children are five times more likely.[7] Racial segregation, in combination with a concentration of poverty and growing economic inequality, results in increased isolation of poor minority households.

Concentrated poverty and racial segregation produce and exacerbate a range of problems and privileges within different neighborhoods and populations. The effect of concentration contributes to a clear divide in terms of access to much needed and deeply valued community resources, institutions, and infrastructure, such as decent housing, medical facilities, employment, safe neighborhoods, and well-resourced schools. The average white student attends a school where poor students account for one-quarter to one-third of overall enrollment. The typical black or Hispanic student, in comparison, attends a school where nearly two-thirds of their peers are low income.[8] Not surprisingly, on every tangible measure—from qualified teachers to curriculum offerings—schools serving greater numbers of students of color have significantly fewer resources than schools serving mostly white students. Racial and economic segregation not only shapes opportunities that have an impact on one's life chances, but the impact is transferred across generations. Increased inequality divides us both socially and physically.

Educational Dimension of This Ecology

As we discussed above, the impact of increased isolation leads to disparate access to valued resources and institutions, including educational opportunity. The result is a widening of achievement gaps. The gap, based on standardized test scores, between children from high- and low-income families born in 2001 is roughly 30 percent to 40 percent larger than among those born in 1970s.[9] As well, the college-completion rate among children from more affluent families has grown sharply in the last few decades, while the completion rate for students from less affluent families has remained almost stagnant.[10] And students from more affluent families make up an increasing percentage of the enrollment at the most selective colleges and universities, even when compared with students from less affluent families with similar test scores and academic records.[11] The connection between poverty and academic achievement has never been so plain.

To understand the achievement gap, we must consider a whole range of factors in children's lives beyond the quality of schools that contribute to "unequal growing up." These factors include access to high-quality preschool, enrichment activities, medical care, housing stability, trauma, and more. The growth and concentration of child poverty dramatically increase the need for educational interventions and supplemental services, thereby increasing the cost of improving student outcomes.[12] In areas with concentrated poverty, additional resources are often limited. And in recent years, there has been declining political support for dedicating those resources to building the capacity of school- and youth-serving organizations in high-poverty communities.[13]

Following on these dismal statistics, the national Equity and Excellence Commission has issued a scathing indictment of our schools: "America has become an outlier nation in the way we fund, govern, and administer K–12 schools, and also in terms of performance. No other developed nation has inequities nearly as deep or systemic; no other developed nation has, despite some efforts to the contrary, so thoroughly stacked the odds against so many of its children. Sadly, what feels so very un-American turns out to be distinctly American."[14]

Access to Learning Opportunities Beyond School Hours

Growth in income inequality means that more affluent families now have far more resources (money, *time*, and knowledge), relative to less affluent families, to invest in their children's development and schooling. Research demonstrates that more affluent families are increasingly investing their resources in providing cognitively stimulating experiences from early childcare, preschool, through high school and beyond. Economists report that the amount of money high-income families spend per year on enrichment activities for their children (e.g., weekend and afterschool sports, dance and music lessons, tutors, etc.) has increased at a greater rate than the amount spent by low-income families: a $2,700 difference per year in the early 1970s, compared to a $7,500 difference in 2006. In 1972, Americans at the upper end of the income spectrum were spending five times as much per child as low-income families. By 2007, that gap had grown to nine times as much per child.[15] A more recent study found that the wealthiest top 10 percent of households, after adjusting for inflation, tripled their total spending on expanded learning opportunities for their children, from $3,000 in the early 1970s to $9,000 in 2010.[16] In contrast, spending among households in the bottom 20 percent increased by $152 in inflation-adjusted dollars from the early 1970s to the early 1980s, and has remained at this level since that time.[17]

Similarly, since 1975, the amount of time that college-educated parents spend with their children has grown twice as fast as it has among less-educated parents.[18] Children from high-income families will spend as many as thirteen hundred more hours, between birth and age six, than children from low-income families on enrichment activities such as music lessons, travel, and summer camp.[19] While less affluent families are also increasing the time and money they invest in their children, they cannot keep up. A generation ago, children under age six from working-class backgrounds actually had slightly more time with their parents than children from upper-middle-class families. Today, that trend has reversed and the gap has grown to nearly an extra hour per day spent by higher-income parents with their children compared to lower-income parents. Lower-income families, which are now more likely than ever to be headed by a single parent, are increasingly stretched for time.

The learning time gap continues to grow well beyond the early years of life. Estimates indicate that students from middle- and high-income families will have spent six thousand more hours in learning activities by the time they reach sixth grade—reading with their family, in preschool, weekend day trips, summer camp, and afterschool activities—than students from low-income families.[20]

Indeed, few parents have afternoons and summers free to provide the safe, supportive places that their children need to study, explore, and pursue their passions under the supervision of caring adults. While many middle- and upper-income families create effective "workarounds," buying and negotiating afterschool and summer experiences rich with extra learning opportunities like academic tutoring, music and art lessons, computer classes, organized sports, and more, less advantaged young people are left scrambling. A total of 11.3 million children (including 3 million elementary and middle-school-aged children) are without supervision between 3 p.m. and 6 p.m., the hours in which young people are more likely to be engaged in risky behavior—either as victims or perpetrators. The unmet need for programs that would support their children in the risky hours after school and during the long summer months is greatest among low-income, black, and Hispanic families.[21] Already facing many hurdles to achievement and healthy development, poor children are further disadvantaged as the opportunity gap between them and more advantaged young people grows wider.

POTENTIAL SCHOOL-BASED CONTRIBUTIONS TO MITIGATING THE EFFECTS OF POVERTY AND INEQUALITY

While the compounding effects of segregation, wealth inequalities, and diminished learning opportunities have demonstrably constrained the ability of schools to increase social equity, evidence indicates that time in school can still make a difference. For example, research shows that although the income achievement gap is already large by the time children enter kindergarten, it does not grow substantially during the school years. In fact, data demonstrate that schools may actually narrow academic achievement gaps.[22] Research shows that the gap narrows for kindergarteners and first graders when they are in school, and widens in the summer between kindergarten and first grade, when students are not in school. While the research can't speculate whether the trends hold for students in later grades, the data suggest that schools may reduce inequality. This finding is consistent with smaller studies that examine "summer learning loss."[23]

Research also confirms that equitable access to learning opportunities can be advanced when educators are empowered to redesign how they organize work and time across the day and year. Based on a longitudinal mixed-methods analysis of over two hundred public schools in Chicago, researchers were able to identify a discrete set of school-based practices that promote student learning and improve organizational conditions for learning in high-poverty schools. Specifically, they found that schools that focused on professional and leadership capacity building, aligning student supports to academic learning goals, and on improving social conditions (parent-community partnerships, student-centered learning climate) experienced substantial growth in measures of student learning compared to those schools that did not attend to these organizational elements.[24] Providing educators with the time and space to actively engage in the establishment of learning goals and pedagogical strategies—through collaboration, the sharing of ideas, learning from others, and leading—contributes to these conditions.

Likewise, at the district and state levels, the research of Michael Fullan and others has elaborated on the importance of policy reforms that focus on fostering the professional capital and intrinsic motivation of teachers and students. Policies that build the capacity of teachers and school leaders to engage in continuous cycles of data-driven inquiry can positively reshape teaching and learning. Researchers are accumulating evidence that these types of reforms are the "right drivers" that yield demonstrably better organizational- and student-level outcomes for all students.[25] These processes and practices require redesigning and rethinking the school day and year to support professional capacity building.

These reform advances notwithstanding, the national Equity and Excellence Commission's own review suggested that schools, while an important part of the equity solution, cannot be expected to solve the problem alone.[26] Nor can we expect schools to solve the problem within our current conception or confines of the "traditional" school day. The US public education system's six-hour day and 180-day year fall far short of what most students need. This schedule provides far too little time for young people to meet the escalating educational requirements of work and citizenship. It is also woefully out of sync with the lives of twenty-first-century families. This finding is not new. More than two decades ago, the National Education Commission on Time and Learning concluded that learning in America was "a prisoner of time," where public schools "held time constant and let learning vary."[27] Our prevailing school calendar was designed for a bygone era. As a consequence, the types of important advances in professional capacity building, effective teaching, and integrated student supports that we have previously described remained shackled to a nineteenth-century design. The consequences are felt most acutely in high-poverty neighborhoods, where even highly dedicated teachers and talented school leaders struggle to narrow the opportunity gap between their students and those from more affluent families.

In 2005, the Education Commission of the States revisited the National Education Commission's 1994 report and found that the context surrounding public schools continued to change rapidly. Profound shifts were occurring in student demographics, technology, and the economy. The family was also experiencing rapid change as more women entered the labor market and more children were living in homes where both parents worked, or where the home was headed by a single working parent. Yet within schools, despite the shifting context, little has changed with respect to the way time for learning is conceived and organized. The nineteenth-century structural shackles remain firmly in place and gaps in complex, meaningful, and deeper learning opportunities between children in wealthy and poor neighborhoods continue to grow.[28]

PUBLIC SCHOOLS AND BEYOND: TOWARD EXPANDED AND BETTER CONCEIVED LEARNING TIME

Following on the review of the Equity and Excellence Commission, the education system we need must broaden what counts as learning and move beyond core academics to reach the social, emotional learning, and mind-sets that make for lifelong success. We also need a policy environment that engages the resources of entire communities and families in the task of transformative learning. According to researchers, adolescents are more likely to become fully engaged in their learning when they have the opportunity to immerse themselves in an area of interest, gain mastery in the interest area, and apply their learning in meaningful and authentic ways.[29] Students become engaged and learn at deeper levels, when they are invested in their learning, form personal connections to the school community, and see educators as collaborators and mentors who model the principles of learning. Further, students become engaged in their learning when they identify educators both within and outside the school setting and are given an opportunity to learn in real-world settings where they can take on a variety of roles and responsibilities. Giving youth a chance to learn in these real-world settings allows them to develop essential career and life skills (e.g., leadership, responsibility, critical thinking, collaboration, persistence, problem solving, communication skills, emotional skills, etc.). Importantly, students' acquisition of these skills and knowledge readies them for success in the adult world. This kind of learning can give them a wide range of postsecondary options and mobility. These skills provide the capacities to function effectively in the complex and changing world; they foster important social competencies and promote economic mobility. An education that fosters these relevant skills enables youth to be more effective within all aspects of their lives, including college, career, and community participation.

The chapters in this volume make the case that what we need are concerted, whole-community efforts to make expanded learning time the "new normal" in neighborhoods of concentrated poverty. Schools, local public agencies, nonprofit community partners, researchers, advocates, and policy reformers must work together to create longer, better school days and years—making every minute count to close the opportunity gaps and address the learning needs of young people and the lives of their families.

SHIFTING POLICIES FOR EXPANDED, REDESIGNED LEARNING TIME FOR YOUTH IN POOR NEIGHBORHOODS

Unfortunately, during the last decade, the policy focus on standardized testing often undermined efforts to broaden learning opportunities, particularly for students in low-performing schools. High-stakes accountability testing pushed many schools and teachers to teach to tests and focus on basic skills, even when these practices conflicted with educators' beliefs about the best approaches for student learning. This effect has been particularly intense for teachers in low-performing schools where pressures to raise test scores and avoid sanctions are highest.[30] As schools became more test focused, students had fewer places to turn for this critical skill development and enrichment. These policies widened the opportunity gap even further as they stood in stark contrast to what research from across a range of fields has demonstrated or reconfirmed: that students learn best through active, meaningful socially mediated activity.[31]

By the time the Education Commission of the States revisited the *Prisoner of Time* report in 2005, the policy environment for expanded learning time had begun to shift in important ways. Community-based organizations (CBOs) and nonprofits in different parts of the United States were organizing and taking action to develop new models of community-school collaboration to expand learning opportunities for low-income youth. Leveraging philanthropic support from such groups as the Annie E. Casey Foundation, Charles Stewart Mott Foundation, the Wallace Foundation, the W. K. Kellogg Foundation, and The Atlantic Philanthropies, afterschool advocates were able to persuade Congress to build afterschool funding into the No Child Left Behind law in 2001. Funding for afterschool programs jumped from $40 million to approximately $1 billion in the first year and grew to an average of $1.9 billion in federal grants to the states between 2002 and 2007. In California, this public investment was accelerated with the passage of Proposition 49 in 2002, which provided a dedicated funding stream for afterschool programs independent of the annual education budget. In the high school space, small-schools grants from the Gates Foundation, as well as from regional funders like the James Irvine Foundation, began to support the incubation of new college- and career-ready schools in partnerships with CBOs and local employers. More recently, the Obama administration—with backing from grantees of the Ford Foundation's More and Better Learning Time initiative and others—helped to champion the Full-Service Community Schools program (2009) and Promise Neighborhoods (2010), bringing them into the federal budget and cementing expanded learning time as a centerpiece of national education equity policy. In California, policy makers similarly moved to embrace funding for expanded learning time through the creation of the California Career Pathways Trust (2014), and new support for community schools through the 2016 amendments to the Learning Communities for School Success Program.

A related development in support of expanded learning time strategies is the broad definition of learning in the new Every Student Succeeds Act of 2015 (ESSA), as well as the new law's wide inclusion of schools, families, and out-of-school partners in shared accountability for advancing student learning. This change in federal law represents a clear departure from the approach to school reform that prevailed in the two decades between 1994 and 2015, which focused almost exclusively on student proficiency in English language arts and math.

Beginning in 2010, and in response to the negative consequences of No Child Left Behind (NCLB) reforms on low-income minority-serving schools, forty-five states (and six major California districts) received NCLB waivers to voluntarily develop comprehensive plans designed to improve educational outcomes for all students, increase equity, and aim for universal college, career, and civic readiness. This shift, cemented in the 2015 ESSA reforms, reflected a growing consensus that if young people were to achieve their full potential, they needed to develop a range of skills, competencies, and academic knowledge. Policy makers have begun to recognize that while academic mastery is important, so too are certain social and emotional dispositions and mind-sets associated with learning, such as growth mind-set, intellectual openness, self-management, and empathy.[32] As well, full human development and the more specific demands of college, career, and civic readiness require competency in transferring or adapting what one learns in school to a lifelong series of new social and work-based situations, problems, and creative challenges. This last set of learning objectives requires the cultivation of more complex and deeper learning skills related to critical thinking, problem solving, creativity, and effective communication.

A NEW SCHOOL ACCOUNTABILITY PARADIGM: LOCAL FLEXIBILITY, CONTROL, AND CAPACITY BUILDING

In addition to adopting college and career readiness as the guiding star for student performance, the ESSA signals a shift in federal policy to allow states, school districts, and local educators greater flexibility in how they may use federal program funds to support state and local school improvement efforts. In California, for example, state leaders followed suit and have begun to design a resource-allocation and school accountability strategy that banks on greater local control over how district and school leaders may use fiscal resources to promote innovation and advance equitable student access to more meaningful and deeper learning opportunities. An important outcome of this shift to local control is that federal and state policy makers are no longer bypassing county and district leaders to impose reform demands directly on schools. Now, district offices are being asked to take a central role in planning for change and in devising strategies for school improvement. These new federal and state rules (e.g., the Local Control and Accountability Plan in California) require the engagement of families and local community stakeholders in the design and execution of district-led reforms through new review processes designed to promote shared accountability.

This new decentralization policy comes with additional or more flexible resources to support and scale up the work of expanded time partners who engage with schools across the school day and afterschool hours. ESSA Title I dollars, for example, can now be more flexibly spent to support expanded learning and early-learning strategies that focus on equitable results. And, pending a policy reversal by the Trump administration, new or more flexible assistance is also being made available to school partners through the reauthorization of the 21st Century Community Learning Centers, the Promise Neighborhoods programs, and the Full-Service Community Schools initiative in conjunction with ESSA.

IMPLICATIONS FOR EXPANDED LEARNING TIME, INTEGRATED STUDENT SUPPORTS, AND EQUITY

The policy focus on universal college, career, and civic readiness and the broad learning objectives that it implies is a game changer. Most obviously, the understanding that college, career, and civic readiness require a range of skills beyond academic mastery has been a long-standing cornerstone of the movement to expand learning opportunities though the combined efforts of school and community partnerships during and beyond the typical school day. In this sense, the policy community has finally caught up. Likewise, the move in many districts across the country (e.g., the California CORE districts) to expand formal accountability systems beyond academic mastery promises to bring schools and their community-based partners under a single accountability umbrella. By including measures such as social and emotional learning and school culture and climate, schools and partners focus on shared learning objectives. This has positive implications for joint efforts at professional and program development that bring teachers and community partners into common learning spaces. State and federal efforts to provide more dollars and flexible spending rules for schools in low-income communities mean new opportunities for expanded and differentiated programming to meet the needs of diverse communities and to advance equitable access to deeper learning opportunities. As the new Trump administration takes the reins in Washington, the outlook is for a continued trend toward local control, albeit with a new emphasis on resources for local innovation through charter schools and market-based mechanisms.

In sum, expanded learning time strategies are now in the mainstream of the new accountability discussion. This represents great opportunity and responsibility for all who care about the education of our youth and the perfection of our democracy through education. And finally, local control (or flexibility) means that districts and schools will need to build system-learning capacity. They will need to pivot away from a reflexive focus on data use for state and federal rule compliance, and move toward data use that is linked to local strategies and that supports their continuous learning about how best to expand opportunity for low-income and minority youth. This new focus offers the opportunity for districts, school leaders, and their community partners to take local context and needs into account as they fashion policy solutions, especially in the area of student supports that require attention to local demographics, economic conditions, and opportunities.

CREATING AN ECOLOGY OF EXPANDED LEARNING OPPORTUNITY

Grounded in new and existing research, this book features practical models, political strategies, and cultural shifts that contribute to reorganizing work and time in public schools. A central focus is the conditions that enable high-poverty schools to provide learning experiences comparable to those of more advantaged students whose life experiences and schools make high achievement likely.

We have organized the chapters into three sections. The chapters in the first section provide examples of what is possible when school and system leaders look beyond the traditional school day and year to meet the needs of all students. Those in the second section explore why approaches that expand and reorganize time have the potential to support the learning that all students deserve—learning that is meaningful, complex, deep, and engaging. The authors investigate how the strategies introduced in the first section of the book more accurately conceptualize students' learning, and how these approaches can achieve more equitable outcomes by bringing together K–12 schools, community organizations, and a range of partners. The chapters in the final section delve more deeply into the technical, cultural, and political obstacles facing expanding learning time approaches. Together, the chapters in this volume provide evidence that giving students more and better learning time can support increased learning for a diverse student population and can respond to our pressing societal need to address growing inequalities. The question is, are we willing to move beyond the traditional day or year to provide students with the opportunities they need to become fully engaged in their learning, tap into their interests, and ensure their preparation for college, career, and civic life?

A CALL TO ACTION

The impact of "unequal growing up" has serious consequences for young people, their families, communities, and our nation by exacerbating social inequalities. In a society that promises poor children little more than a public school education, we must turn to the school infrastructure, alongside community services, to provide opportunities to improve their lives and life chances. We are not naive about the ability of schools to buffer children from the harms of poverty, isolation, and discrimination, but providing more and better learning time is a place to begin.

The chapters in this book provide examples of more and better learning time in practice; they offer theoretical and empirical explanations for why and how these ways of using time "work." Together, they supply a set of evidence-based principles to guide policy makers, educators, and community leaders as they develop and sustain innovations that exploit time as a key resource for equitable and effective schools. With this knowledge and the new flexibility in ESSA, it's time to move forward, bringing these principles to scale by creating local instantiations of more and better schooling that give the nation's least advantaged children opportunities to learn and thrive.

Yet moving this work forward will require courage and persistence. As propitious as this moment is, in terms of readiness and momentum, it could be lost. Some see the pendulum swing of the Trump administration as a death knell for comprehensive, public efforts to disrupt poverty and advance equity. As this book goes to press, we've had a good first look, in the form of the president's first budget proposals, at the values and principles that will drive the administration's agenda for education policy and social policy more generally. Those budget proposals are not encouraging. In addition to calling for deep cuts to the US Department of Education, the proposals turn dramatically away from a willingness to battle inequality with federal authority and dollars. It makes clear the Trump preference for private- over public-sector solutions; individual, rather than collective responsibility; and the elimination of school-related services for poor children (such as meals and afterschool programs) that can't be tied to the efficient production of specific outcomes. On the chopping block, for example, is $1.2 billion for the 21st Century Community Learning Centers program, which has been at the heart of providing expanded learning time opportunities. These specifics of the initial budget proposals may not survive, but the less-than-generous spirit behind them surely will.

Policy makers, educators, and equity-minded community leaders cannot yield to this view. So in addition to sharing the knowledge we and the chapter authors have gained over the past decade of good and hard work, we must also share our commitment to continue. We intend to work locally and through state policy to secure the gains that have been made and to press ahead, knowing that the American people believe in the promise of an outstanding education as a pathway to better lives and a better country. We call on readers of this book to join us and persist.

BROADENING OUR VISION OF LEARNING TIME

In this first section of the book, our authors focus on emerging models of expanded learning. Each model is designed to address social and economic inequalities by increasing access to high-quality learning opportunities in neighborhoods of concentrated poverty, so that students are prepared equitably for college, career, and civic participation. The authors are researchers or field leaders who have guided local, state, and national efforts to implement the idea of expanded and reconceived learning time as an equity strategy.

In chapter 1, Jennifer Davis and David Farbman document efforts by the National Center on Time & Learning to spark a movement to extend the traditional school day and year. By moving beyond the traditional six-hour school day and 180-day school year, the approach they outline attempts to provide all students with time to engage deeply in their learning, make connections across the curriculum, identify a clear purpose in learning activities, develop meaningful relationships with adults, and experience other cognitively stimulating activities in and out of school. This approach transcends the simple addition of time to the school day by focusing on *how* students spend time in schools. While there is no one way to provide students with more and better learning opportunities, the authors shed light on the efficacy and promise of innovative structures, including built-in collaborative planning time for teachers and strategic, fully integrated partnerships with other public agencies and community organizations.

In chapter 2, Jessica Gunderson, Jennifer Peck, and Katie Brackenridge give us an insiders' perspective on the development and professionalization of California's large afterschool sector. Making the school day and year longer is only one of many ways to provide high-quality expanded learning opportunities in safe spaces with support from caring and knowledgeable adults. Creating a well-coordinated system of afterschool and summer programs is another. The authors explain how afterschool and summer programs share learning goals with other efforts to expand the school day and year. They also emphasize the unique contributions of community-based partners whose staff is often more linguistically and culturally diverse in ways that are consonant with the demographics of school communities. They demonstrate how the full range of academic, social, and emotional learning goals can be shared and reinforced across school and out-of-school settings. The key concepts in this chapter focus on how to achieve coherence and integration through *partnership* and *collaboration* across the school and nonprofit youth-serving sectors.

In chapter 3, Kendra Fehrer and Jacob Leos-Urbel bring their researchers' lens to the study of the community school movement as it finds expression in Oakland, California. Oakland's ambition is to become a community school district, where each of its schools is adapting a community schools approach to the needs and unique cultural resources of diverse neighborhoods. Oakland's community schools build on the insights of the first two chapters but challenge traditional notions of schooling by exploring how authentic family engagement strategies build trust and advance student-school connectedness. The authors examine how school partnerships with behavioral and physical health agencies address student barriers to learning. These collaborations can also build instructional capacity in schools and classrooms. Fehrer and Leos-Urbel are part of a long-term research-practice partnership between Stanford University's John W. Gardner Center for Youth and Their Communities and the Oakland Unified School District. Their work aims to demonstrate the value of university-community partnerships. They focus on data-informed research for organizational learning and addressing persistent problems of practice in education.

In chapter 4, Michael McAfee and Jessica Pizarek shift the focus from individual schools or programs to the organizational processes, arrangements, and norms that would support a youth-sector approach to expanded learning opportunities in high-poverty communities. The Promise Neighborhood approach takes the school as an anchor, but posits that fully addressing the challenges of poverty, segregation, and time requires the coherent and results-focused collaboration of all youth-serving organizations in a geographic zone.

These partnerships include schools, families, community-based nonprofits, and health agencies. They also extend to preschool providers, parks and recreation, law enforcement and probation departments, grassroots advocacy organizations, and every other agency that seeks to support positive youth development from cradle to career.

In chapter 5, Gary Hoachlander, Tameka McGlawn, and Brad Stam take on what is arguably the most change-resistant institution in the public education sector: the American high school. In their chapter, they discuss the Linked Learning approach to expanded learning time. At the heart of their argument is growing evidence that the best path to ensuring that all students have equitable access to a college- and career-ready education is to link every technical, vocational, or career-focused pathway in the high school to a rigorous college preparatory academic curriculum. In addition, every student needs to be linked to workplace learning and to comprehensive supports that span the school and community and align to academic and technical learning goals. Linked Learning is growing quickly across California; estimates indicate that Linked Learning strategies will soon be available to approximately one-third of the state's high school students.[1] Linked Learning is also gaining momentum in Houston and Detroit. Linked Learning schools and systems use varied strategies to provide students with expanded learning and development opportunities. These approaches allow students to see a clear purpose in learning activities and play an active role in constructing and making connections. They also give teachers time to learn from other educators and offer opportunities to engage families and integrate community partnerships.

Ultimately, the models reviewed here share common policy elements. Each model:

- includes all students at the school in expanded learning opportunities
- prioritizes students in neighborhoods of concentrated poverty or students vulnerable to academic failure, including English language learners
- insists on a culture of high expectations
- engages strong partners (both internal and external, including teachers, parents, and community-based organizations)
- provides dedicated time for teachers and community-based partners to collaborate, engage in data-driven inquiry, and improve instructional effectiveness

- shares student outcome goals and mutual accountability across internal and external partners
- supports the development of principals, leadership teams, teachers, and school partners
- uses data to individualize support, track progress, and assess effectiveness of interventions

The authors in this first section offer compelling evidence that expanded and redesigned learning time based on these elements has real benefits for student achievement and growth. Teachers would have more time to collaborate and to personalize instruction, working families would have a better match between their busy lives and their children's school lives, and community organizations would have more opportunities to participate in youth development. A common theme is that time is a critical learning resource. Educators are not just adding more hours to the day. They are using time to drive whole-school reform, turning troubled schools and neighborhoods around, and inventing a more effective delivery model for teaching and learning. These positive effects can reach the most vulnerable students, such as English language learners, when the extra learning time provides students with personal attention and opportunities to explore new interests and develop new skills, as well as more effective academic support.

School, district, and system leaders may well ask how they can afford expanded time and learning activities in the current budget climate and within the constraints of large bureaucratic systems. The authors in this section demonstrate the possibilities by illustrating how regular school leaders are elaborating scalable and sustainable proof-of-concept efforts in some of the most challenged urban school districts. Indeed, some schools show how to make these changes without spending more money or withdrawing from public school districts. Moreover, because reforms are shaped by local context, these place-based models illuminate how to achieve sustainable change in a variety of contexts with the engagement and support of parents, educators, and business and civic leaders.

CHAPTER 1

SPARKING AN EDUCATION MOVEMENT

Expanding Learning Time to Raise Achievement,
Empower Teachers, and Enrich Education

JENNIFER DAVIS AND DAVID FARBMAN

OVER THE LAST ONE HUNDRED YEARS, the American education system has struggled to shift from one designed to educate the elite few to one that offers every child a high-quality education. This struggle springs largely from the instinct to overlook or downplay the reality that the needs of students are incredibly diverse, and that the old factory model of education will not adequately prepare all students for the world of the future. Consider one of the most entrenched and uniform features of our public education system: the time provided for teaching and learning. Still operating on the century-old calendar of 180 6.5-hour days, the vast majority of schools are trapped in a structure that is inflexible and often unable to adequately meet the needs of today's learners.

The first public acknowledgment that the traditional calendar stood as a major impediment to achieving our lofty educational ambitions came in 1983 with the release of the National Commission on Excellence in Education's report, *A Nation at Risk*. Commissioners did not hold back their criticism, describing American public schooling as suffering "the rising tide of mediocrity." Aside from urging the revamping of the teaching profession and the establishment of more rigorous and measurable academic standards, the commission recommended expanding school time. In its plain words, "School districts and State legislatures should strongly consider 7-hour school days, as well as a 200- to 220-day school year."[1]

A decade later, Congress convened the National Education Commission on Time and Learning with a mandate to conduct "a comprehensive review of the relationship between time and learning in the nation's schools." That commission's report, entitled *Prisoners of Time*, drew the unambiguous conclusion that the United States would never achieve universal high-quality education with the current school calendar in place.[2] More learning time was, in short, an essential component of an education system built on high standards.

Thus, by the turn of the twenty-first century, the pressing need for more learning time in our nation's schools had been acknowledged without reservation at the highest reaches of the American educational establishment. Yet, as persuasive as the rhetoric may have been, one hundred years of established practice would not be undone simply by recognizing its flaws. The challenge that lay ahead was how to furnish the policy incentives and resources to help educators and families break out of routines and expectations that were firmly rooted in a school day of 6.5 hours and a calendar year of 180 days. Expanding the schedule for all students would constitute nothing less than a revolution that would need to play out over and over again at each individual school.

To illustrate the scope and contours of the challenge, this chapter will review the history of one of the leading organizations to develop the state and federal policies that enabled new resources to support district schools in breaking free from the conventional schedule. This same organization also became the foremost provider of technical assistance to district schools undertaking this transformation, guiding local educators to put in place the structures and the practices that would allow them to optimize not only the additional time, but the whole school day. Formed in Boston in 2000, Massachusetts 2020 (later, the National Center on Time and Learning) drove an effort to find both practical and far-reaching ways to provide urban students more time in quality education. Through its experience, we can better grasp how expanding school time in America is a national question that continues to require relentless efforts at the federal and state policy levels, and most importantly, at the local district level.

MASSACHUSETTS 2020: THE EARLY YEARS

Massachusetts 2020 was animated by a simple, if stunning, fact: in modern America, students spend only 20 percent of their waking hours in school. Learning time—which research from several studies has shown to be one of the strongest predictors of academic success—seems in all too short supply. This fact was particularly troubling given evidence that learning time can begin to close the achievement and opportunity gaps between affluent students who benefit from expanded learning experiences afterschool and during the summer months (e.g., summer camps, tutoring, enrichment classes) and their less affluent peers, who too often do not have access to these supplemental learning opportunities.

Research suggesting the influence of time on learning includes a review of a large data set from students in California and a smaller study of Wisconsin students.[3] Indeed, it is this research, combined with the strong evidence that the academic achievement gap grows over the summer, that has led one group of scholars to conclude that school is actually an equalizing force and, in turn, that economically disadvantaged children spend relatively too little time there to narrow the gap.[4] The many social ills that conspire to work against success in school—from physical health to family instability to inadequate housing, all of which are more likely to be found in the lives of poor children—detract from students' learning time. Our national ambitions to adequately prepare *all* students to thrive in an increasingly complex society ignore the reality that universal proficiency cannot rest on a system that treats all students alike and fails to recognize vast inequities in our society that tend to lead to enormous disparities in the ability to achieve in school.

To address this shortfall, Massachusetts 2020 (which quickly became known as "Mass 2020") seeded several major initiatives in Boston and throughout the state to expand and strengthen afterschool programs. Through these programs, Mass 2020 hoped to supplement and support the education provided through public schools. The leaders of Mass 2020 leveraged their relationships with local philanthropic and political communities to coordinate significant new investments in the afterschool sector. In doing so, they began to popularize the idea that these programs were not simply safe places to "house" children and teens during their nonschool hours, but rather were key to ensuring that students receive the well-rounded educational experiences they needed and deserved.

As successful as these ventures were—serving thousands more students in Boston and throughout the state over five years and raising the quality of programming and, importantly, drawing public attention to the issue of afterschool learning—the leadership of Mass 2020 understood the limitations of trying to add a second layer of educational programming on top of the primary one. Voluntary afterschool programs clearly lacked the mechanisms to ensure consistently high quality and steady enrollment. Put another way, too many children who needed access to afterschool programs that could effectively supplement school-based learning did not have it. The solution actually lay in expanding school time itself. So, beginning in 2004, Mass 2020 made a definitive shift to focus almost exclusively on reforming public schools to redesign themselves around a longer, stronger day.

Mass 2020's first foray into this policy area came with an amicus cur-iae brief filed in support of the plaintiffs in a Massachusetts school financing case, *Hancock v. Driscoll.* The *Hancock* plaintiffs had sued the state, arguing that schools serving proportionally more poor students were unable to offset the ill effects of poverty on learning without a significant boost in dollars to enhance these schools' capacity to educate children at risk of falling behind academically. The plaintiffs averred that public school funding should not be based on a principle of equal treatment of students who entered school on an unequal footing, but rather on the broader concept of equity.

The Mass 2020 brief extended the plaintiffs' argument by making the compelling case that the inequity of resources in the educational system was not simply a matter of money. Time, too, was a resource required in greater quantities in schools populated with more poor students. Indeed, the money paying for schooling was essentially spending for learning time. In the words of the brief, "To meet its constitutional obligation to provide all children with the level of education to which they are entitled, the state must ensure adequate learning time for all students, especially those at risk of failing, by expanding the time public school children spend in productive learning environments."[5]

Among Mass 2020 leaders and staff, the urge to generate change did not mean simply making a strong case, however; they also harbored the strong desire to act. Mass 2020 aspired to implement concrete initiatives that would both help bring more learning time to real students and schools in need and, equally important, prove that changing traditional school systems was indeed possible. Mass 2020 leaders began to espouse a vision and a plan for trans-forming the seemingly fixed, standard school schedule—a structure that, they believed, held back our public schools from achieving to our expecta-tions—into a vestige of the past. The new norm should instead be a school schedule that meets the true learning needs of contemporary students, espe-cially those from disadvantaged backgrounds. Thus, Mass 2020 set off on a new course to expand school time in as many schools as possible.

THE EXPANDED LEARNING TIME INITIATIVE

Mass 2020 first ventured into the field of education reform in its home state by spearheading an effort to pilot expanded time in district schools. The model was straightforward, albeit replete with political and even cultural challenges: provide state funding to support the additional costs of operating a school with substantially more hours. Mass 2020 then began efforts to work with the governor and state legislature to put such a program into place.

To help navigate through the policy and political complexities of public education, Mass 2020 first formed an advisory board comprising political, legislative, philanthropic, and union leaders. Parlaying the backing of this advisory board, Mass 2020 persuaded legislative leaders to support a relatively trivial budget line item ($500,000) for planning grants to schools to develop whole-school plans for adding 30 percent more time to the school year. The grant authorized districts and schools to determine how they would allocate the three hundred hours (e.g., longer days, longer years, or some combination), and how they would use that time within the expanded schedule. The only broad requirement was that the additional planned time had to be dedicated to three distinct areas: (1) student academic support; (2) enrichment programming; and (3) more opportunities for teacher collaboration and development embedded within the school day. By funding only a planning process—not the far more costly implementation—the legislature sanctioned a way to test whether there was demand and will among public school educators, students, and their parents for schedule expansion. The planning process involved outreach and involvement of parents and youth, including forums, surveys, and parents serving on the planning committees. Soon, it became clear that several school communities were eager to seize the opportunities that more and better learning time in school promised.

After a year of planning, seventeen schools applied for implementation support. With demand thus demonstrated, Mass 2020 was able to persuade the legislature to fund the implementation of a majority of the plans. Designating the funding level at $1,300 per child, the legislature allocated a total of $6.5 million to program implementation, meaning that up to five thousand students in district schools would be provided three hundred more hours of learning the following year. Thus began the Expanded Learning Time (ELT) initiative with a cohort of ten schools, a group that became the first in the country to participate in a statewide effort to expand learning time in district schools. In subsequent years, the legislature allocated more funding to the program, eventually doubling funding to $13 million and participation to twenty-two schools.

ELT planning and implementation were complex, considering that breaking from the conventional school schedule demanded significant changes to teacher contracts, budgets, and transportation logistics. Further, the resistance among some families, students, and teachers to such a dramatic disruption in the patterns of daily life was real. Recognizing the depth of these challenges, Mass 2020 worked very closely with the pilot schools and districts to help navigate these uncharted waters. Mass 2020 not only tried to help educators surmount inevitable roadblocks, but also to assist school leaders and teachers to advance a positive vision of a redesigned school. Such efforts included holding many community meetings to discuss plans for redesigned school days.[6] Over time, those on the front lines of education reform—together with parents and students—came to see the additional three hundred hours as a tremendous opportunity to better meet the academic and enrichment needs of students and teachers.

Mass 2020 became the de facto provider of technical assistance support to the implementing schools, as well as the chief policy and political advocate for the initiative's continuation and growth, while the state's Department of Education selected the schools that would participate, provided oversight, and administered the state funding.[7] Throughout the rollout and continued implementation of the ELT initiative, Mass 2020 and the Massachusetts Department of Education maintained a deep collaboration. They formed a unique public-private partnership that grew out of mutual recognition that, for this innovative education reform to succeed, both agencies had to work side by side and, at the same time, play their unique, independent roles.

Surely, this intensive technical assistance and the dynamic initiative oversight helped to bring about the successes of some schools in the ELT initiative. Still, the overall impact on student outcomes was less than anticipated in the early years. A five-year external evaluation found that, on average across all eighteen schools included in the evaluation, students registered few significant gains in academic achievement. Despite this finding, which might be characterized as disappointing, the evaluation also showed impact in areas that were harder to measure, per se, but that were no less meaningful. For example, the evaluation confirmed that students in ELT schools benefited from substantial new enrichment programming and that teachers in ELT schools reported real enhancements in their students' academic experience.[8]

The conclusion that academic gains—narrowly measured by test scores—seemed to be slower to take hold than expected prompted Massachusetts 2020 to investigate even more deeply the question of what organizational and instructional elements might lead to higher achievement on standards-based assessments. After reviewing practices of the higher-performing schools and comparing them to the lower-performing schools, it became clear that school leaders' ability to use data to help focus the whole school on a small number of instructional priorities was essential. Fortified by this finding, Mass 2020 reintensified its technical assistance approach by pressing each school to first identify an "instructional focus" based on student needs and then organizing internal systems in ways that would build instructional coherence by aligning all activity around this shared focus.

Mass 2020's continued advocacy for and intensive work with schools in the ELT initiative have helped ensure its continuation and some real success stories. Eleven years after the first cohort expanded its schedules, the ELT initiative is still going strong, with twenty-two schools now participating and ongoing funding by the state at roughly $14 million each year.

Closing Opportunity Gaps

From the outset of its effort to reshape the American school calendar, Mass 2020 was committed to increasing learning time not only so that less afflu-ent children could be better able to catch up academically to their more af-fluent peers, but also so that they could have greater access to the kinds of enrichment that fills the lives of middle- and upper-middle-class young peo-ple. Indeed, the "opportunity gap" between children of lower and upper so-cioeconomic backgrounds is well documented. As just one marker of this gap, consider that since the 1970s, the difference in spending on out-of-school pro-gramming between the lowest and highest quartiles has more than tripled.[9] Of course, improving access to quality afterschool programs is a worthy strat-egy in helping to address this inequity, but as research in the early days of Mass 2020 revealed, very often the students most needing this programming outside of school were not accessing it. As such, in its work with schools that were expanding schedules, Mass 2020 consistently and aggressively asserted that some of the additional time needed to be devoted to furnishing robust enrichment opportunities to *all* children in the school.

The ELT schools in Massachusetts represented the first coordinated ef-fort to integrate enrichment programming into the core of the school day. Indeed, as noted, allotting time for noncore academic courses and/or activ-ities was required of grant recipients. The result of these efforts meant that elementary students in the ELT schools were, on average, participating in enrichment for 20 minutes per day (or 1.7 hours per week) and middle-school students for 30 minutes per day (2.5 hours per week), an amount more than quintuple what students in non-ELT comparison schools received.[10] The outcome was not just quantitative, but qualitative. In this cohort, students could partake of classes in karate, drama, robotics, or dance, to name just a few. In many cases, these enrichment opportunities were facilitated through deep partnerships with community-based organizations and other institutions and businesses that supplied experts to serve as instructors. Partners in the Massachusetts schools ranged from the YMCA, Tenacity, and CitySprouts to Massachusetts General Hospital, Genzyme, and the Boston Ballet.[11] The longer day, in essence, served as an ideal platform on which schools and external providers could collaborate toward the mutual objective of better serving students. As Mass 2020 eventually expanded its work beyond Massachusetts, it maintained the same commitment to providing a "well-rounded education."

GOING NATIONAL: LAUNCHING THE NATIONAL CENTER ON TIME & LEARNING

From the outset of the ELT pilot project, Mass 2020's leaders considered the pilot program as a model that could be replicated in other states. True enough, Massachusetts may have had a somewhat more advanced policy environment and funding structure in place to support public schools than many other states, but Mass 2020 leaders harbored little doubt that if district schools could leverage public dollars effectively to expand school time in Massachusetts, such a process could take root in other states as well. All that was needed were sufficient resources and ample will.

Mass 2020's leadership also knew that there were already plenty of examples of public schools across the country that had successfully broken from the conventional calendar. Most of these came in the form of charter schools. Charters stood independent from the conventional policies and structures of most public schools and, thus, constituted the first large-scale challenge to the uniformity of the public school calendar. Indeed, charter school networks, like KIPP and Achievement First, were organizing a robust education program including a substantially longer school day and year—up to 50 percent more annual learning time. But charters were not the only instances where educators did not simply accept the standard school schedule as immovable. Schools such as Achievable Dream Academy in Newport News,

Virginia, or the Plus One elementary schools in Volusia County, Florida, had also added significant hours to their academic years.

Ambitions to spread the ELT initiative beyond the borders of Massachusetts took a leap forward when, in 2007, Senator Edward Kennedy and his education team visited the Edwards Middle School in Charlestown, Massachusetts, to highlight the urban school success story. Senator Kennedy found the Edwards story—and the ELT policy initiative that brought it about—compelling, and he and his team encouraged Mass 2020 leaders to launch a national agenda. With support from philanthropies with a national scope, Mass 2020's leaders created the National Center on Time & Learning (NCTL) to take on this enlarged mission.

Launched at an event in Washington, DC, NCTL began auspiciously. Kennedy announced the introduction of the Time for Innovation Matters in Education Act (TIME Act), legislation that supported the replication of the Massachusetts ELT initiative in up to five additional states. Though not passed in successive congressional sessions, the TIME Act set a benchmark for future policies that emerged to incentivize schools to expand learning time.

The true breakthrough in creating more schools with substantially more time came when Barack Obama became president in 2009. As is often the case in driving education reform from the federal level, the central entry point for the Obama administration's support for expanded-time schools was through additional money. In this case, the American Recovery and Reinvestment Act (ARRA), also known as "the stimulus," poured a groundbreaking onetime amount of $100 billion into education through both traditional entitlement programs as well as through new and newly revamped programs aimed at turning around the lowest-performing schools and helping states "race to the top." Most important for the cause of expanding school time was the makeover of the School Improvement Grants (SIG) program, which allocated $4 billion to states that would, in turn, fund schools to implement one of four turnaround models.[12] Two of the models—Transformation and Turnaround—required "increased learning time" as one component of the improvement plan.

These ARRA policies were momentous for the expanded-time movement, for they represented the first time that ELT became enshrined in federal law. No doubt, NCTL's own advocacy, together with several former aides to Senator Kennedy who then went on to hold leadership posts in the Obama administration, were key voices in turning this bold idea into reality.

In addition to the SIG funds, efforts to expand school time were enabled through other federal programs as well. Another large-scale Obama administration initiative to spark substantive education reform, for example, was the Investing in Innovation Fund (i3), which gave schools, districts, and other education organizations three-year grants to replicate practices or programs that had proved effective. Several of these i3 grants went to proposals that included an expanded school schedule as a core element (e.g., the KIPP network of charter schools). NCTL, in partnership with Boston Public Schools, was successful in securing an i3 grant to replicate the early successes of the Edwards Middle School in two additional Boston middle schools.

Meanwhile, Obama's Department of Education instituted in 2012 a waiver process to help states bypass the perceived deficiencies of the No Child Left Behind Act, a process necessitated by Congress's failure to reauthorize the Elementary and Secondary Education Act. One new option the waiver enabled was for states to request the authority to direct dollars from the 21st Century Community Learning Center program—a $1.2 billion fund that had previously been limited strictly to supporting voluntary out-of-school-time programs—to supporting high-quality expanded learning time for all students in a school. Twenty-one states opted for this flexibility. This option, in particular, created tensions with the afterschool community concerned that funding for afterschool programs would be diverted to schools. Only a handful of states actually took advantage of the waiver option in those early years. By 2011, several leaders in the afterschool sector, including The Afterschool Corporation (now ExpandED Schools) and Citizen Schools, had come to embrace the expanded learning approach, seeing the benefits of the deep integration of community partners and schools through new school designs with expanded time.

GROUNDBREAKING PARTNERSHIP
WITH THE FORD FOUNDATION

With these solid policy victories opening new opportunities for district schools all over the country to break from the conventional schedule, NCTL sought to develop a support infrastructure that might provide the technical assistance these schools would need to make such a conversion successful. Years of helping schools in Massachusetts to overcome the significant hurdles inherent to the conversion process—for example, logistical, educational, and fiscal issues—convinced NCTL that schools were unlikely to manage through the challenges without considerable third-party guidance. Consequently, NCTL sought to find a philanthropic partner that could help to underwrite the development of this technical assistance infrastructure and, moreover, would prioritize the mission to expand learning time in low-performing schools.

In their early meetings in 2010 with the new president of the Ford Foundation, NCTL leaders found their partner. Their first project together would be the creation of a grassroots advocacy campaign to raise the national visibility of the need for children to have more time to succeed in school. This campaign, named the Time to Succeed Coalition, included over two hundred high-profile leaders, including union presidents, district superintendents, and over two hundred leading education thinkers. Eventually, this campaign gathered over twenty-five thousand signatories who all agreed that children need "more and better learning time."

The partnership deepened when in 2011 the foundation launched the More and Better Learning Time initiative. One of the early Ford investments was in the TIME Collaborative, NCTL's five-state effort to leverage federal funding to support the conversion of conventional district schools to expanded schedules. The TIME Collaborative would achieve its objectives by building the state and district capacity necessary to facilitate successful implementation of the redesigned school days in Colorado, Connecticut, Massachusetts, New York, and Tennessee. As in the original ELT initiative in Massachusetts, the TIME Collaborative focused on adding time to achieve three goals: increasing academic support, broadening enrichment opportunities, and expanding teacher collaboration and development opportunities. NCTL's focus was ultimately on the quality of the added time, not just the quantity. Over the next four years, the TIME Collaborative grew to include forty schools in nineteen districts that together served over twenty thousand students. (See the box "Guilmette Elementary School" for a description of a TIME Collaborative school in Lawrence, Massachusetts.)

To support the schools undergoing conversion, NCTL developed a three-year detailed technical assistance process—intensive planning in year one, implementation of school-identified priorities in year two, and a focus on teacher collaboration and development and student interventions in year three. The technical assistance was structured such that school practitioners could track their own progress toward the expectations that had been outlined in their planning process and then receive direct coaching in those areas where implementation fell short of expectations.

Guilmette Elementary School

When the Lawrence Public Schools became the first district in Massachusetts taken over by state authorities to address its chronic low performance, many worried that little would actually change. But when the new superintendent (or "receiver") Jeff Riley took the helm in 2012 and outlined his plan for the district, the scope and depth of the reforms became apparent. In addition to cutting the staff of the central office by 25 percent and redirecting resources and decision-making powers to individual schools, Riley was also firmly committed to providing substantially more time for teaching and learning. All K–8 schools instantly increased their annual hours by two hundred, and four joined NCTL's TIME Collaborative in order to add three hundred more hours a year. Guilmette Elementary School, headed by dynamic principal Lori Butterfield, was one of those four, and Butterfield and faculty together undertook a dramatic remaking of its school.

So what does a redesigned day look like at Guilmette? Running from 7:30 a.m. to 3:35 p.m., the schedule now includes several key elements that together help ensure that students have the supports they need to achieve to high standards. Perhaps the most vital of these is the daily "Learning Lab," where struggling students receive targeted interventions from instructional coaches and special education teachers. To make sure that each student is in the appropriate group—and there are several small groups within the Learning Lab, depending on students' specific learning needs—teachers review student data weekly, regrouping and adding supports where they are most needed. During this same period, students who are learning at grade level take part in accelerated studies, like debate teams or math club. More than just having a personalized learning system in place, this dedicated time for intervention support preserves a well-rounded curriculum, including science and social studies, for all children. In the past, students who had struggled in reading and math were taken out of science and social studies to receive additional help, a compromise Guilmette educators had been forced to make for lack of sufficient time.

A second core component of the longer day focuses on what is commonly known as the enrichment programming that makes up a "well-rounded education." In addition to daily experiential learning classes, like arts or music, Guilmette now offers all third and fourth graders an array of enrichment activities held at the local Boys & Girls Club on Friday afternoons. For two and a half hours, students choose from activities like karate, swimming, arts, dance, and environmental exploration. (Students in first and second grades remain in the school while community organizations come in to run those classes.) And while students are engaging with high-quality community partners, teachers meet for a concentrated block of professional development, including collaborating in grade- or content-level teams to review student data, plan lessons, and learn from each other about effective teaching practices.

After four years with a redesigned day, the Guilmette Elementary School continues to see impressive gains. From 2012 to 2015 (the last year for which data are available), the percent of students achieving proficiency on state assessments grew by over 15 points in English language arts and 25 points in math. And these gains are in a school where more than 90 percent of students receive a free or reduced price lunch and nearly 40 percent are non-native English speakers. The staff and leadership at Guilmette are not satisfied, however, and each year continue to make adjustments to better meet student needs and help all students succeed. The school stands as yet another example of how the infusion of more time—and optimizing use of time across the entire school day—can breathe new life into learning.

The creation and use of NCTL's continuous improvement (CI) system (formerly known as a progress monitoring system) emerged over time as the most powerful accelerator to catalyze focused improvement efforts at the TIME Collaborative schools. The CI framework was built around seven essential elements: (1) high-quality instruction; (2) targeted interventions and acceleration; (3) purposeful teacher development and collaboration; (4) strategic and effective leadership teams; (5) high expectations in a supportive culture; (6) engaging enrichment opportunities; and (7) data-driven systems for continuous improvement. Within each of these elements, NCTL itemized seven to ten indicators to delineate how schools and educators should bring them to life. Twice each year, in partnership with local district leaders and school partners, NCTL coaches conducted a full-day review of each TIME Collaborative school to assess to what degree it lived up to expectations within the framework of effective practice. Coaches then used these ratings to make recommendations for schools that school leadership teams could readily digest and act upon. The framework emphasized that high-quality implementation was not a destination, but an iterative proceess of data-driven inquiry that focused on helping school teams improve over time and to ensure that the ELT design was effectively adapted to the specifics of local needs and contexts.

From the beginning, both Ford and NCTL had intended that the TIME Collaborative spur not just effective implementation in the participating schools, but also policy changes in the targeted states that would lead to the seeding of even more expanded-time schools. Since 2011, NCTL published a biennial national policy report (called *Learning Time in America*) to outline the fast-shifting policy landscape. In addition to federal policy shifts, the report described a number of state policies that have enabled expanded-time schools to take root. These include New York, where Governor Andrew Cuomo launched an ELT initiative based on the Massachusetts model, and Connecticut, where providing more and better conceived learning time became an integral element of the turnaround strategies of the thirty Alliance School Districts. Florida, meanwhile, can boast of perhaps the largest state-wide effort to expand time when it allocated (in fiscal year 2015) $75 million to lengthen the school day by one hour in the three hundred lowest-performing elementary schools so that they could increase literacy instruction. NCTL also tracked an emerging trend in the field of education policy that holds the potential to seed even more expanded-time schools: innovation districts (and/or schools) that empower educators at the local level to make decisions on school time, budgets, and staffing. In a number of states, these new autonomies are leading to many more schools expanding their day and year.[13]

A LASTING LEGACY: THE FIELD
OF EXPANDED-TIME SCHOOLS IN 2016

At its founding in 2007, NCTL set a goal to ensure that by the year 2020, one million American students would be enrolled in ELT schools. In the organization's biennial review of the state of the field of expanded-time schools in the 2013–2014 school year, NCTL discovered that the nation had, in fact, achieved this milestone well ahead of schedule. What started out as little more than a compelling idea tucked into a 1983 commission report had become reality for over two thousand schools in America, nearly double the number in the review in 2012. Perhaps even more impressive, most of the growth in the field had occurred not through charter schools—which, as noted earlier, were the early adopters of the longer day and year—but through regular district schools that overcame the challenges of implementation to make real substantially more learning time for their students.

How did this happen? Big-city mayors in Chicago, Boston, and New York launched initiatives to add more time for learning. Every school in New Orleans and all schools serving K–8 students in Lawrence, Massachusetts, offered expanded time. Midsized cities, including Newark and Elizabeth, New Jersey; Springfield, Massachusetts; Syracuse and Rochester, New York; Nashville and Memphis, Tennessee; and many more have "school innovation zones" comprising low-performing schools that, as part of their turnaround plan, added more time for learning. Policy momentum around adding time was clearly building, even if these efforts did not always generate the improvements in achievement scores that education leaders hoped for—in large part because the added time was too easily separated from deeper matters of strengthening schools.[14]

Massachusetts provides a compelling example of how the idea and reality of expanded-time schools has spread. Eleven years after the launch of the ELT initiative, Massachusetts hosts over 140 expanded-time schools enabled by many different policies and funding streams—federal, state, charter, pilot, turnaround. While Massachusetts continues to lead the way in achievement and innovation on school time, other cities and states are just beginning to explore the reform.

Meanwhile, new school models, including Summit Schools, are revolutionizing education through a personalized learning approach allowing students to progress at their own pace, thus breaking away from the traditional "seat time" model. And technology is enabling anytime/anywhere learning to be available more broadly—for those who have access.

In the late twentieth century, the notion of unlocking our schools from the "shackles of time," as the National Education Commission on Time and Learning put it, seemed aspirational, perhaps even fanciful. But, two decades later, the fact that over one million children attend schools that are no longer bound by the somewhat arbitrary calendar of 180 6.5-hour days means that the value of more learning time in driving a richer, broader educational experience in schools has become accepted and, in so many cases, the reality. Indeed, in policy and education circles, expanded learning time is now seen as a fundamental component of a high-quality education for disadvantaged children. The cost of this innovation, however, continues to mean that states and districts with minimal per pupil investments find it difficult to afford. Some states are exploring innovations through staggered teacher scheduling, the blending of funding streams, and the utilization of federal funding for new turnaround strategies as options to implement expanded time for students.

Not all efforts to expand learning time in schools will look like the ELT initiative started in Massachusetts. As this review has made clear, even with Massachusetts 2020 and the NCTL playing a leading role in pushing such a model, expanded learning time has always taken a variety of forms. Regardless of the specific policy or funding mechanisms that increase opportunities for students to learn, however, the most essential truth is that absent these expanded learning opportunities, schools will be simply unable to provide the kind of deep and broad education that today's students—especially those from disadvantaged backgrounds—need and deserve. With the passage of the Every Student Succeeds Act of 2015, states once again have primary responsibility for putting in place the necessary structural changes, support systems, and financial investments to ensure all students can succeed.

In 2016, NCTL itself went through a transition. In light of shifts in the national funding landscape, the leadership of NCTL determined that the expanded learning time agenda would be best advanced through deep partnerships. In Massachusetts, expanded learning time had become an integral part of the state and district school turnaround requirements. One of the leading state organizations supporting that shift was Empower Schools, founded by one of NCTL's cofounders. As of 2016, NCTL's Massachusetts policy, ELT network, and technical assistance team merged with Empower Schools.

NCTL's national advocacy operation is now embedded within the Education Redesign Lab at Harvard Graduate School of Education. In so doing, more learning time has become a core component of an ambitious agenda focused on aligning diverse funds, missions, and agencies—schools, public health, mental health, community organizations, and more—into a coordinated and focused endeavor to mediate the ill effects of poverty in communities across the country.

Local approaches to "collective impact" will clearly be critical in the years ahead as our nation struggles with deep divides. More than ever, the future prospects of our children are in the hands of local community leaders, mayors, and superintendents. We are hopeful that local leaders will embrace the successful educational and youth development strategies identified over the last twenty years. Our collective future depends on it.

CHAPTER 2

BEYOND THE SCHOOL DAY

The Necessary Role of Expanded Learning
Opportunities in Closing the Achievement Gap

JESSICA GUNDERSON, JENNIFER PECK,
AND KATIE BRACKENRIDGE

It turns out that the learning that happens in the 80 percent of waking
hours that are spent out of school (between ages of 5–18) has as much
to do with achievement gaps that show up in school as anything in the
school. We can't expect a 20 percent solution to solve 100 percent of the
problem; we've got to address the inequalities of enrichment and stim-
ulating activities outside of school.[1]

—PAUL REVILLE, professor, Harvard University
Graduate School of Education,
and founding director, Education Redesign Lab

INTRODUCTION

One of the biggest challenges and opportunities in public education lies in the
stark difference between how low-income students and their higher-income
peers spend time beyond the formal school day. While we often focus on
school financing and quality teaching as the primary factors to educational
inequity, equally important is the time students have for exploring, learning,
and developing skills outside the classroom. These out-of-school hours are a
rich resource for all students to deepen their growth and interests. Families
who can afford to pay for additional classes, sports activities, and camps will
invest a great deal in these opportunities to advance their children's educational and social development. For children from low-income families, however, the unequal access to expanded learning experiences beyond the school
day and year results in a widening opportunity gap. As amply demonstrated
in the opening chapter to this book, the research is clear that the way kids
spend their out-of-school hours is essential to addressing this opportunity gap
and, consequently, to improving their educational and social outcomes. Yet,

as Paul Reville has observed, schools cannot tackle the learning-time opportunity gap alone.

Given the way schools are currently organized and funded, there is not
enough time or resources in the traditional school day and year to provide
for every student's needs, and there are certain experiences that are not best
suited for delivery during the school day. However, the school day has a complementary partner in out-of-school expanded learning programs. Publicly
funded afterschool and summer learning programs have a robust infrastructure serving families who could not afford these services on their own and are
uniquely suited and proven to improve and expand students' learning opportunities and outcomes. In particular, publicly funded afterschool and summer
learning programs expand students' social and emotional learning—including interpersonal and self-management skills that assist students in meeting
their educational and life goals.[2] Significant opportunities are missed when
education leaders and afterschool and summer program partners fail to leverage and collaborate to expand learning opportunities for all youth, in support
of a shared vision of student success.

The Partnership for Children & Youth (PCY) is a California-based advocacy and capacity-building organization focused on providing access to
high-quality learning opportunities for underserved youth. We believe that
schools cannot and should not do the work of educating children by themselves; the skills, relationships, resources, and contextual understanding that
community-based partners bring to a student's learning experience are essential. For over fifteen years, PCY has worked directly with schools and
community-based organizations to improve practices in afterschool, summer, and community school initiatives, and has served as a bridge to policy
makers to ensure that funding and policies support quality programming.
As a capacity builder, PCY trains, coaches, leverages resources, and builds
coalitions that support quality improvement, which in turn produce better
outcomes for students. As an advocate, PCY develops and fights for legislative and administrative policy that supports expanded learning opportunities in California. For example, PCY leads a statewide coalition working to
increase funding for California's After School Education & Safety (ASES)
Program. PCY is a member of Every Hour Counts, a national coalition of
expanded learning intermediaries, and a founding member of the California
Afterschool Advocacy Alliance, a coalition of California providers and advocates that serve hundreds of thousands of students and families daily. Based

on our experience as advocates and capacity builders, this chapter describes out-of-school expanded learning opportunities, how they work to narrow the opportunity gap, and the lessons learned and policy implications from our work in California.

WHAT ARE EXPANDED LEARNING OPPORTUNITIES?

In the California context, expanded learning refers to before and afterschool, summer, and intersession learning experiences that develop the academic, social, emotional, and physical needs and interests of students. As further defined by the California Department of Education (CDE), "[e]xpanded learning opportunities should be hands-on, engaging, student-centered, results-driven, involve community partners, and complement learning activities in the regular school day/year."[3] Afterschool and summer programs have a rich and deep history in the United States that extends as far back as the late nineteenth century. Many of the longest-standing US community-based organizations have provided afterschool and summer programming for well over a century, including New York City's settlement houses, 4-H Clubs, YMCAs, and Boys & Girls Clubs.[4] As the role and function of these programs have evolved, so have the terms that describe them: boys clubs, afterschool programs, out-of-school-time programs, youth development, extracurricular activities, enrichment, and many more. For the purpose of this chapter, we use the CDE definition (provided above) because it reconceives summer and afterschool initiatives as expanded *learning* opportunities. This vocabulary best encompasses where the field is today and its ongoing potential. These programs can and should be working in concert with school leaders and other educators to expand learning experiences and to support more positive outcomes for students.

As reflected by the field's evolving terms and characteristics, the impact of these programs are far-reaching and diverse. Research over the last several decades shows that high-quality afterschool and summer learning programs have demonstrated a range of positive academic and well-being outcomes, including improved math and language arts achievement; improved student engagement and school attendance; stronger social-emotional skills; reduction of risky behaviors (e.g., dropout, drug and alcohol use, and juvenile crime); and improved physical fitness and nutrition.[5]

As the substantial research base over the last thirty years has grown, so too have levels of participation in, and focus on, out-of-school expanded learning programs. According to national survey data, participation in after-school programs increased annually over the past ten years.[6] Today, nearly one in four families (10.2 million) have a child enrolled in an afterschool program, though the demand for these programs far exceeds the current participation rates (two in five, or 19.4 million children, would participate if programs were available).[7]

With the growing demand and demonstrated impact, policy makers have intentionally invested in expanded learning programs beyond the formal school day. The primary federal funding for these programs is through the US Department of Education's (USDOE) 21st Century Community Learning Centers (21st CCLC). These 21st CCLC funds are granted to state education agencies to provide low-income students academic and enrichment supports and opportunities. The $1 billion annual investment serves approximately 1.6 million children and youth, 70 percent of whom are in the K–8 grades and 30 percent in high school.[8] In addition to the 21st CCLC program, expanded learning strategies have increasingly been incorporated in and supported by broader education policy reform efforts such as the Full-Service Community Schools program, grade-level reading efforts, and federal STEM initiatives. As Davis and Farbman note in chapter 1, many public schools, including but not only charters, have also explicitly embraced and modeled different schedules and strategies to expand learning time after school and in the summer.

Among the fifty states, California stands apart, having invested $550 million per year in state dollars for afterschool programs, more than all other states combined. There are 4,500 publicly funded programs serving nearly 500,000 students daily across the state, the majority of which are supported by the state's ASES Program.[9] These school-based programs promote collaboration between school districts and community-based nonprofit providers, ensuring student access, leveraging the use of facilities, and creating a clear system of oversight and accountability. As outlined in the preceding chapters, research has shown that expanded learning opportunities are needed to address both the opportunity gaps and the achievement gaps experienced by children and youth in low-income communities.

LESSONS FROM CALIFORNIA

As noted earlier, the size and intensity of California's public investment is unique. Given the geographic, economic, and ethnic diversity of the state,

California's experience can inform the policy and practice of district, regional, and statewide efforts throughout the United States. Indeed, policy makers and advocates across the country look to the promising practices and lessons learned from California's experience as they strive to expand learning opportunities for students beyond the traditional school day and year.

Defining and Building Consensus on High-Quality Expanded Learning Programs

In 2012, PCY and other leaders in the out-of-school expanded learning community formed a partnership with CDE to build consensus on a set of principles that would define high quality and help to institutionalize systems of quality improvement for afterschool programs.[10] Adopted by CDE in 2014, California's Quality Standards for Expanded Learning Programs define best practices that align well with the learning strategies and conditions found to be most effective in developing social-emotional skills.[11] Of the twelve quality standards, five are particularly targeted to the learning experience and the interaction between children and staff, where much of the social-emotional learning takes place. These standards include:

- *Safe and supportive environment.* Quality expanded learning programs create a safe, orderly environment that is fun, honors individual differences, and celebrates successes. At the same time, they hold participants to high expectations for behavior and achievement.

- *Active and engaged learning.* Project-based, experiential learning is a mainstay of expanded learning programs, requiring students to explore, think, and create collaboratively and actively.

- *Skill building.* Staff members are intentional about the scope and sequence of learning opportunities. Participants have the flexibility to move at their own pace and to dive more deeply into skills and content that interests them.

- *Youth voice and leadership.* Expanded learning program participants are given opportunities to express their opinions about the activities they do, hold leadership roles, and see their preferences and interests reflected in program offerings.

- *Diversity, access, and equity.* The program creates an environment in which students experience values that embrace diversity and equity regardless of race, color, religion, sex, age, income level, national origin, physical ability, sexual orientation, and/or gender identity and expression.

Together, these point-of-service and program quality standards help to support the creation and scaling-up of opportunities and environments where young people are continuously building and deepening their sense of self, connection to others and community, and confidence as learners.

Providing Learning Opportunities Critical for the Development of Social-Emotional Skills[12]

A broad body of research substantiates what common sense and parents have long known—social and emotional skills contribute to, and are interdependent with, improved outcomes in school, work, and life.[13] Most of us are familiar with these types of programs because we and/or our children have participated in them. For example, theater classes where children create, write, and read scripts based on stories that interest them. In these classes, students work in constant collaboration to build sets, create costumes, rehearse, and design invitations; the opportunities for students to learn and model communication, negotiation, and compromise skills are endless. Or, the activity might be focused on science, where students are using their hands and minds to solve a critical question through experimentation. Together, students and the teaching staff ask questions, suggest solutions, and try out their ideas—the chance to experience the learning process can spark curiosity, confidence, and a heightened sense of agency. Or, the activity could take place on the sports field, where soccer practices include a mix of fitness, individual skill building, group drills, and scrimmages, culminating in the opportunity for full field competition. Children are motivated to work hard, respond to their teammates, and sometimes, are challenged to overcome losses with grace and renewed motivation.

Parents recognize that skills such as the ability to manage one's own behavioral impulses in different settings, to work collaboratively with others, or to persist through challenges are vital to lifelong learning and success. Consequently, parents who are financially able tend to invest substantially in opportunities for their children to build these skills.[14] Children develop social-emotional skills over time and through a variety of experiences. By their design and structure, high-quality afterschool and summer programs as described above have key features that have frequently been linked to social and emotional development.[15] These features include projects and activities that are collaborative in nature; they keep learning active, using students' bodies and minds; have meaning and relevance to students based on their interests and values; and broaden students' horizons by exposing them to new ideas, experiences, and people.[16]

A 2015 report by the University of Chicago describes a setting in which young people can develop social-emotional skills. Its framework identifies categories of experiences—involving action and reflection—that are similar to the types of activities provided in high-quality expanded learning programs (see figure 2.1). These activities are accessible over time and are rooted in relationships with caring adults, a fundamental aspect of quality programs discussed in the next section.[17]

Increasing Access to Caring Adults and Mentors

In quality expanded learning programs, the relationships between staff and young people are one of the field's greatest assets, given the intentional focus on creating a culture and community of mutual respect. Staff members in these programs reflect the diversity of the communities they serve and often

FIGURE 2.1   Developmental experiences require action and reflection

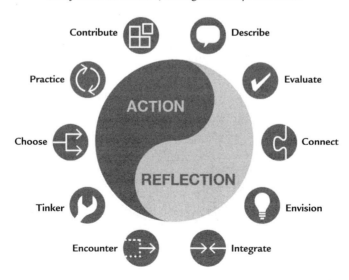

Children learn through developmental experiences that combine **Action** *and* **Reflection**, *ideally within the context of trusting relationships with adults.*

Contribute · Describe · Practice · Evaluate · Choose · Connect · Tinker · Envision · Encounter · Integrate

ACTION

REFLECTION

Source: Jenny Nagaoka et al., *Foundations for Young Adult Success: A Developmental Framework* (Chicago: University of Chicago Consortium on Chicago School Research, 2015). Used with permission from the authors, Jenny Nagaoka and Camille Farrington.

come from similar backgrounds and experiences as the youth. A 2012 labor market analysis showed that the out-of-school expanded learning workforce in California is staffed by approximately 70 percent people of color, and a similar percentage is under the age of twenty-nine, as compared to the California teaching workforce, which is currently comprised of less than 35 percent educators of color.[18] A recent 2014–2015 survey of approximately 2,000 staff from LA's BEST (an expanded learning provider serving 25,000 students in Los Angeles on any given day) found that 90 percent identified as Latino/Hispanic or black/African American, over 50 percent lived in the communities they served, 20 percent were LA's BEST alumni, and 68 percent were currently enrolled in college (33 percent plan to become teachers and 39 percent plan to become human services workers).

Young adult expanded learning staff can be natural and valuable role models who are deeply trusted by students and help them understand a broader set of possibilities for their own futures. In many cases, expanded learning staff members have made a series of choices—about academic effort, graduation, and college—that young people can emulate. They may also have made poor choices from which they've recovered, showing young people the value of learning from mistakes and the ongoing possibility for resilience. Practically speaking, staff members have information about college (applications, financial aid, and admission tests) and about work (résumés, interviews, and references) that young people in families with limited connections may otherwise have difficulty finding.

Beyond the personal connections, quality out-of-school expanded learning programs also introduce young people and their families to organizations and resources in their communities with which they might not otherwise be familiar. These connections can be simple or more enduring. For example, the Jamestown Community Center, located in San Francisco's Mission District, takes children to Ocean Beach on public transportation in the summer. Most of the participants have never been to the beach and have no idea that it is accessible for a $1 bus ride. Afterschool and summer programs frequently build partnerships with local libraries, where children get their first library card, access to the Internet, and a quiet, safe place to do their homework. According to the California State Library, the launch of summer learning programs in Fresno resulted in 86 percent of their students acquiring a library card, compared with 22 percent before the summer learning program began. The afterschool and summer programs for older youth can connect them to job opportunities, often through publicly funded youth employment programs or even within their own programs.

These connections are more likely to occur, and are more enduring, when school-based expanded learning programs partner with community-based organizations. These organizations are often deeply embedded in the communities where the families live and have an extensive network of partner organizations and city agencies with whom they collaborate frequently.

Targeting Children Whose Families Cannot Afford Access to Additional Learning Opportunities

Public investment allows low-income youth to access expanded learning programs. Nearly three-fourths of the students that participate in federal 21st CCLC–funded programs receive federal nutrition assistance (federal Free or Reduced-Price Meals program [FRPM]) and over half of attendees are African American and Latino.[19]

In California, these programs are located in schools where the average FRPM participation rate is 80 percent, nearly double the state average. These schools have more than double the average percentage of English language learners.[20] A recent analysis of four of California's largest school districts, including Los Angeles, Sacramento, Oakland, and Fresno, found that the ASES programs serve a greater proportion of black and Latino students than the districtwide population averages for these subgroups.[21] Similar statistics are true across the state.

The California expanded learning infrastructure works best when it leverages the public investment of both the in-school and out-of-school systems in service of better student outcomes. Students who participate regularly in federally and state-funded afterschool and summer programs in California can gain 90 to 115 additional days of learning time, which translates to a 50 percent increase or more above the average 180-day school calendar. When educators and partners collaboratively work toward shared learning goals, the educational impact of these additional learning hours can be significantly greater than the sum of the individual parts.

Aligning School Day and Expanded Learning Program Goals

National and statewide K–12 policies and systems have broadened their definition of student success to encompass more than standardized test scores, promoting the opportunity for more authentic partnerships with expanded learning programs. Until recently, the education system's driving vision of student success was narrowly focused on academic achievement. This affected expanded learning policy; in the early years of ASES implementation, programs were expected to be held accountable for student test scores.

In addition, state and federal categorical programs have long divided student and school needs into siloed interventions, with academic, school safety, and expanded learning initiatives defined by different accountability and funding mechanisms. This division often undermined partnerships and opportunities to maximize both community and school resources to provide support to the most underserved schools. The passage of the Every Student Succeeds Act of 2015 has provided an opportunity for a more explicit recognition of the importance of school climate and growing unanimity across many education sectors about addressing the needs of the whole child. As well, school-day educators are remaking classroom instruction to adapt to the Common Core State Standards, which require a solid foundation of social and emotional skills. These shifts are more in line with research showing that when schools and community organizations partner collaboratively, program quality improves, resources are leveraged more effectively, and goals and curricula are better aligned.[22]

California is leading many of the efforts listed above. That includes implementing a more equitable financing formula, known as the Local Control Funding Formula (LCFF), aimed at closing the opportunity and achievement gaps.[23] Alongside increased resources for historically underserved student groups and more local flexibility in how these dollars can be spent, California is seeking to create an accountability system that recognizes multiple measures, including student engagement, school climate, and college and career readiness.

Similarly, California's publicly funded expanded learning programs are working to improve quality and to effectively support social-emotional learning. They are strategically based at school sites, where coordination across strategies and instructional practices offers a real opportunity for consistent student supports. In California and across the country, it is an important moment for rethinking how our education system can best utilize all the hours and resources at our disposal to effectively educate *all* students.

POLICY IMPLICATIONS AND RECOMMENDATIONS

Given the conditions and opportunities described above, the time is ripe for state and local leaders to prioritize equitable access to high-quality expanded learning programs. There are several investments, actions, and policy incentives that can be put in place now to increase access to, and the quality of, expanded learning while also increasing coordination of these programs with the formal education system. These recommendations are based on California's experience, where much work has been done to invest in and build quality programming at scale, and where lessons are still being learned from the ongoing challenges and successes. In 2014, PCY released a report, *Time Well Spent*, which looked at best practices of systemic coordination between expanded learning providers and eight diverse school districts (ranging from 300 to 46,000 students).[24] The recommendations below and the case study examples are drawn from report findings.

1. Increase Access to High-Quality Out-of-School Expanded Learning Programs

State policy makers should invest funding to serve more children in afterschool and summer expanded learning programs. While there is a robust existing infrastructure, the unmet need of expanded learning programs for low-income students is still significant across the country. Only twenty states have a dedicated funding source for expanded learning (with varying levels from $50,000 to $550 million), and the primary federal funding stream has been decreasing over the past ten years.[25] In California, even with ASES funding, 41 percent of low-income schools do not have a publicly funded afterschool program.[26] Schools that do have ASES grants are only funded to serve a small portion of their low-income student population.

State policy makers and agency leaders must ensure that student-level data are collected and accessible to stakeholders. Collecting and utilizing data are critical steps in ensuring that students most in need are being served by expanded learning programs. Data are also a powerful tool that can be used to identify gaps in service, effectively target resources, and sustain political will to continue investments in these programs. California law currently requires that data for students in publicly funded expanded learning programs and the school day be linked through a common statewide data system, and CDE will soon be implementing this statutory requirement. Data from the largest state system in the country will be useful nationwide to demonstrate the opportunity for expanded learning programs to operate at scale and to inform other states' system-building efforts.

Local leaders must demonstrate commitment to expanding access by investing local funds. Cities and school districts can also play a key role in growing access to expanded learning opportunities by serving as the hub to ensure that all community resources, including parks and recreation, libraries, and violence prevention funds, are being leveraged to meet the needs of all students. In cities across the country—New York, Boston, Nashville, Oakland, and San Jose, for example—the city or school district directly funds afterschool and summer programs through grants to community-based organizations that partner with schools.

In San Francisco, for example, city leaders announced a $1.8 million expansion of summer program funding to eliminate waiting lists in San Francisco's publicly funded summer programs. The funding represented a 55 percent increase in the number of spaces available at thirty-one school-based, fifty community-based, and fifty recreation and park–run summer programs.[27] The funding was generated by a successful ballot initiative that authorized a property tax be set aside to support education and youth-related programs. A variety of city agencies were involved in making the program slots available, including the Department of Children, Youth and Their Families; the Recreation and Parks Department; San Francisco Unified School District; San Francisco Public Library; and public housing sites. School leaders in the Franklin-McKinley School District (San Jose, California) have used LCFF dollars to serve more students in afterschool programs after parents successfully petitioned for more slots, given the lengthy waiting list.

2. Focus on Program Quality Improvement

States must invest in building the quality of programming to maximize its return on public investment. Research has clearly demonstrated that if programs are of low quality, they do not have the positive student impacts outlined earlier.[28] Though California's investment exceeds that of most other states, the state is still far off the mark in meeting the cost of quality (or even covering the most basic operating costs). Research has shown that the cost of a quality program ranges from $21 to $24 per student/per day.[29] In contrast, California provides $7.50 per student/per day—a rate that has remained the same for a decade. During the same time period, labor costs in California have gone up 33 percent (due to new minimum wage laws) and the consumer price index has increased by nearly 20 percent.[30]

States need to incentivize quality through the establishment of quality improvement systems. High-quality programs do not happen by chance; it takes intentional policy and resource prioritization. This work includes the establishment of quality standards, mandated quality improvement processes, and technical assistance to help providers meet higher standards. The California standards were based on existing standards in other states and were vetted through an inclusive statewide process of stakeholder input. The statewide process of co-creating these standards with afterschool leaders serves as a model for the development of professional standards. The state has also mandated participation in quality improvement processes that are low stakes and locally determined to ensure authentic buy-in from participants.[31] California's commitment to quality started at the top, with state agency leadership prioritizing the effort, which was essential to ensuring that resources were in place and that a common vision was collaboratively developed and communicated.

State leaders can ensure quality by supporting workforce development and retention strategies that help programs find and keep highly qualified staff. A 2016 survey of California providers in over two hundred school districts reported that 86 percent of providers found it very difficult to recruit and retain high-quality staff; this is the field's number-one challenge.[32] State leaders can address this challenge by formalizing connections between state universities and expanded learning programs. The majority of out-of-school expanded learning staff members are young people enrolled in higher education or are of college age. Expanded learning programs, school districts, higher education systems (community colleges, state colleges, and universities), and their students would benefit greatly from partnerships and pathways between these learning institutions. Furthermore, many students are eligible for federal work-study funds that help offset the cost of staffing. If established statewide, local programs and districts would have an existing system to tap into for their staffing needs and to access this federal support.

The expanded learning workforce is young, diverse, and experienced in working with young people in underserved communities, providing a well-matched career pathway to address the teacher shortage many states are facing and diversify the teaching profession. There are successful career pathway program models that promote the transition of expanded learning workers into the teaching profession. The California Teaching Fellows Foundation

(CTFF) is one such example that involves partnerships between school districts and higher education institutions. CTFF employs undergraduate students in community college or university in teaching internships where they are able to get hundreds of hours of firsthand teaching experience while leading afterschool programming—and get paid while doing it. CTFF's graduates then have several years of direct experience working in diverse and underserved school communities before they ever reach the classroom. CTFF partners with forty school districts to staff programs in Fresno, Madera, Merced, and Tulare counties, serving more than thirty thousand students each day. But these types of models remain few and relatively isolated and should be brought to scale through state-level, systemic investments.

Local leaders must embrace quality improvement as a core strategy. The use of quality assessment and improvement tools has been effective in building better programs. To support these efforts, local leaders need to invest in, and provide time for, professional development for both management and direct service staff. Given the central role of staff, most quality improvement plans require professional development. Districts and their partners struggle to find time and resources for this work because many staff are part-time and stretched to capacity. In Oakland, the district's After School Programs Office puts together its own comprehensive schedule for year-round professional development that includes quality assessment linked to training and coaching. In service of quality improvement, the district has shifted away from one-day trainings to offer a variety of learning communities for staff cohorts with a focus on areas such as restorative justice, literacy for English language learners, STEM learning, and others. Programs that are serious about quality find the time through creative structures including Saturday academies, evening classes, and the appropriate alignment of work and training schedules.

3. Support Goal and Operational Alignment Between In-School Efforts and Expanded Learning Programs

With public education policy and funding aligned around a broader vision of student success, there is a great opportunity to create more systemic coherence between the school day and out-of-school expanded learning programs. State policy and guidance have a clear role to play in communications, technical assistance, and funding priorities to ensure that public investments are being maximized for all students.

State leaders should ensure that expanded learning programs are prioritized by their own organizational structure, messaging, and leadership. In California, CDE has elevated expanded learning by creating a new, unique division for these programs, and the state superintendent proactively supports the policy to expand access and improve program quality. Administratively, state education departments can issue guidelines, examples, and technical assistance outlining the allowable and effective use of state and federal dollars for expanded learning programs and community partnerships. A great example comes from the states' role in providing guidance on the new, more flexible Every Student Succeeds Act dollars. CDE's most recent guidance on Supplemental Education Services, for example, points to out-of-school expanded learning: "It is recommended that Local Education Agencies (LEAs) implement alternative supports consistent with the following guiding principle: leverage existing programs that currently provide successful expanded learning opportunities for students, such as the After School Education and Safety Program."[33]

State leaders can require or incentivize partnerships between schools and expanded learning programs through requests for proposals (RFPs) or other mechanisms that provide funding. RFPs are a powerful tool for communicating priorities and values, and for creating incentives to shift practice. This approach can prioritize or give more weight to those proposals that include community partners and expanded learning strategies. For example, in California's 21st CCLC grant process, extra points are awarded to applications that include community partners as well as those that provide students with year-round learning opportunities. Similarly, as states invest in new technical assistance and capacity-building supports for districts, they should ensure that out-of-school expanded learning programming is included.

States can support increased alignment by encouraging data collection and data sharing across partners. Data on student achievement, behavior, and demographics—which can be used to understand access and quality at the state and district levels—are a much more powerful tool when all entities are able to use them (with, of course, the appropriate and clear privacy guidelines). Shared data also provide opportunities for joint evaluation, planning, and technical assistance between LEAs and their community partners. The state and federal government should provide guidance and best practices on data-sharing agreements and memorandums of understanding between schools and their community partners, drawing on successful models.[34]

4. Build and Support Strong and Authentic Partnerships

To achieve alignment, the school district and/or city must set the vision that expanded learning is part of the core work of public education. Through word, deed, and funding, local leaders need to communicate their commitment to building strong community partnerships in support of out-of-school expanded learning. In Oakland, for example, the district's five-year community schools plan explicitly includes out-of-school expanded learning programs as core assets for improving student outcomes, and the district has invested millions of dollars, which increased the quality and access of their summer learning programs over the past several years. In Chula Vista, the superintendent (who sits on the board of the local YMCA, which operates the district's after-school program) communicates that community partnerships are a priority. This is accomplished by requiring that the district's cabinet leaders be active in community boards and organizations (the district pays for necessary membership fees).

Once the vision is set, local leaders must sustain authentic partnerships through shared planning and management. To create these deep collaborations, the district first needs to take a critical look at contracts, policies, and procedures to ensure that they encourage rather than obstruct partner relationships. The district also needs to identify the right people to coordinate these often-complicated partnerships, champion expanded learning, and represent each entity's point of view. It should also give those people sufficient time and resources to do the work. Across the eight diverse districts in *Time Well Spent*, coordinators consistently needed to have decision-making power, connection to district leadership, and semi-regular communication with principals in order to effectively coordinate systems.

Local systems must have the right balance of empowering school site administrators to create and sustain effective programs. Ultimately, school sites are where effective, well-coordinated expanded learning programs take place. Districts that expect to see quality programs in action need to give principals and site coordinators responsibility and support. The majority of districts in the *Time Well Spent* report provided school sites with a basic memorandum of understanding that the site then customized to address issues such as access to technology, space, and custodial services. In the most coherent expanded learning programs, school day and afterschool staff work side by side for at least a portion of the day, and school site administrators have the flexibility to share resources on both formal and informal levels. Officials can help create this environment by working to make sure that their personnel policies and union contracts support collaborative staffing. Districts, schools, and providers can ensure that joint professional development and training opportunities are available. The YMCA in Chula Vista requires that site leaders go through training with school and district staff to build relationships and acclimate to district culture and policies. At South Bay Union, the district has increasingly relied on afterschool staff to also work in part-time classified positions (library, playground, classroom aides, etc.). This dual staffing reinforces the integration of schools and expanded learning.

CONCLUSION

Research, experience, and common sense tell us that our education system must assertively adjust its practices to reflect the realities of how students learn best and what they need to be successful. While affluent families ensure that needed opportunities are in place for their children, many less affluent students do not have access to these opportunities and networks. System leaders are increasingly talking about educational equity; we must expect that their actions follow their words. Leaders and stakeholders at every level of the education system must recognize that the moment is here to ensure *all* children have positive learning opportunities throughout the day and year. Educational leaders and policy makers must leverage this chance for new partnerships and increased effectiveness using the same kinds of innovation, creativity, and collaboration that we aspire to instill in our students. Working together, across the organizational lines of formal schooling and out-of-school learning time, is essential to the development of socially conscious, engaged young people who are well prepared for twenty-first-century careers and citizenship.

CHAPTER 3

MORE AND BETTER LEARNING IN COMMUNITY SCHOOLS

Lessons from Oakland

KENDRA FEHRER AND JACOB LEOS-URBEL

Our kids come to school with so many stories. Maybe they're hungry. Maybe they're homeless. Maybe they saw mom get arrested. I had one student who saw his dad get shot right in front of him. They've seen domestic violence, neighborhood violence, custody battles, drugs, foster care. They've gone through so much, as seven-year-olds and eight-year-olds, that no adult should ever have to go through . . .

As teachers, we see our kids every day. When we hear about what's going on with them, we ask ourselves, how can we keep from losing them? How do we help them succeed? I've been in schools where teachers cared a lot about kids, they screened kids about what happened, but they had no place to put it. If that cycle doesn't complete—if you don't have anywhere to go—it can just deplete you as a teacher. Because nothing feels worse, if you care about your kids and you suddenly have this information, and you don't know what to do with it. That's going to burn you out . . .

I think being a community school allows you to say to a student, "Here, eat something. Here, come to therapy. Here, let's manage some of this. But we need you here every day. We need you in the classroom. We need you paying attention." The partners are critical, because if we didn't have partners, the school couldn't do it. We couldn't do it and we couldn't fund it. All this support stuff needs to happen to get the learning to happen. The thing that we're really after is the learning, and the kids just getting to be students.

—OAKLAND TEACHER

INTRODUCTION

The community schools approach posits that the traditional school model, including time, resources, and personnel, is not sufficient to address the role of poverty in equitable access to learning.[1] To this end, community schools partner with community-based organizations to deliver integrated services that comprehensively address student barriers to learning and increase the amount of time available for instruction and enrichment. Beyond expanding the amount of time for learning, community schools can improve the quality of learning by increasing student readiness to learn, allowing teachers to increasingly focus on teaching, and by aligning school-day and afterschool activities to shared learning goals. Further, community schools help build relational trust among families, partners, and school staff, a critical ingredient of strong schools.

In this chapter, we first discuss community schools as a strategy to promote more and better learning time generally, then focus on lessons from the full-service community school initiative in the Oakland Unified School District (OUSD).[2] We provide an overview of the Oakland context and the district's community schools initiative. Then we outline how OUSD community schools are reorganizing and leveraging time and resources to promote equitable access to learning and build school capacity for improvement. Finally, we close with a discussion of the promise of community schools as a strategy to redress educational inequalities, as well as some of the complexities and challenges.

The Community School Model: Leveraging Time and Resources to Promote Equitable Access to Learning

Well-functioning community schools build on the traditional school model in important ways. While instantiations of community schools vary somewhat from place to place based on local context, at their core is a focus on the whole child and the aim to reduce barriers to academic learning through an array of integrated services and supports. Community schools leverage the resources of the community to improve student achievement through partnerships with community-based organizations (CBOs), while often also serving as a hub for services and other resources for community members more broadly.

The Children's Aid Society's National Center for Community Schools that has developed, coordinated, and studied community schools in New

York City and beyond since 1992 stresses the importance of core instructional programming, expanded learning opportunities, and comprehensive student supports, including health and wellness services. Other elements often include family engagement strategies, as well as alternative approaches to discipline, such as restorative justice.[3] To scaffold the integration and alignment of these expanded services, community schools (and their stakeholder constituents) must also develop a set of core organizational capacities, such as: (1) the capacity to offer programs that comprehensively address the needs of the whole child (e.g., health, mental health, enrichment activities) and also respond to the student's family and community context; (2) the capacity for collective action of multiple stakeholders working to achieve shared goals not possible without the efforts of each other; (3) the capacity to develop shared goals, agreement on the standards and nature of the work, and ongoing assessment and alignment of efforts; and (4) the capacity for long-term buy-in from key stakeholders to make permanent changes in institutional practice and arrangements, including the required human and financial resources.[4]

THE OAKLAND CONTEXT
Inequality and Opportunity

Oakland is home to one of the most demographically diverse populations in the United States, with residents of different racial, ethnic, national, linguistic, and other cultural groups. White, African American, and Latino residents each represent about one-quarter of the population, and Asian residents make up 16 percent. About four in ten residents speak a language other than English at home and more than one-quarter of Oakland residents were born outside the United States.

Within Oakland, there are considerable disparities in opportunity and outcomes largely along racial and geographic lines, with severe concentrated poverty in places, especially for Oakland's children. Among Oakland families with children, 12 percent live below the federal poverty rate ($24,300 for a family of four). However, given the high cost of living in the Bay Area, estimates of the income a family of four needs for self-sufficiency are much higher than the federal poverty threshold, and 38.1 percent of Oakland households fall below this self-sufficiency index.[5]

Those born in some Oakland neighborhoods are much more likely to suffer from poor nutrition, be subject to violence, and lack adequate health care. For example, according to an often cited 2008 report from the Alameda County Public Health Department, compared to a white child born in the affluent Oakland Hills neighborhood, an African American child born in West Oakland is seven times more likely to be born into poverty, four times less likely to read at grade level by grade four, and 5.6 times more likely to drop out of school. Additionally, as an adult, that same African American child will be at least twice as likely to die of heart disease, stroke, or cancer.[6] Further, Oakland has experienced considerable demographic shifts in recent years, attributable in part to both increasing immigration as well as increasing gentrification as housing costs continue to rise across the San Francisco Bay Area. Between 2000 and 2010, Oakland saw increases in the number of Latino and white residents, and decreases in its African American population.[7]

Oakland also is home to tremendous cultural diversity and civic engagement. Birthplace of the Black Panther Party, a longtime stronghold of organized labor (for example, Oakland port workers' International Longshore and Warehouse Union), and a creative center of multiracial and multi-issue organizing, Oakland has a long history of community activism. Beginning as early as the Black Panther Party free school hot breakfast program in 1969, civic organizations have played a critical role in the struggle for more just and equitable access to high-quality education for the city's poorest residents. Not surprisingly, many of today's organizations that serve and advocate for Oakland's children and their families have played a critical role in the community schools initiative.

Oakland Unified School District

OUSD serves a diverse population of approximately 37,000 students across eighty-six district-run schools.[8] Within these schools, Latino (44 percent) and African American (27 percent) students make up the majority of the population, followed by Asian/Pacific Islander (15 percent) and white (10 percent) students. Nearly three-quarters (72 percent) of the student population qualify for Free or Reduced Price Meals and three in ten are English language learners. These demographics have changed considerably over time, mirroring the changes in the larger community. For example, over the last decade, the number of African American students decreased by 34 percent, while the Latino student population experienced a 30 percent increase.[9]

OUSD has a complex history that includes a range of initiatives to address the barriers to educational success that many students face, as well as notable challenges in doing so. In 2003, after declaring bankruptcy, OUSD was placed under state receivership and received a $100 million bailout from the state.[10] With a return to local control in 2009, OUSD's board regained autonomy to make decisions on behalf of the district. In 2010, Superintendent Tony Smith initiated a massive, communitywide strategic planning process that involved students, parents, school and district staff, and CBOs.[11] This process pointed to full-service community schools as a central strategy to redress systemic inequality in student outcomes and opportunities. Additionally, a concurrent investigation by the US Department of Education's Office for Civil Rights into disproportionate suspensions of African American students resulted in a voluntary agreement by the district to employ several strategies to reduce suspensions of young people of color—including implementing restorative justice practices—that would become integral to services offered at OUSD community schools.[12] In 2011, OUSD announced its intention to become the nation's first full-service community school district.

OAKLAND'S COMMUNITY SCHOOL INITIATIVE

Since 2011, OUSD has been transforming its schools into community schools. With the support of numerous partners—including the city of Oakland, Alameda County, multiple health providers, myriad community groups, and CBOs serving the children and youth of Oakland—and substantive philanthropic and public investment, the district has expanded and deepened its community school initiative. As of the 2016–2017 academic year, the majority of OUSD high schools are considered community schools, and the district continues to expand the number of elementary and middle school community schools. The first cohort of community schools included high schools with established, school-based health centers and/or sites located in high-poverty communities with strong existing partnerships.[13] Subsequently, two additional cohorts have been established through an application process, prioritizing schools in high-need communities. In all, approximately one-third of OUSD students now attend community schools.

Although most district schools offer at least some of the programmatic elements of the community school model (e.g., afterschool programming, mental health services), to be an official district community school, a site has to have a designated community school manager (CSM). This funded position manages and integrates the additional functions of the community school (e.g., partnerships, family engagement activities, etc.). CSMs are responsible for introducing the community schools model to the school community; identifying gaps in programs, services, capacity, and assets; managing and maintaining the quality of school site partnerships; supporting students and families through coordinating services and other programs; and supporting youth, family, and staff leadership and engagement. Often, the CSM is deeply involved in school leadership and decision making, participating in culture or climate and even instructional leadership teams, working with the principal to ensure partners are aware of instructional goals, and engaging families in school improvement initiatives.

While OUSD community schools vary in how they adapt the model to their local contexts and are at various stages of development and implementation, they are well positioned to ameliorate the effects of poverty and inequality by expanding and enhancing the time students spend learning. At the core of these efforts are three programmatic pillars: integrated student supports, expanded learning time, and family and community engagement.[14] We describe each of these elements below.

Integrated Student Supports

In partnership with CBOs or public agencies, OUSD community schools offer a wide range of on-site integrated services and supports far beyond what the school would be able to provide on its own. These services and supports aim to address student barriers to learning and increase the amount of time available for instruction and enrichment. These include primary health care, dental and vision services, mental health counseling, health insurance enrollment, social services, peer conflict resolution (e.g., restorative justice circles), chronic absence intervention, and other health and behavioral health supports. All community school high school sites have on-site health clinics, as do some middle schools. The district is currently encouraging sites that do not have on-site clinics to partner with nearby clinics to facilitate access for students and families. Community schools implement a range of strategies to integrate health into school culture, including class visits to health clinics with short screenings for all students and health education classes offered by health and wellness providers on campus.

Most community schools also have structures and systems in place for identifying students in need of support services. Health and behavioral health partners, school administrators, and the CSM meet regularly to identify and address individual students' health and behavioral health needs in a structure known as a coordination of services team (COST). While the district encourages all school sites to use COST, community school staff often attribute the effectiveness of their COST teams to two factors: the valuable administrative role of the CSM in facilitating COST, and the strong collaborative relationships with partners. Both are key attributes of the OUSD community school model. Many community schools have instituted "attendance teams" to identify students at risk of chronic absence; teams include partner agencies (often a partner-funded family liaison or CSM), along with school administrative staff.

Given widespread student experiences with trauma in Oakland schools, community school staff noted that behavioral and mental health services were an essential support, as well as one of the greatest remaining needs. OUSD community schools have offered a number of behavioral health interventions, including restorative justice circles, Positive Behavior Interventions and Supports (PBIS) programs, and subgroup-specific identity and leadership development programs (e.g., an African American male achievement initiative, the Latino men and boys program, and the African American female achievement initiative). School staff note that the increased availability and integration of these services on campus can help lessen the stigma of students' participation and increase utilization; on-site behavioral health services ensure that students get supports needed to function better in school, while minimizing class time missed.

Expanded Learning Time

Expanding the time available for learning is a key component of the OUSD community school model. OUSD community schools partner with CBOs to offer year-round and full-day programming for students, including morning care and enrichment programs, afterschool programming, and summer learning opportunities. The specific opportunities vary widely across schools, but may include morning art classes, academic tutoring, intensive literacy instruction, credit recovery, robotics or science clubs, youth leadership development, internship placements, core subject classes, English language development intervention, and summer camp placements. Many OUSD elementary and middle community schools have one core partner agency that provides primary afterschool services, though multiple partners may provide more specialized programming to smaller targeted groups of students (such as literacy classes for dual language learners or dance classes for interested students). For many OUSD high school community schools, expanded learning consists largely of connecting students to other opportunities within or outside the school, such as the school's Linked Learning pathways, external internships, or other college preparatory activities, like SAT prep courses or AP classes.

While all OUSD schools may offer expanded learning opportunities for students, community school staff are able to elicit high levels of participation in expanded learning activities, as well as alignment and integration between expanded- and school-day programming. In one community school, nearly all students (99 percent) participated in expanded learning time activities outside the traditional school day. As the principal explained, "We don't call anything afterschool; there's no such thing as afterschool; everything is part of what you do." In this school—where almost all middle school students stay after the traditional school day for activities such as STEM, coding class, and Folklorico (dance)—the afterschool program is called eighth and ninth period, and activities provided by CBOs are included in students' daily school schedules. Any student earning less than a 3.0 GPA is required to participate in afterschool time; most students choose to participate.

In addition to expanding the amount of time students spend learning, OUSD community schools are helping to increase the *quality* of instructional time by aligning and integrating expanded learning programming with the school-day curriculum. Through articulating clear school goals, meeting regularly with partners to share goals and assess progress, and creating opportunities for collaboration, community schools seek to enhance the time students spend learning. For example, in one OUSD community middle school, a long-term partner agency's afterschool academic mentors rearranged their working hours to allow them to participate in students' classrooms during the day (referred to as "push-ins"). This allowed the mentors to understand their students' school-day assignments and align their afterschool supports accordingly. Additionally, the presence of the mentors provided teachers with extra assistance during class time, allowing for extra academic support to individuals or groups when needed, as well as assistance addressing behavioral issues. Further, the subsequent relationship building fostered ongoing opportunities for collaboration and alignment of instruction between school-day and afterschool staff. In this site, and others, community schools are reorganizing adult time to create opportunities for teachers and partner staff to communicate about students, align lessons, and discuss goals, including common monthly faculty meetings and shared professional development.[15]

Family and Community Engagement

OUSD community schools recognize that learning happens not only in the classroom, but also in the home and community. Yet in many communities of high poverty and/or with large immigrant populations, school-community relationships are fragmented, characterized by disengagement and sometimes even distrust. OUSD community schools are reconfiguring traditional school-community relationships by prioritizing engagement with families as critical stakeholders in the school community. Schools offer resources to support family needs and strengths, design innovative ways to engage parents in their children's academic learning and goals, and involve parents in leadership and advocacy for school improvement.[16] Together, these initiatives help to expand learning time by creating meaningful home-school relationships, aligning two of the most important spheres of a child's life.

Most OUSD community schools offer family resources and supports dedicated to addressing family needs, from adult literacy classes and food assistance programs, to legal aid and tax assistance. Given high levels of violence, trauma, poverty, and other instabilities in many Oakland neighborhoods, ensuring students' equitable opportunities to education means addressing these circumstances. Working to support families' needs is an important strategy to address student barriers to learning. In the words of one district staff member, "We know that our students and families are achieving inequitably . . . So it's not just [about] equality—providing the same thing to everyone—but really [about] meeting students and families where they're at when they come through the door. What does this particular student or family need, or what does the school community need given that they're located in this particular neighborhood that has X, Y and Z going on."

Most community schools have family resource centers that offer parents support, as well as multiple staff with titles such as family liaisons or family engagement specialists, dedicated to engaging and supporting families. District staff importantly note that while some Oakland neighborhoods may have a multitude of needs, they also have strengths—for example, caring families, strong cultural identities—sometimes invisible to traditional school staff. One of the tasks of the community school, then, is to leverage community assets as well as respond to community needs that reduce barriers to learning and strengthen student resilience.

Many OUSD community schools are also intentional about engaging families with their students' academic learning and success. This includes parents participating in students' learning (in school and at home), expanded learning or enrichment opportunities, college or future plans, attendance, and discipline issues. For example, at one school, parents are supported in navigating a complex application process for a college-track summer program. These types of supports are critical for families, because seemingly minor errors, such as misunderstanding the application due date, can present real barriers to access. At another school, the principal described adopting an innovative approach to parent-teacher conferences that scaffolds conversations between teachers and parents. This practice has led to better teacher-parent collaboration, especially among some teachers who felt limited in their ability to meaningfully communicate with parents from different cultural and linguistic backgrounds about their children's in-class learning.[17] Lastly, at another school, family advocates were immediately informed if a child was absent and communicated with the parent as part of a coordinated initiative to decrease chronic absence. Engaging families in their children's academic decisions, school learning, and school participation can ensure students are in class and have access to expanded learning opportunities, and can enhance learning by aligning at-home practices with school learning goals.

HOW DO COMMUNITY SCHOOLS CREATE MORE AND BETTER LEARNING TIME?

Taken together, community school activities and initiatives—integrated student supports, expanded learning, and family/community engagement—function to reduce barriers to learning, allow students to spend more time learning, and ensure that existing learning time is better leveraged. The overwhelming majority of staff we spoke with at community schools reported that community school interventions have positively affected student readiness to learn, increased the quantity and quality of class and learning time, and improved the conditions for teaching. We discuss some of the most prominent themes referenced by school principals, teachers, and staff below.

Reducing Barriers to Learning

Staff at community schools consistently underscored the importance of meeting students' basic needs as a precursor for classroom learning. By providing *all* students access to services and supports (e.g., health and mental health needs), community schools foster equitable access to learning. As one teacher succinctly noted, "Kids who are healthier physically and emotionally are more likely to be able to concentrate and absorb the academics." Staff also cited numerous examples where perceived behavioral or academic issues turned out to be health issues (e.g., a student who wasn't doing the homework didn't have glasses that he needed to be able to read the whiteboard). As one partner stated, "Too often an assumption is made that a student's medical and behavioral health, and basic needs are being met. And if that's not happening, then it's much harder for them to succeed."

More Time in Class

Community school staff noted that enhanced health and wellness services, increased attendance supports, and alternative disciplinary practices had a direct impact on increasing students' time available to learn. For example, on-site wellness services allowed students to miss only one or two classes for basic medical needs, rather than being sent home for an entire day. Attendance support—often through the efforts of dedicated partner staff—was also cited as producing steady improvements in learning time. As one principal stated, "We've had a partnership with [a CBO] . . . and through them we've had an attendance team here. So, [we were able to go] from 15 percent chronic absent down to 5 percent; kids are in school more, so that's going to help with their academics because they're in class."

Expanded Time for Learning

In addition to missing less class time, students at community schools are offered more time for learning through extensive, expanded day programming. Staff members across schools we visited discussed seeing noticeable improvements in students' academic learning, which they traced, at least in part, to increased expanded learning opportunities. CSMs and other partners work together to identify opportunities for students—summer internships, coding classes, dance programs, science camps. Community school afterschool programming is often aligned and integrated with school-day programs. Engaging with students' parents about their learning can also increase support for learning at home. At the high school level, expanded learning opportunities—such as a Linked Learning pathway—can provide students opportunities for engaged, rigorous instruction. As one teacher at a community school high school shared, "At the end of [the students'] freshman year, one of our most rigorous teachers could see a drastic difference in our students that were in the [Linked Learning] pathway and our students that weren't."

By engaging with strategic partnerships and cultivating practices to align and integrate those partnerships with core school instruction, community schools can offer students increased access to rigorous and meaningful instruction.

Higher-Quality Class Time

School staff—especially teachers—observed that the increased use of alternative disciplinary practices (e.g., restorative justice circles) and behavioral health supports (e.g., PBIS) is helping to create much less disruptive classroom environments. The improved referral systems (e.g., COSTs) also made it easier for teachers to refer students to needed social and academic supports, further ensuring that individual students receive the help they need to enhance quality class time. Across the community schools we visited, teachers described the support they experienced as instructors. Specifically, they cited that community schools improve the conditions for teaching by reducing the number of hats that teachers have to wear, giving them more time for instruction and fostering a better classroom environment due to student supports. As one teacher stated, "You don't have to be social workers or coaches. You don't have to worry that you don't have those resources, because we have partners." Improved conditions allow teachers to focus on providing higher-quality instruction.

REORGANIZING TIME AND RESOURCES

Effectively reorganizing time and resources requires intentional efforts to bolster school capacity. In other words, becoming a community school requires more than simply adding services to a school site.[18] As OUSD community schools work to support more and better student learning time, they develop critical organizational capacities to offer expanded services, foster collaboration, build coherence of programs and initiatives, and cultivate long-term commitment. Together, these strategies shift relationships among schools, families, and community to ultimately reorganize time and resources, and expand and enhance learning time for students. OUSD community schools are learning to:

- *Integrate new stakeholders.* Being a community school means expanding the boundaries of who is considered part of the school community. OUSD community schools involve families, partners, and the CSM as integral actors in the daily functioning of the school.

- *Building relational trust.* Relational trust in a school context can be understood as "all parties understand one another's expectations and their own obligations, and the actions of all parties (e.g., principals, teachers, parents) validate those expectations."[19] Across the OUSD community school sites we visited, staff spoke about high levels of trust among the principal, the CSM, core partner agencies, and families. In many cases, this did not occur immediately, but was the result of working together over multiple years, communicating effectively, understanding their respective roles, and working together toward common goals.

- *Shared leadership and decision making.* Community school leadership requires including a wider group of stakeholders in school leadership and decision making than that in traditional schools. At most OUSD community schools, the CSM acts as a high-level administrator, sharing responsibilities with and supporting the principal. Schools also include partners in institutional leadership positions, such as a school culture-climate team, the COSTs, or even instructional leadership team. Nearly all schools develop ways to involve parents in school leadership, through parent-advisory councils and parent-action teams, allowing families to play an instrumental role in directing school resources and shifting culture.

- *Developing structures and practices to facilitate collaboration.* In addition to decentralizing leadership and decision making, community school staff members also need structures and practices to facilitate their shared work. These include exchanging information about each others' goals, resources, and needs; participating in joint meetings; co-planning events and activities; and even sharing planning time and professional development. Undergirding these activities is a clear understanding of common purpose and goals. Simply participating in meetings together or co-planning events is unlikely to promote meaningful collaboration. However, the substantial structures outlined above provide opportunity for the types of daily interactions in which a shared agenda and understanding of the work may be forged. When taken in tandem with building trusting relationships and sharing leadership and decision making, these structures and practices provide opportunity to foster a culture of collaboration and, ultimately, more effective work toward common goals.

- *Establishing a shared vision.* OUSD community school principals are tasked with establishing a shared vision across the school community.

At the heart of this work is a commitment to, in the words of one principal, "listening to the community and having this be an inclusive process." Principals and CSMs often held meetings and consultations with parents and partners to review school and student data, discuss hopes and dreams, and set priorities for the work ahead. Partner agency staff at traditional schools are often marginally engaged in school visioning and goals. One principal reflected that the experience helped ensure that "all the partners knew where we're going as a school site and how their work aligns within our strategic plan, which was huge. It was something we've never done before." A staff member at a newly emerging community school stated, "I think our partners do really hard work just because they know it's important, without knowing the bigger 'why' behind it. But I do believe it's time for them to start knowing the bigger 'why.'" At community schools, an inclusive visioning process can be particularly important in setting the groundwork for reorganizing resources—especially partner resources—to support school priorities.

- *Aligning resources to school goals.* Developing a shared understanding of the purpose and nature of the work allows staff across the school to align practices and resources.[20] As OUSD community schools aim to develop a clear vision, priorities, and goals, staff members work to align partner and community resources in support of these goals, which range from academic to culture or climate. For example, one school worked with a literacy partner to provide targeted intervention for students to help meet that year's goal of improving reading scores, including collaborating on additional fund-raising to ensure sufficient resources. Another school leveraged its family resource center staff to help meet its attendance goal of reducing chronic absence by 10 percent: through establishing an attendance team that included core partner staff, engaging with families, and diligently reviewing the district-provided data, grade by grade, week after week, and providing targeted interventions, the school decreased its chronic absence rate. The CSM often played a critical role in these efforts, facilitating shared meetings, communicating with school staff and partners, building relationships, and helping adults at the school see their part in the big picture.

- *Assessing partnerships in terms of alignment with school goals.* Assessing partnerships in terms of their alignment with and contribution to school goals sets an expectation that the partner's role is to contribute to the core goals of the school, rather than to simply provide stand-alone services. For example, one principal described working closely with a new partnership to "figure out how it aligns to our school values, what they're going to be able to put into place." Another principal explained assessing prospective partnerships: "We made it really clear what our objectives were, like our schoolwide site plan. Our three big rocks are literacy, safe and secure school climate, and teacher effectiveness. If you're not partnering with us on these three, then this is not going to work." Principals and CSMs use a quality partnerships rubric developed by the district for setting expectations with partners and engaging in ongoing dialogue to reflect on the partnership. For example, one CSM mentioned sitting down with partners to ask, "Where do you think you are? Where do I or the school think you are? And where do we want to be?" Ongoing dialogue and data-driven assessment help ensure that partner resources are being best harnessed to remove barriers to learning and expand or enhance learning time. In some cases, schools let go of partnerships that did not seem to be supporting school goals. However, most differences were resolved through productive communication about priorities, shared goals, and expectations.

Even the best-intentioned school reforms often fall short when they fail to recognize that policies are carried out by real people in real places.[21] To facilitate community school implementation that makes a difference for students, the school must do more than simply adopt new programs and policies. It must also make intentional efforts to shift organizational culture and practice. The strategies described above outline key strategies that OUSD community schools are utilizing to help reduce barriers to learning. These strategies are also helping to realign school-community resources to expand and enhance student learning.

Although community schools in Oakland report meaningful changes for students, teachers, and the school community, this complex initiative has faced persistent challenges. Collaboration across stakeholders from diverse institutional backgrounds requires relationships and trust that often take time to build, especially if time is needed to repair prior relationships of distrust. This process may be slowed by frequent turnover in school leadership, which is not uncommon in urban school districts. Further, OUSD as a district is implementing a multitude of initiatives aimed at improving student achievement, presenting a challenge of competing organizational priorities at both district and school levels. District community school staff have aimed to portray community schools not as a program in competition with other initiatives, but rather as complementary framework for serving the whole child that is consistent with other district efforts to, for example, promote social emotional learning, increase family engagement, or better serve English language learners. School site staff have received support from the district in financing the community schools' work—especially the CSM role. However, as schools are asked to increasingly contribute funds from their own budgets, the sustainability of the work will require a continued belief in its effectiveness as a strategy for promoting learning.

CONCLUSION

Across the country, decades of reform have not adequately addressed the opportunity and achievement gap for the nation's poorest and most vulnerable students. Education reform efforts are often short-lived and one often cedes to the next.[22] Lessons from research in the field show that efforts at school improvement often fail due to poor implementation, policy fragmentation and incoherence, and/or lack of broader, systemic approaches.[23] In Oakland, the full-service community schools initiative is still early in its trajectory. Today, four years since the initiative's inception, the district has sustained its commitment to community schools through multiple changes in leadership, as well as expanded the number of schools to include nearly a third of all schools in the district. While more empirical evidence is needed, promising reports from OUSD school and partner staff suggest that community schools are bolstering student readiness to learn, increasing the quantity and quality of time learning, and improving the instructional environment.

Educators know that meaningful reform must consist of more than simply piecemeal additions to existing practice in order to make a difference in the classroom and in students' lives.[24] Community schools offer a comprehensive framework for school transformation that presents a compelling model for redressing systemic inequalities by incorporating new stakeholders, expanding services and supports to students and their families, and developing key organizational capacities for integrating and aligning those services with the school's instructional goals. Together, these efforts reduce barriers to student learning, and expand and enhance the time available for students to learn. The community school initiative presented in this chapter offers an opportunity to learn about the development of an equity-focused district reform strategy that expands more and better learning time as it evolves and matures.

CHAPTER 4

PROMISE NEIGHBORHOODS

*Expanding Opportunities to Learn and Succeed
from Cradle Through Career*

MICHAEL MCAFEE AND JESSICA PIZAREK

INTRODUCTION

A fifteen-minute drive northwest of downtown Minneapolis will take you past old stone churches, quaint Craftsman-style homes, schools of all sizes, and lawns green in the late summer light. Along the way, colorful signs pop up outside homes celebrating the college graduation dates of the North Minneapolis scholars who reside there. But they are not proclaiming the impending commencement of college students; most of these dates are more than a decade away. That is because, in North Minneapolis, every child is a scholar, and every scholar will graduate from college. A quick jaunt down a business corridor delivers you to the doors of the Northside Achievement Zone (NAZ). A high school and expanded learning center are down the block; the community's prized theater sits next door; a locally run radio station shares upstairs office space. Residents—many of whom are also staff—chat outside as the local bus drops off and picks up new passengers. Inside, phones hum as the same staff—first and foremost, proud North Minneapolis residents— check in and connect with their family teams and scholars. As described by its residents, North Minneapolis residents are strong, connected, committed to, and concerned for each other. The North Minneapolis community is a family.

Two thousand miles away, residents of Chula Vista, California, chat and grab an early-morning cup of coffee as they find seats in the auditorium of Castle Park Middle School. They have gathered for a Resident Leadership Academy meeting, during which they celebrate peers who have dedicated significant hours of service to the Promise Neighborhood and caucus with their mayor about upcoming community initiatives and ballot measures. They are a proud and commanding group, actively supporting and celebrating one another. These parents, grandparents, and neighbors are connected. They are unified to ensure that their students and their community are seen, and that their voices are heard and incorporated into the systemic decisions that are shaping their city and schools. Their demeanor emits *familia*—not just a feeling, but an act of family. Chula Vista sits just seven miles from the US–Mexico border, and for many residents, a shared past experience of having been excluded from access to education lingers. Like North Minneapolis, Chula Vista is a community marked by social and racial stigma as well as systemic underinvestment, pitting residents in a fight against inequitable schools, food deserts, and an alarmingly prohibitive housing market. These challenges do not phase them, though. Outside the walls of this auditorium, the same buy-in is occurring in schools, homes, and offices across the neighborhood. Residents own the community's educational future and are fighting to ensure that every student receives the educational opportunities needed to succeed.

The Northside Achievement Zone (NAZ) and Chula Vista Promise (CVP) are building an integrated set of interventions that address the most pressing needs of families and scholars living in their zones. NAZ and CVP formally launched after receiving Promise Neighborhood funding from the federal government, but the communities' commitment to improving life outcomes for children and families is not new. As in many underinvested neighborhoods, North Minneapolis and Chula Vista residents continue to experience the disparate effects of historically racist and elitist policy making that has shaped how infrastructure, public education, and economic development have inequitably developed in their communities. Despite these disparities, and a history marked by implicit and explicit racism, North Minneapolis and Chula Vista are thriving epicenters of change. Each Promise Neighborhood is catalyzing the local energy of its community and a rich network of partners to reverse the egregious disparities experienced by its students, fundamentally reshaping the ecosystems in which they live. This means that simply "doing good work" is no longer acceptable. Every child is not just a student; she is a scholar who will go to college. Parents are not passive observers of their children's education; they are the utmost authority on their scholars' progress and success. Consequently, Promise Neighborhood staff and providers act with families and scholars as teammates on equal footing with the same goals for each student and the tenacity to see each student achieve those goals. NAZ and CVP expanded learning time interventions are designed to recognize that learning does not just take place within school-based and out-of-school programming, but in family homes and in all social settings of the neighborhood. Improving local schools and educational opportunities is an invitation for all community members to rebuild equity into their communities. North Minneapolis and Chula Vista residents believe that change is possible, but only through hard work.

Promise Neighborhoods seek to reverse the cycle of generational poverty by improving the educational and developmental outcomes of children from cradle to career. In this chapter, we illustrate how local leaders in two communities are working with families and multisector stakeholders to build comprehensive and integrated systems of support for children and their families. Promise Neighborhoods in Chula Vista, California, and Minneapolis, Minnesota, are forging sustainable partnerships to implement student-centered expanded learning time opportunities that improve learning outcomes during school hours and beyond. The Promise Neighborhoods Institute at PolicyLink (PNI) is supporting leaders in both communities to use a disciplined approach for moving from talk to action and holding themselves accountable for achieving shared goals. The individual elements of expanded learning time initiatives will vary from place to place, but our experience with these and other Promise Neighborhood sites has convinced us that the implementation process of continuous organizational learning, improvement, and mutual accountability employed in Chula Vista and Minneapolis is replicable. It can advance the quality, effectiveness, and scale of programs aimed at addressing social and economic inequalities at the neighborhood level across the United States.

During a rally in 2008, then-Senator Barack Obama promised children and families across the country that, if elected president of the United States, he would strengthen learning opportunities for every child, regardless of race, class, or zip code. That US senator won the faith of the American people and, as president, secured bipartisan congressional approval to implement a suite of place-based initiatives to build opportunity into all communities so that all children can thrive, from cradle to career. Among these federal initiatives is the Promise Neighborhoods movement—a strategy for addressing persistent inequities by building wraparound systems of academic, health, and social supports for students and their families, with strong schools at the center. Across the country, Promise Neighborhood leaders are strengthening educational systems that have failed generations of children and youth—primarily low-income students and students of color—by using a results-driven framework to support organizational learning within youth-serving institutions. Part of this strategy includes expanding learning opportunities for target populations at every age, inside and outside the classroom. Within each Promise Neighborhood, expanded learning opportunities include, but are not limited to before-school, afterschool, summer learning, and extended day/expanded learning time programs.[1] Promise Neighborhoods also support parents and other family members, as well as improve the overall quality of life within the neighborhood. By doing so, Promise Neighborhood partners are collectively improving their organizational effectiveness and reimagining access to more and better learning time as a means for achieving more equitable educational outcomes.

PROMISE NEIGHBORHOODS: A PLACE-BASED APPROACH TO ACHIEVING EDUCATIONAL EQUITY IN COMMUNITIES OF OPPORTUNITY

Inspired by the Harlem Children's Zone, the US Department of Education's Promise Neighborhoods program is designed to provide children who live within a defined geograpic footprint or neighborhood with a seamless pipeline of supports and wraparound services from birth through college and career. Every Promise Neighborhood commits to using a common results framework (see table 4.1) organized around ten goals and fifteen corresponding indicators associated with positive developmental outcomes for students and their families. This results framework acts as a beacon, providing Promise Neighborhood leaders with a clear way of measuring outcomes; a means for aligning partners and solutions; and a common language for communicating progress with families, residents, partners, funders, other Promise Neighborhood leaders, and the general public.[2]

Within this framework, leaders are encouraged to expand opportunities to learn and increase learning time for their students as one positive way to achieve results. As outlined in the federal notice for Promise Neighborhoods, this means "using a longer school day, week, or year to significantly increase the total number of school hours" during which a child learns. Promise Neighborhood leaders, school officials, and partners are encouraged to consider various strategies targeting (1) instruction in core academic subjects; (2) instruction in other subjects and enrichment activities that contribute

TABLE 4.1   Education Indicators and Results They Are Intended to Measure

Results	Indicators
Children enter kindergarten ready to succeed in school.	• # and % of children from birth to kindergarten entry who have a place where they usually go, other than an emergency room, when they are sick or in need of advice about their health. • # and % of three-year-olds and children in kindergarten who demonstrate at the beginning of the program or school year, age-appropriate functioning across multiple domains of early learning as determined using developmentally appropriate early learning measures (as defined in the Federal notice). • # and % of children, from birth to kindergarten entry, participating in center-based or formal home-based early learning settings or programs, which may include Early Head Start, Head Start, child care, or preschool.
Students are proficient in core academic subjects.	• # and % of students at or above grade level according to State mathematics and reading or language arts assessments in at least the grades required by the ESEA (3rd through 8th and once in high school).
Students successfully transition from middle school grades to high school.	• Attendance rate of students in 6th, 7th, 8th, and 9th grade.
Youth graduate from high school.	• Graduation rate (as defined in the Federal notice).
High school graduates obtain a postsecondary degree, certification, or credential.	• # and % of Promise Neighborhood students who graduate with a regular high school diploma, as defined in 34 CFR 200.19(b)(1)(iv), and obtain postsecondary degrees, vocational certificates, or other industry- recognized certifications or credentials without the need for remediation.
Students are healthy.	• # and % of children who participate in at least 60 minutes of moderate to vigorous physical activity daily; • # and % of children who consume five or more servings of fruits and vegetables daily; or • Possible third indicator, to be determined (TBD) by applicant.

continues

TABLE 4.1 *Continued*

Results	Indicators
Students feel safe at school and in their community.	• # and % of students who feel safe at school and traveling to and from school, as measured by a school climate needs assessment (as defined in the Federal notice); or • Possible second indicator, TBD by applicant.
Students live in stable communities.	• Attendance rate of students in 6th, 7th, 8th, and 9th grade.
Families and community members support learning in Promise Neighborhood schools.	• Student mobility rate (as defined in the Federal notice); or Students live in stable communities. • Possible second indicator, TBD by applicant. • For children birth to kindergarten entry, the # and % of parents or family members who report that they read to their child three or more times a week; • For children in the kindergarten through eighth grades, the # and % of parents or family members who report encouraging their child to read books outside of school; and • For children in the ninth through twelfth grades, the # and % of parents or family members who report talking with their child about the importance of college and career; or • Possible fourth indicator TBD by applicant.
Students have access to 21st century learning tools.	• # and % of students who have school and home access (and % of the day they have access) to broadband internet (as defined in the Federal notice) and a connected computing device; or Students have access to 21st century learning tools. • Possible second indicator TBD by applicant.

Source: Promise Neighborhood Initiative, US Department of Education, http://promiseneighborhoods
.ed.gov/content/results-framework.

to a well-rounded education (e.g., physical education, service learning, and experiential work-based learning opportunities); and (3) teacher collaboration, planning, and engagement in professional development within and across grades and subjects.[3] Using the result-based framework, PNI and other technical assistance providers support local leaders to employ a mix of systems-change approaches to fundamentally improve the ways in which children learn. These approaches, such as evidence-based programming, family engagement strategies, and policy advocacy, have led to early successes beyond those in North Minneapolis and Chula Vista:

- Since 2012, the kindergarten readiness scores in the Berea Promise Neighborhood in Kentucky (including Clay, Jackson, and Owsley counties) have increased from 16 percent to 42 percent.
- In San Antonio, Texas, absenteeism in the Eastside Promise Neighborhood has decreased by 15 percent among sixth graders as well as 16 percent among seventh and eighth graders.
- Academic Performance Index (API) scores of the eighteen Los Angeles Promise Neighborhood target schools increased an average of eighteen points from the 2011–2012 to the 2012–2013 school year, with eight schools increasing by more than thirty points. During the same period, the overall statewide average API decreased by two points.

The PNI Approach: Implementation That Supports Effective Expanded Learning Time Opportunities at Scale

Although the community-change field has made significant progress in improving holistic outcomes for individual groups of students at discrete ages, we have yet to create lasting, widespread, equitable change for whole populations of students and families.[4] Rebuilding school and community systems so that they set all students on a course for lifetime success is the goal of Promise Neighborhoods—a vision that has required intentional, explicit focus on building the right systems to create pathways to opportunity. Community and school leaders in Promise Neighborhoods are gaining important insights into how to balance long-term accountability for system changes that will yield improvements for entire populations of students with their real-time commitment to the essential day-to-day work of expanding learning time and opportunities in schools. As they build their cradle-to-career initiatives, these leaders are demonstrating replicable strategies for achieving population-level outcomes from the entry point of a program (in this case, Promise Neighborhoods) by steadily moving from scope, to scale, to sustainability:

1. *Scope.* Can you articulate and build out a comprehensive and integrated cradle-to-career system?
2. *Scale.* Can you begin to move beyond small-scale responses to building the necessary infrastructure to meet at least 60 percent of the need among your students?
3. *Sustainability.* Can you sustain this infrastructure over time by developing new leadership behaviors, improving collaboration, restructuring existing capital, and attracting new investment?

Based upon the experience of the Harlem Children's Zone, it could take a minimum of twenty years for an effective pipeline to be built within a community. In order to help leaders move from scope to scale to sustainability and achieve population-level results, PNI uses a coaching system focused on providing technical assistance that ensures acceleration, builds evidence, and supports partners in reaching scope and scale.

Acceleration. Acceleration focuses on a system of support that enables partners, schools, and teachers to achieve results for their students faster than they otherwise could on their own. Building an infrastructure to support the required system changes can be a massive organizational burden for local leaders, potentially distracting them from their main goal: scaling up a full array of programs and services to meet the needs of as many children and families as possible. To help ease this pain, PNI designed a replicable system of foundational supports to help local leaders get their programs up and running. As described below, these supports focus on the collection of data that can ensure continual improvement, and emphasize a mix of solutions and strategies.

- *Results-based accountability (RBA).* PNI works with local leaders to implement the RBA management tool to build a foundational infrastructure for the results-driven culture they seek in their partnerships. Case management data, constructed by linking participation and service delivery records from each collaborating partner, are routinely analyzed to evaluate the effectiveness of existing programs. This shared system enables leaders to determine the greatest areas of need, service gaps, and opportunities to address them. As Promise Neighborhood initiatives grow, leaders, stakeholders, families, and students engage in continuous communication and analysis of progress toward shared goals. They use case management data to understand the answers to these essential questions: *How much are we doing? How well are we doing it? Is anyone better off?* As part of these conversations, strategies are revisited and adjustments are made.
- *Data infrastructure.* Student performance data, disaggregated by race, ethnicity, and English learner status, are a critical tool for facilitating the implementation and results accountability process.[5] PNI helps leaders build longitudinal case management systems and analytic data

dashboards that allow them to track how coordinated services have an impact on student outcomes throughout their geographic footprint. Using this case management data, for example, local leaders can better understand if and how expanded learning time interventions are improving community well-being.

- *Skills to Accelerate Results (STAR)*. In partnership with the Annie E. Casey Foundation, STAR was designed to help community leaders understand how to put RBA into action as they build their data infrastructure and solution plans. The program provides space, time, resources, and direct coaching for local leaders to develop the competencies that will enable them to implement these tools.

- *The right mix of solutions*. While it is important that Promise Neighborhood leaders capitalize on the existing strengths of community partners, the cradle-to-career wraparound supports they pursue must include families in defining problems and solutions. In addition, the partners must address needed change in public policies and systems that will support or hinder progress. A portfolio of disparate programs will not create dynamic change. To save communities time and resources, PNI makes this mix of strategies readily available by regularly providing Promise Neighborhood leaders with evidence-based solutions and successful examples from the cradle-to-career field.

Evidence. Building evidence that illustrates how better coordinated efforts and a cradle-to-career approach can achieve population-level change is another core area of technical assistance. The Promise Neighborhoods initiative has been conceived and implemented to establish proof points across the nation that can support the approach. To this end, PNI has been chronicling the quantitative and qualitative success of Promise Neighborhoods' cradle-to-career systems through rigorous case studies, data dashboards, and case management systems—all of which are telling a powerful, emerging results story.

Scale and sustainability. Scale and sustainability are achieved by providing consistent coaching to help local leaders identify and correct failing leadership behaviors, find new avenues for collaboration, realign existing resources and capital, attract new public and private investment through advocacy and fund-raising, and ensure that policies and systems result in improved outcomes for children and their families. This work ensures that leaders are crafting solutions commensurate with the scale of the problem and is sustained from cradle through career.

EPICENTERS OF CHANGE

Northside Achievement Zone (NAZ): Reimagining the Cradle-to-Career Ecosystem

In North Minneapolis, an evolving results-based culture is yielding improved outcomes for children and families who participate in expanded learning time programs. But it didn't happen overnight. Although the North Minneapolis community had been pursuing equity for children and families for decades, too many scholars were still struggling when NAZ received Promise Neighborhood implementation funding in 2011. Students needed supports inside and outside the traditional school day. Despite collaboration with more than fifty organizations and schools, only 54 percent of students were graduating from the local high school. In a representative study of the neighborhood, NAZ found that of all third- and eighth-grade students living in the zone, 76 percent and 72 percent, respectively, were performing below grade-level proficiency in mathematics and language arts. Forty-five percent of parents surveyed had a school-aged child who did not have afterschool supports. Two-thirds of scholars were not connected to a mentoring program, although the majority of parents expressed that they wanted their child to have that opportunity. NAZ scholars needed more than just programs; they needed a supportive ecosystem.

Reimagining systems to meet the holistic needs of children and their families was no easy task. It required reimagining and taking on the systems that had disregarded North Minneapolis students in the first place. The ecosystem had to be rebuilt as one that honored the student as scholar and the family as experts on their own strengths and needs, and aligned services and providers accordingly. Anyone involved in NAZ, therefore, had to be invested in the scholar and in his or her family. In North Minneapolis, this meant that a scholar and supporting adults became a team that included parents, teachers, school administrators, in- and out-of-school providers, and mentors. Participating organizations needed to reorganize themselves around the scholar, around the result they were pursuing for that scholar, and around the ways they were going to pursue that quality of life together. They were embracing RBA as a working framework.

The community accomplished this, using the results it desired for its scholars as a North Star. After collectively studying student academic needs, NAZ created a suite of afterschool and summer expanded learning programs offered by seven different partners. These strategies, known as ExL, emphasized skills building in reading and academics, scholar engagement (e.g., study skills, time management, goal setting, connection to community, etc.), and integration with family supports offered throughout NAZ's system.

Partners engaged in the implementation of expanded learning must work together, share best practices and strategies with one another (based upon their outcome data), regularly review outcome data, and actively seek resources and partnerships to fully ensure accelerated outcomes for scholars. This focus and intentionality is paying off in major ways. Fifty-five percent of elementary grade students in expanded learning programs are achieving at least one year of growth in reading during four months of participation in afterschool programming during the summer.

With a sixty-two-year legacy of supporting the neighborhood, the Plymouth Christian Youth Center has become an integral partner in the expansion of learning time and opportunities for scholars living in the zone. When NAZ was created, PCYC recognized the initiative's collaborative model as an opportunity to further its own mission of serving scholars, guided by the same vision of dramatically improving well-being. With that mission, PCYC has become a collaborative partner in developing the suite of supplemental academic and socio-emotional services to students throughout the NAZ footprint.

In addition, PCYC has relinquished its autonomy in recruitment and enrollment in order to align with the NAZ case management system. NAZ family coaches have become the first point of contact for students enrolling in PCYC. This ensures that every student and his or her family are coordinated with every source of support they might benefit from. For PCYC, this partnership has been a huge asset, but also a great challenge: trying to serve the same kids through two different organizational lenses can be difficult for staff, especially when they are so personally invested in each scholar's life. Each staffer's investment in the common goals for each child, however, offers saving grace and reunification. Participants say that this has led to a sense of unity within the initiative; PCYC staff members are NAZ staff, and vice versa. In the words of a PCYC leader, the beauty of it all looks like this: a scholar who is struggling to reach benchmarks in reading, math, or another area preventing his or her learning comes into the program. With that, his or her family signs on to having PCYC become a big part of their lives. Importantly, PCYC's programs are not childcare. They are set up to support scholars to meet academic, social, and emotional goals with the understanding that there will be multiple staff, coaches, and teachers interacting with each family and scholar to navigate the entire pipeline.

This progress cannot be achieved without data collection and disaggregation. Every Promise Neighborhood uses a common case management system is designed so that the outcomes of scholars who participate in multiple services can be tracked against the result areas and indicators of the initiative. Partners are expected to contribute their data to this system and participate in regular assessment about how their services are contributing to student outcomes. Using the common case management system, school staff and Promise Neighborhood partners and staff can gain greater common appreciation for the lived experience of a child across the ecosystem. Through data analysis, mentors increase their understanding of how to create a better learning environment for each scholar. It allows a family coach to look at partner input on how a scholar is progressing inside and outside the classroom. That person can then diagnose what works and what doesn't work for that child.

The data system is complex, but necessary. It becomes even more complex when partners already using individual data systems are incorporated into the main system. But when the data are complete, they enable partners to change the way a scholar experiences school. According to the chief operating officer at NAZ, when staff, partners, families, students—whoever makes up a student's team—hit a brick wall, they "all come together and have a team meeting and determine what strategies are working collectively, what strategies are not having impact or great enough impact, and how every member of the scholar's team can better align."

Data stop shaming and blaming within these conversations. All partners are rooting for the success of the family and student in different ways, but when everyone's contributions come together through the common case management system, it creates a space for greater alignment. Data facilitate tough conversations, and partners stay at the table. As one NAZ staffer described it, "NAZ Connect [NAZ's data system] helps people stick to the facts about what's going wrong, what the situation is, and how to move forward." RBA provides avenues through which service providers, families, and partners can understand how best to plug in and contribute their expanded learning services in the most effective combinations and dosages. Their expertise in delivering high-quality learning opportunities is honored and effectively aligned with the contributions of their peers.

Orienting community change around a new framework, approach, or tool is a balancing act, especially when honoring the wisdom already present within a community. This approach requires Promise Neighborhoods and expanded learning partners to embrace individual organizational change as they coalesce into a mutually accountable and aligned collaborative. Staff in each community will attest to the difficulty of this transition. This level of synchronization simultaneously demands patience and diligence, as well as robust trust. When these human behaviors falter, however, staff and partners regularly come back to the central concerns: *How much are we doing? How well are we doing it? Is anyone better off because of what we're doing and how we're doing it?*

As the commitment, language, and application of a results-based frame seeps throughout a Promise Neighborhood's partners and the wider community, the process crystalizes. In North Minneapolis, the first step in achieving this was to help all partners understand the framework, followed by practice and coaching from PNI and its partners to engage all stakeholders in a disciplined shift in organizational culture. This shift was achieved as NAZ adopted bits and pieces of the framework that resonated most with what was already working in each community. As one NAZ partner stated, "Frameworks should be used in service of, not in place of, community expertise." Leaders must grasp the concepts of a results-based approach and then adapt it to their community needs. In Promise Neighborhoods, frameworks are tools; they are systemic catalysts that sharpen and quicken effective practices for improving learning as identified by the people who know their community best. Through a results-based lens, everyone involved is trying to serve the same scholars with the same goals but through unique, additive contributions.

Chula Vista Promise (CVP): Influencing Systems Change in Schools

When CVP applied for Promise Neighborhood implementation funding in 2012, all five schools in its footprint were in Program Improvement status under federal regulations of the No Child Left Behind Act for failing to meet Adequate Yearly Progress standards for three years or more. Neighborhood schools were under-resourced and struggling to fully meet the needs of their students, a situation all too common in districts serving predominantly low-income students and students of color. CVP began tracking how high school students in the neighborhood were accessing postsecondary opportunities after graduating from high school. They found that fewer than 63 percent of students were enrolling in either a two-year or four-year college or university. An initial survey of the neighborhood had led CVP leadership to believe that the majority of parents were talking to their students about the importance of enrolling and completing college. When staff members explored this further, however, they found that parents, while supportive of higher education for their children, were nonetheless concerned about the cost of applying to and enrolling in college, lacked familiarity with the application process, and feared separation from their children.

Community leaders often know what they want for their students and families, but may not know how to move from vision, to planning, to implementation with successful results. CVP knew that it wanted to provide rich, supportive learning environments so that all students could be college-bound and job-ready. To craft the right mix of solutions to meet their needs, CVP used data to identify those students who would benefit most from interventions. To help students successfully transition out of high school, CVP took the mystery out of preparing for, applying to, and enrolling in college. This effort even extended to readying them to graduate from college and to join the workforce.

As CVP planned to embed supports inside and outside of classrooms, it looked for service delivery gaps that it could strategically fill with complementary supports and resources. Every student has an academic advocate—a CVP staff member who works closely with school staff, administrators, and counselors, utilizing case management data to ensure that students are reaching academic goals, remaining on track to graduate from high school, and planning for college. CVP's academic advocate program continues into college. It promotes college persistence and completion by checking in regularly with students and connecting them with resources on campus. This work is supported by *promotoras*—residents of the Castle Park community who provide intensive outreach to families around CVP's larger pipeline of solutions. *Promotoras* ensure that a student and his or her family are connected to any health, housing, or financial supports that might be critical to ensuring that students enroll and succeed in college. Together, advocates and *promotoras* assist students and their families in navigating high school graduation requirements, entrance examinations, college applications, and financial aid.

Partner organizations like Manpower offer additional programs to help students prepare for the workforce and self-sufficiency by placing students in virtual scenarios. Scenarios force students to navigate the potential stressors of adult life inside and outside college, including securing a job, budgeting and paying bills, and securing housing. Current Hilltop High School senior Gustavo Aguayo took Manpower's Career Academy course as a junior. Gustavo's main interests were in IT and architecture. At the completion of the three-week course, Manpower and CVP staff were able to connect him with two architects in the Eastlake area, where he was able to complete a forty-hour paid internship. Well versed in several programs this firm used, Gustavo was able to work on real projects for its customers. Juan Quemada, the lead architect, said, "We are very happy with him and his work ethic." In response, Gustavo reportedly said, "The course I completed with Manpower through CV Promise really prepared me to know what to expect in the real world of work."

Building this system required CVP to internally examine how it operates as a lead agency for the Promise Neighborhood initiative. The RBA framework, along with an understanding of how to put the framework into action through the STAR program, provided the time and resources to help staff think strategically about aligning their efforts with the results framework. Having difficult conversations about which efforts were working and which weren't allowed CVP to gain clarity and better alignment by weeding out the activities that were not effective and were detracting resources from solutions that demonstrably worked better for students. The investment in becoming more systematic internally as an organization has had huge payoffs. Staff members feel that they aren't spinning their wheels and are effectively contributing to students learning. The data support this. In a conversation about the evolution of CVP, staff people joked that they had probably gone through twenty iterations of RBA and their case management system, and each time they learned more about what was and wasn't working. RBA helped them to get organized.

CVP began to adopt results-driven behaviors, such as the systematic use of data to inform action, which changed the ways in which it operated internally as an organization. As well, a culture shift began to occur in the way it partnered with families and the school district. It saw the potential of schools as spaces for engagement and aligned contributions to improve educational opportunities and outcomes. This approach had the potential to permanently change the way that students and families experienced and contributed to the education system in their community.

But implementing a plan with a partner is not always a clear-cut process. Entering into schools can be especially sensitive and territorial, creating angst. To achieve a culture of mutual accountability for goals, new, more connective, and sometimes more formal infrastructure needs to be built with local schools. All partners, the school district included, have to commit to the common results and share responsibility for the outcomes that align to their work. In the case of CVP, formal data-sharing agreements were created to give CVP staff access to critical information on how students were doing academically. This involved gaining legal Family and Educational Rights and Privacy Act clearance for CVP to receive these data and building the infrastructure for the district to actually share data with CVP's case management system. These arrangements were a result of a lengthy process of negotiation and trial-and-error implementation to achieve the needed reallocation of budget, staff time, and resources among all the CVP, district, and school-level partners. But their commitment to shared goals has helped these partners persist and prevail.

The Promise Neighborhoods approach provided the *how* for developing the mutual commitment to results, continuous communication, and adaptive leadership necessary to achieve the larger CVP vision. Being intentional and focused on *How much? How well? Is anyone better off?* meant that the work was different. This then meant that communication had to be different, too. CVP's implementation of classroom tutoring support provides one important example. CVP staff people had to adjust how they worked with schools and school staff in real time, recognizing that teachers were already so taxed by the immediate needs of their students that their ability to teach effectively was often strained. With adaptive leadership tools from PNI and STAR, CVP realized that the teaching and tutoring roles needed to be clarified—CVP staff are meant to be complementary to school staff, filling important programming gaps that many schools cannot afford to fill on their own. This requires clear, continuous communication to ensure that contributions are aligned, not threatening.

As CVP continues to move from scope, to scale, to sustainability, it is adapting the Promise Neighborhood framework to achieve lasting systems change within the local school system so that every child is served, regardless of whether or not she or he lives within the bounds of the Promise Neighborhood footprint. Analicia McKee oversees postsecondary supports for CVP and is an academic advocate herself, working with a cohort of fifty high school students in the zone. In 2015, McKee and her colleagues saw a need for expanding benefits of college-going counseling among students in CVP schools. McKee wanted to pursue a solution that could be scaled and offered to non-CVP students in order to expand the college-going culture. Guided by this vision, she worked with a cohort of students to found Club U, a student-run effort in which student leaders offer their peers opportunities to learn more about preparing for, applying, and transitioning to college. During a retreat at UCLA, student leaders received leadership training, and learned more about the history of educational barriers for Latinos. This opportunity helped them to recognize how far they and their peers have come and confirmed the need to continue addressing barriers that keep their peers from succeeding. "We're trying to change a community," McKee explained.

In partnership with her students, McKee is doing her part to ensure that CVP's future constituents are prepared to continue rethinking educational equity in their neighborhood. Through this hard work, CVP and its schools are aligned. CVP staff and partners are on campus at every school and in many classrooms. In addition, the ripple effect of CVP's influence is benefiting students who do not live within the Promise Neighborhood footprint but attend CVP schools. Since 2012, the four-year high school graduation rate for both high schools in the CVP footprint has improved to 99.6 percent.

CONCLUSION

Educational inequities in our nation are daunting, and our history of tackling those disparities can be uninspiring. Low-income children and children of color, especially, do not have the basic tools to succeed: effective opportunities to learn and sufficient time to do it. We do ourselves a disservice when we are tempted to believe that any single theory, approach, or tool will solve systemic challenges, or that any one thing can be effective in all communities across the country. We know from decades of evolving work that holding an expectation that a single solution can tackle the enormity of the challenges we face is laughable, and even irresponsible. To achieve equity in all schools, the education system itself will have to change. To truly understand how we will build equity back into public education, we have to be comfortable with the complicated nuances of systemic inequity that affect students.[6]

The Promise Neighborhoods approach on its own will not achieve educational equity. However, Promise Neighborhoods as a strategy is a significant pathway to it. In Chula Vista and North Minneapolis, local leaders are fostering a culture of results and creating the infrastructure to support that vision. Each community is building a cradle-to-career pipeline that maximizes efficiency and effectiveness (scope), is yielding improved results for at least 60 percent of its population (scale), and is creating an operational standard of leveraging diverse resources to support the continued expansion of the pipeline (sustainability). The key to moving toward substantial outcomes for our children and families lies not so heavily in the "what" but in the "how": *How much are we doing? How well are we doing it? Is anyone better off because of what we're doing and how we're doing it?*[7] What matters is that a group of multisector actors commits to a results-based culture, moves from talk to action with discipline, and uses data for learning, continuous improvement, and shared accountability. This is the experience of Promise Neighborhoods communities attempting to expand the realms of learning and opportunity for their scholars and families, both inside and outside school.

CHAPTER 5

LINKED LEARNING

Making the Best of Time for All Students

GARY HOACHLANDER, TAMEKA MCGLAWN, AND BRAD STAM

A DETROIT SCHOOL STORY

The Benjamin Carson High School of Science and Medicine was founded in 2011 on the campus of the Detroit Medical Center with the mission of helping all students graduate, attend college, and prepare to enter the science and health professions. "We wanted them to be able to touch and feel science and medicine differently than if they were enrolled in a school down the street," says founding principal Brenda Belcher, who is now the high school network lead for the Detroit Public Schools.

What was needed at Ben Carson was a curriculum and a program of study that would help students connect their learning to the real world and a professional pathway. Linked Learning provided a framework for realizing that goal. With Linked Learning, teachers at Ben Carson were able to craft a more coherent offering of academic and technical courses. They introduced real-world multidisciplinary projects, strengthened connections between the classroom and the workplace, and attended to the student supports that helped create a caring school culture more focused on what each student needs to achieve success in further education and career. Linked Learning expanded the modes, contexts, environments, and the *time* needed for all students at Ben Carson to learn.

Today at Ben Carson, one class period each term is dedicated to the technical courses in the health and science career pathway—health careers, anatomy and physiology, and microbiology. Soon, all students will graduate with a skills certificate in pharmacy, phlebotomy, nursing, or another medical area. The school's location on the medical campus makes it easy for students to do internships and experience what medicine is like day to day, watching open-heart surgery, shadowing doctors, or spending time in the emergency room. Each year, the teachers produce a curriculum that integrates a community-based, health-related project into every academic class. For example, ninth graders are working with the Detroit Food Policy Council, and tenth graders are investigating high-risk teen behaviors with a local teen center.

Students, who wear green scrubs to class, are enthusiastic about the projects. Asia Nixon and Tayebah Chowdhury, tenth graders, both want to become pediatricians. Christoph Brown is interested in genetic research, and Hafizur Rahman hopes to become a psychiatrist. Last year, their challenge was to create a marketing campaign for a healthy beverage for the youth of Detroit. Students presented their marketing plans to Dr. Reginald Eadie, head of Detroit's school board and three hospitals, who chose the most effective presentation.

Hafizur said he liked doing the project because it had a real impact on other people. "I felt I was doing something for others instead of myself for once," he explained. His group, which advocated drinking green tea instead of soda, created social media content and a video comparing the side effects of drinking soda and artificial juices with green tea. In Tayebah's group, students did a science experiment demonstrating how much sugar is in soda if you boil away the water. Christophe liked the way he learned things in every class that would contribute to the project: "In history we learned histories of health and what to eat and drink, in math we looked at data and results and took surveys, and in science we did sampling sizes that helped us with the surveys."

Math teacher Michelle Schwendemann says the students are much more involved in their work with project-based learning than with quizzes and worksheets: "When we apply learning to real-life situations, the students see the significance and why they need to know it, so their engagement increases tremendously—and so do their test scores." Typically, each year, schools look for a one- to two-point growth in state college readiness scores; last year, Ben Carson High School had a four-point increase. More students were motivated to apply to college; while the school is open enrollment with no academic standards to apply, 92 percent went on to college, and 8 percent to the military.

One of the ways Linked Learning Detroit has supported the school is by helping to create more paid internships and learning opportunities for the students in medical settings. "The students have made great connections to people in hospitals and businesses, and had remarkable experiences," says

Belcher. "It's exciting for them to be able to watch open-heart surgery behind a glass wall. They feel they can be a pediatrician or psychologist because they've talked to the people who do it." Connecting the classroom to the real world has made all the difference in the students' interest levels and energy. "We see the light bulbs go off for kids as they realize the relevance of learning to their real lives," says the principal, Charles Todd.

This chapter examines the Linked Learning approach to high school education as an opportunity to dramatically rethink the use of time *during* and after the school day and throughout the year. As the story of Ben Carson High School demonstrates, Linked Learning allows for a more flexible, comprehensive approach to education that encourages new behaviors of learning and teaching. It also demonstrates how more and better use of time can support those behaviors. We begin by providing a description of Linked Learning, its primary objectives, and promising research on its effectiveness. But Linked Learning is a means, not an end. We turn to the student outcomes—what it means to be college- and career-ready—that Linked Learning pathways are intended to produce.

Central to accomplishing these student outcomes are major changes in learning and teaching, not just modifications in classroom instruction but also strategies for aligning and integrating the opportunities to learn outside the classroom, afterschool, and during the summer. We will explore how Linked Learning can bring greater focus and coherence to how students learn and spend their time, both inside and outside the traditional classroom. Making these changes in learning and teaching is no easy task, so next we will examine how attention to high-quality pathway design and implementation can help support and reinforce these challenging shifts in instruction and curriculum, including more attention to personalized student supports. Finally, we will conclude with a discussion of some of the major challenges and policy implications of realizing the promising potential of Linked Learning, with fidelity and at scale.

THE LINKED LEARNING APPROACH

Started in California in nine large school districts in 2008, Linked Learning embodies a fundamental redesign of the typical American high school. In this approach, the academic curriculum, career-based learning, workplace learning opportunities, and student supports are coherently linked through thematic pathways or academies. Just as important, the school-based learning experience is linked to the school's community and regional economy by providing opportunities for youth to learn in out-of-school workplace settings and by giving access to tutors, mentors, and community-based partners before, during, and beyond the school day.[1] To be sure, Linked Learning promotes proficiency in mathematics, reading, writing, history, and science. But it also emphasizes critical thinking, creativity, collaboration, and communications—qualities that are often more effectively taught through cross-disciplinary problem solving and real-world application.

In short, Linked Learning prepares young people for *both* college and career, not just one or the other. It ignites students' passions by creating meaningful learning experiences through career-oriented pathways in fields such as engineering, health care, digital media, agriculture and natural resources, the visual and performing arts, law, and more. Typically, Linked Learning students are organized into pathways or academies of three hundred to six hundred students in grades 9–12. They attend classes as grade-level cohorts, each served by an interdisciplinary team of academic and career technical education teachers. This organization allows for much greater flexibility in the use of time during the school day, and for much more direct and coherent links to afterschool and summer learning time and opportunities.

This approach makes learning more like the real world of work, responds to student interests, and helps students answer the question, *Why do I need to learn this?* When students love what they're learning, they work harder, dream bigger, and learn more.

In some respects, Linked Learning is not a new idea. A century ago, John Dewey advocated for "learning through occupations," and theme-based high schools (such as Aviation High School in New York City or DeBakey High School for Health Professions in Houston), career academies, and industry-themed small learning communities have been part of the American education landscape for some time.[2] But more often than not, these opportunities have existed in spite of the system rather than because of it. They are products of a few innovative teachers or a visionary principal, and too often when these founders disappear, their innovations do as well.

Additionally, as interest in this pathway approach has grown, the quality of design and implementation has been uneven at best. Frequently, "academies" or "pathways" are little more than names superimposed on traditional curriculum and teaching. All too often, the classrooms look the same as they always have. Teachers work individually behind closed doors. The schedule consists of six or more fragmented, disconnected classes, with bells ringing every fifty minutes. And there are few if any connections between school, afterschool, and summer activities.

Linked Learning, therefore, as a clearly defined field of practice, has four primary objectives that help distinguish it from other seemingly similar approaches. First, Linked Learning begins by focusing sharply on what students need to know and be able to do to achieve more lasting success in both college and career. What do we mean by college and career readiness? A formally adopted Graduate Profile, which describes the skills and dispositions students must possess to be ready for success in college, career, and community life, guides the design of each pathway to produce those outcomes.

Second, Linked Learning seeks to change how students learn, how teachers teach, and how schools organize and use time to support better learning and teaching. Linked Learning promotes interdisciplinary, experiential learning that emphasizes real-world application. It reorganizes time to enable curriculum integration, team teaching, and project-based learning. It brings school to work and work to school by connecting teachers and students to industry professionals who help create authentic projects, assess student work, and work side by side with students through job shadowing, mentoring, and internship experiences. And it blurs the boundaries between school, afterschool, and summer learning by better aligning and connecting what students have traditionally done in these three domains.

Third, Linked Learning seeks to be very clear and specific about what constitutes high-quality pathway design and implementation. While there are different ways to deliver Linked Learning, pathways must embody a comprehensive, multiyear program of study that integrates college-preparatory academics, challenging career and technical education, a range of work-based learning experiences, and personalized student supports.

Fourth, Linked Learning calls for *systemic* implementation throughout a school district and the community surrounding it—a strategy for engaging a wide range of stakeholders in expanding and sustaining a menu of high-quality Linked Learning pathways, accessible to any student wanting this kind of educational opportunity. Systemic implementation does not necessarily mean that every school in the district must offer pathways. Nor does it mean that pathways displace all other instructional approaches. It does mean, however, that the district is committed to making pathways accessible to any student who wants this kind of experience. It also means that pathways are engaging a majority of schools and students in ways that ensure that the approach becomes an integral, sustainable strategy and not just another program that may quickly become marginalized.

There is growing evidence that Linked Learning, when implemented with fidelity to these four objectives, produces better outcomes for students. An independent seven-year longitudinal evaluation of the California Linked Learning Initiative (involving nine large districts) found that the initiative produced important equity-related results. That is, the study presented evidence that better outcomes are achieved across critical student subgroups and that the demographics of pathway participation reflect the demography of the surrounding school, district, and community.

The research has shown that, compared with their peers, students in certified Linked Learning pathways earn more credits during their four years in high school and graduate at higher rates. This has significantly reduced time to a diploma and increased the likelihood of on-time graduation. Increased credit accrual rates also translate into reduced course retaking and remediation. Additionally, students in certified pathways report greater confidence in their life and career skills and say they are experiencing more rigorous, integrated, and relevant instruction. These perceptions reflect a greater sense of self-efficacy, which can translate into better student persistence to graduation and beyond. Evaluation data also show that students who had low achievement scores in earlier grades make significant progress in high school when they participate in Linked Learning, reducing the achievement and equity gap.[3] Most recently, the evaluation of postsecondary outcomes shows that Linked Learning has had a significant impact on the four-year college-going rates of African American students. When enrolling in postsecondary institutions, Linked Learning pathway students with low previous achievement were 6.4 percent more likely to enroll in a four-year institution, and African American students were 12.4 percent more likely to enroll in a four-year institution.[4]

These are promising findings. How do the four objectives of Linked Learning contribute to these results?

WHAT SHOULD STUDENTS KNOW AND BE ABLE TO DO TO SUCCEED IN COLLEGE AND CAREER?

Linked Learning school districts and their communities are beginning the challenging transition from traditional school- and course-based programs of study to a competency- and community-based educational system. At its core, this approach recognizes that the responsibility for educating our children is not simply that of professional teachers and educators. They are critical, of course. But in today's world, we all have a role in teaching—and that includes parents, employers, community-based organizations, postsecondary institutions, and other stakeholders in ways that are much more comprehensive and different from the ways so many of us experienced "school."

Central to achieving this paradigm shift is the development of a district or community Graduate Profile, which describes the skills and dispositions that students need for success in college, career, and community life. There is no single best formulation of a Graduate Profile; it is essential that the profile reflect community goals and aspirations. Figure 5.1 displays one approach at Long Beach Unified School District and its community stakeholders. What is distinctive about the Long Beach framework is the way in which it integrates college and career readiness. None of the five outcomes is distinctly "college readiness" versus "career readiness." Rather, each element defines an outcome that will serve students well in both further education and career. This, in turn, promotes pathway development that integrates and blends college and career readiness rather than encouraging isolated courses and activities that serve one or the other.

The Graduate Profile can provide a common vision that unites key stakeholders in a community, including business and postsecondary partners, and sets the groundwork for a more expansive and flexible environment for learning. The Graduate Profile, if effectively implemented and supported, can become a powerful strategy for focusing and aligning teaching, learning, assessment, and accountability in a district system. When there is a true equity-based commitment to ensuring that all students achieve the outcomes reflected in the Graduate Profile, district and community systems must be reorganized to support and assess students on their individual progress toward college and career readiness. Policies, structures, processes, resource investments, and time are all reorganized in support of Graduate Profile attainment. Ensuring adequate time for professional development and capacity building for teachers, counselors, and administrators becomes paramount as they work collectively, collaboratively, and intentionally to serve all students with the goal of achieving the outcomes identified in the Graduate Profile.

FIGURE 5.1   Long Beach Graduate Profile

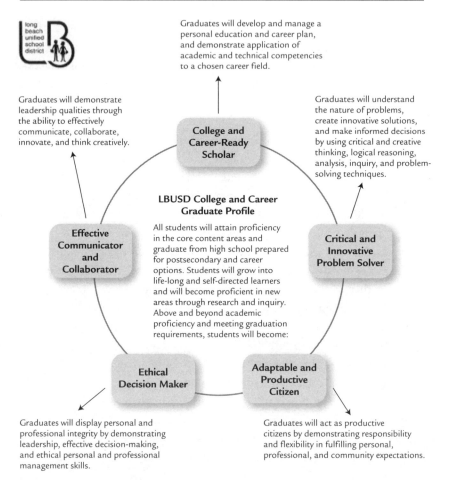

Graduates will develop and manage a personal education and career plan, and demonstrate application of academic and technical competencies to a chosen career field.

Graduates will demonstrate leadership qualities through the ability to effectively communicate, collaborate, innovate, and think creatively.

Graduates will understand the nature of problems, create innovative solutions, and make informed decisions by using critical and creative thinking, logical reasoning, analysis, inquiry, and problem-solving techniques.

College and Career-Ready Scholar

LBUSD College and Career Graduate Profile

All students will attain proficiency in the core content areas and graduate from high school prepared for postsecondary and career options. Students will grow into life-long and self-directed learners and will become proficient in new areas through research and inquiry. Above and beyond academic proficiency and meeting graduation requirements, students will become:

Effective Communicator and Collaborator

Critical and Innovative Problem Solver

Ethical Decision Maker

Adaptable and Productive Citizen

Graduates will display personal and professional integrity by demonstrating leadership, effective decision-making, and ethical personal and professional management skills.

Graduates will act as productive citizens by demonstrating responsibility and flexibility in fulfilling personal, professional, and community expectations.

Source: Long Beach Unified School District. Used with permission.

HOW DOES LINKED LEARNING CHANGE LEARNING, TEACHING, AND THE USE OF TIME?

Traditional secondary school structures have been in place for over a century and were modeled on a Taylorist, or factory model, organization of time within the school day, and a calendar that suspended school during the summer months. Neither of these forms of time organization is particularly applicable or effective in twenty-first-century America, and yet both persist and are pervasive despite consistent critique.

Especially troublesome are the ways in which the traditional school day and calendar contribute to considerable inequities in opportunities to learn, particularly for low-income students and students of color. For example, the traditional school day, broken up into six or seven fifty-minute periods, segregates disciplines and discourages the kind of relevance that can be achieved through real-world cross-disciplinary problem solving. This kind of class scheduling can also lead to over-reliance on lectures and other modes of undifferentiated instruction that many students find disengaging and can leave lower-achieving students behind. Without relevance and opportunities to learn by doing, many students are less motivated to learn, and achievement gaps widen. Further contributing to these gaps is the three-month summer break. For many students, this break produces large amounts of learning loss, requiring significant relearning time when school resumes in the fall, if the problem is even addressed at all.

To help mitigate these problems, federal (and later state) legislation promoted several new compensatory programs, strategies, and practices to shore up student learning through afterschool and summer opportunities. Research has demonstrated the benefit to students.[5] However, the benefit could be magnified dramatically through a rethinking of the uses of time *during* the school day and year, and not only the time surrounding it. Linked Learning allows for this more flexible, comprehensive approach, first by encouraging new behaviors of learning and teaching and second by demonstrating how reorganizing time can support those behaviors.

Linked Learning seeks to introduce behaviors of learning and teaching that dramatically improve student motivation, empowerment, understanding, and achievement. As further elaborated by figure 5.2, in Linked Learning pathways, learning and teaching are (1) collaborative, (2) student-directed, (3) outcome-focused, (4) relevant, (5) rigorous, and (6) integrated.

In practice, these characteristics can assume many forms. Within core academic classes, teachers devote greater attention to how the knowledge and concepts of their particular discipline are used in the industry that is the theme of the pathway. For example, in a geometry class that is part of a pathway in architecture, construction, and engineering, the teacher illustrates or, better yet, allows students to practice ways in which architects, engineers, and

FIGURE 5.2   Behaviors of Learning and Teaching

COLLABORATIVE	Students can be seen . . .
Work With Others	· Regularly working with industry and postsecondary partners as learning resources and project clients. · Practicing teamwork skills in a variety of collabortive teams and settings. · Using industry-specific norms, strategies and technology tools to make their teamwork efficient and effective.
STUDENT-DIRECTED	*Students can be seen . . .*
Work Students Lead	· Designing their interdisciplinary learning experiences and organizing, revising, and self-monitoring a learning plan. · Learning through an inquiry-based approach where their questions, choices, insights, and solutions lead the way. · Pursuing learning through feedback, reflection, revision, and defense of work.
OUTCOME-FOCUSED	*Students can be seen . . .*
Work With a Goal	· Creating, using, seeking feedback on, and revising plans for project work and for their college and career goals. · Explaining how their daily work helps them master project, course, and pathway outcomes. · Completing complex tasks and persevering when facing learning challenges.
RELEVANT	*Students can be seen . . .*
Work That Matters	· Engaging in projects of personal interest that are authentic to an industy sector and matter to external clients. · Using state-of-the-art, industry-specific technologies to produce work that reflects standards of the workplace. · Participating in a devolpmental sequence of work-based learning experiences.
RIGOROUS	*Students can be seen . . .*
Work That Challenges	· Engaging in deep critical thinking using challenging material and industry-specific problem-solving tools. · Designing and publicly defending high-quality project solutions. · Ariticulating how they are mastering the Common Core State Standards and other pathway outcomes.
INTEGRATED	*Students can be seen . . .*
Work That Connects	· Intentionally using concepts and skills from pathway theme courses in core academic courses—and vice versa. · Making connections across core academic and career technical subjects in theme-based interdisciplinary projects. · Engaging in work-based learning experiences that link directly with core academic and career technical courses.

Source: ConnectEd, *Learning, Teaching and Leading Framework: Behaviors of Learning and Teaching* (Berkeley, CA: The California Center for College and Career, June 2014). Used with permission.

builders use geometry to frame a building, construct roof trusses, or design a seismically sound bridge.

Similarly, a team of academic and career and technical education teachers, with input from industry professionals, develops a multidisciplinary project that, over the course of a semester, will engage students in researching a challenging industry-related problem. Such an effort will encourage them to recommend and test solutions, prepare a written report, and defend their findings and recommendations in an oral defense assessed by a panel of teachers and industry experts.

Such a project (especially if the district commits to an expanded school day) might require students to visit workplaces after school, where they can interact directly with industry professionals in tackling various aspects of the problem. Students get to experience directly how adult professionals analyze data, question and talk with one another, speak to clients, and write in a variety of different ways. They get to "think like an engineer" or "diagnose like a doctor." The project, formally or informally, might also serve as one way in which employers assess whether students are ready to benefit from a summer internship that perhaps delves more deeply into selected aspects of the project they participated in during the spring semester.

Let us return to Ben Carson High School for a moment. At that school, all eleventh and twelfth graders participate in the Future DOCS program at the nearby Detroit Medical Center. There, on Saturday mornings, students are paired with medical college student mentors, and together they engage in hands-on workshops organized around various medical topics. They also have the opportunity to earn cardiopulmonary resuscitation (CPR) certification, as well as certification under the Health Insurance Portability and Accountability Act.

These kinds of interactions often lead to profound changes in perceptions and understanding on the part of both students and employers. A teenager who was part of an afterschool internship at a local hospital once said, "When I put on my scrubs, I become an adult." A physician, examining an X-ray of a fractured tibia with a student, said with obvious disbelief: "Wow, you really know a lot about anatomy and how bones mend." The elevation in mutual respect can be palpable.

Enabling this kind of learning and teaching requires that schools and teachers use time differently. The deeper learning that occurs through multidisciplinary projects depends on students and teachers having more than fifty minutes to engage in research, analysis, design, prototype construction, and assessment. Block scheduling and other strategies for reorganizing the school day can help create larger chunks of time more conducive to project-based learning and learning labs. Dual enrollment—the opportunity for schools to expand their course offerings through related academic and technical, college-level courses offered at a nearby college campus—not only gives students the opportunity to experience college culture and expectations directly, but also gives them a leg up on earning college credits that can reduce their time to a postsecondary degree. And an explicit commitment to making the time for afterschool and summer internships as a part of students' learning can dramatically shift the way students, teachers, and parents think about how a student experiences high school.

More flexible scheduling also supports common planning time for teachers. This time creates opportunities for better curriculum alignment and project planning, allows teachers to jointly examine the progress of students they share in different classes, and gives educators the chance to take more immediate and coordinated action to address emerging problems immediately. Further, common planning time provides teachers with collegial support that contributes to their satisfaction and strong teacher relationships.[6] Similarly, new ways of thinking about year-round schooling, rather than simply offering more of the same during the summer, could combine teacher "externships" with student "internships" in workplaces, where both teachers and students have the opportunity to better understand authentic problem solving and workplace norms and cultures.

In short, when established with a focus on quality, when equitable and measurable outcomes for students and adults are defined, when learning and teaching become more collaborative and student-directed, and when time is thoughtfully reorganized to support these changes, Linked Learning demonstrates strong potential for interrupting long-standing educational inequities and delivering on the promise of college, career, and civic readiness for all students. In some respects, many of these practices could be part of any strategy for improving learning and teaching. How, then, does high-quality pathway design and implementation enhance and reinforce these practices?

WHAT IS HIGH-QUALITY PATHWAY DESIGN AND IMPLEMENTATION?

When implemented with fidelity, Linked Learning is student-centered and driven by well-defined student outcomes that, ideally, have been codified in a Graduate Profile developed by a wide range of community stakeholders. Designing a menu of pathways, as well as specific programs of study within each pathway, not only reflects the outcomes articulated in the Graduate Profile, but also leverages diversity by responding to students' individual interests and aspirations. A critical first step in developing a menu of Linked Learning pathways in districts large enough to offer students a range of options is optimizing the mix between student interest and the range of industry sectors and employer interests present in the community.[7]

There are many different ways to deliver the chosen menu of pathways—career academies, small theme-based learning communities, small theme-based high schools, to name a few. But whatever the approach, every Linked Learning pathway must offer students a comprehensive, multiyear program of study consisting of four essential components:

- college-preparatory core academic courses in English, social studies, science, mathematics, world language, and art *emphasizing real-world application* in the industry that is the theme of the pathway
- a cluster or sequence of three or more technical courses delivering challenging technical knowledge and skill (and where appropriate enabling students to obtain some level of formal industry certification)
- work-based learning that enables students to interact with working adults around analyzing and solving real-world problems
- personalized student supports that include college and career counseling, as well as accelerated instruction in reading, writing, and mathematics to raise the proficiency levels of lower-achieving students.

In addition, high-functioning Linked Learning pathways adjust the master schedule to allow students to learn in cohorts and provide common planning time for teachers. Cohort scheduling means, for example, that ninth graders in a biomedical and health pathway will take English 1, Biology, American History, Spanish, and Principles of Biomedical Science together.[8] Cohorting makes it easier for academic teachers to focus on real-world application in the industry that is the theme of the pathway. Cohorting also facilitates cross-disciplinary curriculum alignment, team teaching, more flexible use of time, and more personalized monitoring of student progress and challenges. Importantly, cohorting also contributes to a strong sense of community and respect. When students feel that they are part of a supportive learning environment, they are willing to take academic risks.

In high-quality pathways, work-based learning constitutes a continuum of experiences that may begin in ninth grade, for example, with mentoring and job shadowing, and evolve by eleventh or twelfth grade to entail paid and unpaid internships, employer-generated senior projects, and other kinds of opportunities for students to engage with working adults in authentic problem solving or service learning. These opportunities are provided during and after school, and in the summer.

Personalized student supports, provided during and after the school day, are also essential to promoting equitable access by students to pathways, as well as ensuring opportunity to learn. All too many young people arrive in ninth grade performing well below grade level in reading, writing, and mathematics. Without supplemental instruction designed to accelerate achievement in these core skills, many students will be unable to succeed in pathways that are academically and technically challenging. Equally important are individualized college and career counseling and personalized social and emotional supports.

These kinds of student supports can take many forms. At Ben Carson High School, for example, they include a Summer Bridge Program between eighth and ninth grades that provides an orientation to the Ben Carson medial program of study, assesses basic skills, begins to develop any needed individualized tutoring, and helps students forge friendships with other students and bonds with teachers. During subsequent summers, students at Ben Carson have the opportunity to attend classes at Michigan State University, participate in the Joyce Ivy Summer Scholars program, or engage in other summer institutes.

Fully developed pathways also provide opportunities for dual enrollment whereby students can earn both high school and college credit. Students can enrich their learning by enrolling in college courses during the traditional school day or during after school or summer hours.

To help promote high-quality pathway design and the continuous improvement necessary to achieve and sustain high quality, the Linked Learning field developed and defined "Seven Essential Elements for Pathway Quality," along with a rubric that allows pathway teachers and external reviewers to assess progress toward high-quality pathway implementation.[9] When pathway and district leaders determine that they have met or exceeded specific criteria with respect to each of these elements, they can request a structured external review to determine whether the pathway should be formally "certified" as a high-quality Linked Learning pathway.

HOW DOES LINKED LEARNING NURTURE AND SUSTAIN SYSTEMIC CHANGE TO ACHIEVE MORE EQUITABLE RESULTS?

When pathways are limited to one career academy within a large comprehensive high school or a single, small, industry-themed school among many high schools in a district, they often receive inadequate support and may not even survive changes in pathway, school, and district leadership. For example, if a large, comprehensive high school houses a single career academy that serves only 15 to 20 percent of the school's students, a principal may find it impossible to implement the kinds of changes in the master schedule that enable common planning time, student cohorting, and team teaching. The benefits of this difficult change simply are not realized by the rest of the school and, hence, are not likely to garner the necessary support from staff, parents, or students.

This issue is not simply a matter of sustaining particular pathways or making implementation easier. It is also critical for achieving equity for more students, particularly underachieving students and students of color who all too often are relegated to classrooms and schools that fail to motivate them or provide the additional supports and opportunities that make success more likely. As the evidence mounts that Linked Learning is successful in improving a wide range of student outcomes, ensuring that all students have access to these opportunities takes on more and more importance.

Consequently, one of the distinguishing features of Linked Learning has been close attention to strategies that increase the chance that the approach will serve, within schools and within the district, a critical mass of students. The goal is ensuring that Linked Learning pathways become an integral part of the larger district and community systems, as well as the leadership, culture, and operations of schools where pathways are delivered.

What constitutes a critical mass can vary from school to school and district to district. It certainly does not mean that all schools must offer Linked Learning pathways or that the schools that do require all students within the school to choose a pathway. Some districts do choose to go that route, but others explicitly elect a more hybrid approach that allows different options to thrive. For example, with careful planning, International Baccalaureate programs can easily function in a school or district with a robust menu of Linked Learning pathways.

We are loath to define precisely what constitutes a critical mass. However, in our experience, schools where pathways enroll at least 50 percent of the student body and districts that implement pathways in 35 percent or more of their schools are more likely to implement the changes necessary to sustain and continuously improve pathways. If participation is lower, pathways remain isolated one-offs, more susceptible to partial, lower-quality implementation and collapse when key leaders depart.

Realizing systemic change in a district and the surrounding community is challenging, slow work. While districts that elect to pursue a systemic approach can see immediate benefits, it is likely to take five years or more to implement a deeply rooted, districtwide system of Linked Learning. This is especially true in larger districts with multiple high schools and even greater numbers of feeder elementary and middle schools. We have found that this challenging, but ultimately very rewarding undertaking can be greatly aided by careful attention to six important steps:

1. Creating a core team of district and community partners (employers, postsecondary institutions, community-based organizations) to lead a communitywide Linked Learning initiative.
2. Developing a well-informed plan for designing and implementing a menu of pathways districtwide.
3. Formalizing strong distributed leadership and a communications strategy around implementation.
4. Mapping and dedicating resources to support implementation.
5. Following Linked Learning Pathway Quality Criteria as pathways are incrementally implemented across the district.
6. Assessing progress and continuously revising and improving pathway quality.

While district leaders play a pivotal role in establishing and sustaining the conditions for high-quality, equitable Linked Learning pathways to grow and thrive, deep, lasting success depends on crafting a larger community-based commitment to Linked Learning. Districts pursuing a Linked Learning approach must include in their efforts collaborative engagement with parents, employers, postsecondary partners, economic development and employment training agencies, and community-based organizations. Such a coalition can help break down traditional bureaucratic silos and create a more seamless, flexible, and responsive set of learning opportunities and resources available to all students. This kind of communitywide system building can take many forms, which may include:

- Collaborating closely between the district's academic office, secondary school office, and student support office with local agencies and organizations responsible for afterschool and summer programming to expand and better align and integrate work-based learning.
- Creating a work-based learning officer position in the district to coordinate with employers, locally and regionally.
- Developing explicit policies with respect to school choice and transportation strategies that make it easier for students to participate in pathways in schools outside their immediate attendance areas. Districts could work in collaboration with local and regional public transit agencies to accomplish this.
- Developing succession policies and leadership development strategies that address the preparation, recruitment, and placement of principals and assistant principals well versed in sustaining and improving pathways at the site level.
- Providing district-sponsored opportunities for practitioners directly supporting students to develop an integrated case management approach focused on student success. This kind of model would draw upon the experience of special educators in individualized student learning goals and supports.
- Establishing cross-school, collaborative professional learning communities to conduct an inventory of each district's existing student support programs and activities, including in- and out-of-school time.
- Creating a districtwide integration plan. This plan would establish clear progress benchmarks and accountability for district and school leadership teams to design and implement systemic strategies for integrating student support services with existing effective programs and activities, including high-quality instruction and work-based learning.

District leadership alone is rarely capable of recognizing and implementing these kinds of systemic changes. In a growing number of communities engaged in systemic change, an independent organization assumes responsibility for coalescing key stakeholders and aligning missions, policies, and resources.[10] Promising examples of this kind of strategy include Alignment Nashville, which has spawned a number of similar approaches in other communities around the country. In some communities, the local United Way is taking on this role. In others, regional compacts are emerging, often with support from outside intermediaries such as Jobs for the Future. As is usually the case, there is no single best approach. But without some strategy for systemic implementation, Linked Learning and related initiatives risk regressing to old ways of operating that all too often minimize success and reproduce inequities that have dominated public school systems for much too long.

CHALLENGES TO IMPLEMENTATION

Advancing Linked Learning as a new framework for more and better learning that significantly improves student college, career, and community readiness faces many challenges. School and district leaders seeking change must confront a legacy of decades of unchanged, tradition-based policies and practices grounded in the paradigm of the Carnegie unit and the agrarian calendar, entrenched adult interests, and a lack of will and capacity for innovation. Ironically, perhaps one of the biggest barriers to change is that, in one form or another, we all went to school. Our own experiences, our memories of what worked and what did not, and the ways we encountered privilege and inequity all too often reinforce a traditional mind-set of what school should be.

That mind-set perpetuates resistance to new ways of learning and teaching. It stands in the way of reorganizing the school day and year, and assessing competency and performance rather than just content knowledge. It promotes school funding based largely on "seat time" and rigid rules about in-school and out-of-school activities. In some instances, charter schools and reconstitution of traditional public schools have successfully experimented with new approaches to learning and the use of time. However, even in these cases, community expectations and postsecondary admissions requirements (e.g., primacy of grade-point average, standardized test scores, and completion of discipline-defined courses) often undermine deeper and sustained change.

This traditional mind-set also perpetuates public policies and community norms that continue to view the mission of high school as preparing young people for either college *or* career. Linked Learning unequivocally is about college *and* career, not just one or the other. Linked Learning, by design, rejects the practice of tracking, delivering separate course offerings and programs of study for college-bound versus career-bound students. Linked Learning is crafting pathways that prepare students for the full range of postsecondary options—four-year college, certainly, but also community college, formal employment training, and the military. There is, however, pushback, which comes not only from some proponents of career and technical education wedded to traditional occupational training but also from some equity advocates who fear that Linked Learning's integration of career-based learning will reintroduce tracking that limits postsecondary options.

The inertia of the status quo also hampers designing and implementing new approaches to teacher preparation and certification. Restrictions on the certification of adults to provide credit-bearing instructional minutes to students narrows the range of potential learning opportunities for students within the traditional school day. Greater flexibility in adult certification—particularly in the technical realm—to support student learning would promote a more seamless integration of afterschool and summer learning opportunities with state-mandated minutes for the traditional school day. It would also facilitate expanding dual enrollment, which is often impeded by competing credentialing requirements for secondary versus postsecondary faculty.

Equally important is more innovation and flexibility in training and credentialing administrators. Schools and districts would like to provide greater flexibility for personalized learning, interdisciplinary and work-based learning opportunities, and cohorts for a more personalized, smaller learning community environment. But those seeking to change master schedules to make this possible confront a lack of technical know-how and easily accessible, high-quality examples in practice. Many of the teachers and administrators currently practicing have only known the narrowed curriculum, traditional structures, and conservative policy climate inspired by adherence to the No Child Left Behind Act. The more local and flexible reform models of the 1990s form a distant and hazy memory that only the most veteran educators in the system experienced.

These are some of the challenges to implementing Linked Learning and related initiatives in ways that make significant inroads to inequity and persistent gaps in student achievement and opportunity. They reflect to a large degree the fact that existing district systems have been honed over time to deliver precisely the results they are delivering. In many instances across the nation, resources, opportunities to learn, access to high-quality learning experiences—and consequently student outcomes—reflect the broader inequities and disparities in society. While much rhetorical energy is spent in local, state, and federal policy areas, precious few concerted systemic change efforts have yielded dramatic improvements in equitable student outcomes. Entrenched privilege and a strong disinclination by those benefiting from the current system to support significant change reinforce these disparities.

POSSIBLE POLICY DIRECTIONS IN SUPPORT OF PATHWAY QUALITY AND SYSTEMS CHANGE

As Linked Learning continues to expand in California and other states and with lessons learned from our work in these communities, we offer some concluding policy recommendations that could help expand, improve, and sustain local and regional systems of Linked Learning. Perhaps first and foremost, we need to more carefully examine how the basic framing of public policy—at the federal, state, and local levels—prolongs the isolation of academics from career and technical education, the uni-disciplinary approach to learning and teaching, the separation of in-school and out-of-school learning, and the absence of more seamless articulation between secondary and post-secondary education. At the federal level, defining the nation's major education legislative initiatives along the lines of types of education or populations served contributes to continued resource silos that inhibit innovation, integration, and coordination. For example, legislation specifically and separately addresses elementary and secondary education (i.e., Every Student Succeeds Act), higher education, career and technical education (i.e., the Carl D. Perkins Vocational and Technical Education Act), employment training (i.e., Workforce Innovation and Opportunity Act [WIOA]), adult education, and special education. Many states, for example, despite emphasis on curriculum integration, do not allow use of Perkins funding to support joint professional development for academic and career and technical teachers. Whether motivated by a desire to limit broader distribution of funding or to reduce risk of negative audit findings, many states and localities limit the use of Perkins funds to activities that only support credentialed career and technical education teachers.

Perhaps it is time to consider reconstituting Perkins and related parts of the Elementary and Secondary Education Act, the Higher Education Act, and WIOA into an integrated, comprehensive College and Career Readiness for the Twenty-First Century Act. Such legislation would promote comprehensive college and career pathways, spanning at least grades 9–16. It would require that pathways consist of industry-focused programs of study that are made up of a challenging academic core, aligned with demanding career and technical courses. The programs would also be integrated with a continuum of work-based learning opportunities and provide personalized student supports. This legislation might require, or at least encourage, that students demonstrate college and career readiness through completion of multidisciplinary capstone projects. Panels of secondary and postsecondary educators and industry professionals could assess these efforts. Monitoring such an indicator of college and career readiness with respect to traditionally underserved populations would promote not only equity but also the kind of learning and teaching that is more likely to produce lasting success in college and career for all students, not just the privileged few.

Related state policy would allow districts to give schools greater flexibility and technical support to redesign master schedules and to imagine new learning opportunities for students that blur the boundaries between academic and technical, in-school and out-of-school, the classroom and the workplace, and secondary and postsecondary. State funding allocation systems for secondary and postsecondary education might offer opportunities to use federal and state funding more flexibly. Administrators could braid or combine various funding streams to support locally determined strategies for designing and implementing comprehensive college and career pathways.

Without doubt, pursuing such a policy agenda will require considerably more thought, discussion, debate, and specificity. But doing exactly that would represent the kind of innovation that is needed if we are to deliver on the promise of college *and* career readiness for all.

LINKING OPPORTUNITIES AND OUTCOMES—WHY AND HOW EXPANDED LEARNING TIME "WORKS"

The five chapters in this section shed light on how and why expanded learning opportunities can promote a broad range of learning outcomes, including supportive learning environments and social climates that enable student success. These chapters explicate how expanded learning time can enable all young people to be more effective in all aspects of their lives, including college, career, and community participation. The authors provide compelling existence proofs to demonstrate that quality changes can be made at the school, district, and state levels to create greater alignment between how students learn and how schools and systems are structured.

Written from diverse scholarly perspectives, the chapters illuminate how and why these approaches can be equitable and effective. Authors draw on insights from learning theory, youth development theory, educational psychology, urban planning, and sociology to explore how expanded learning time approaches can more accurately capture what we know about teaching and learning to advance more equitable educational outcomes.

In chapter 6, Ben Kirshner and Rebecca Kaplan integrate evidence and theory from the learning sciences to examine how community schools, Linked Learning, and afterschool youth organizing programs can transform student's educational experiences. Kirshner and Kaplan detail how these expanded learning time approaches draw on fundamental insights about human learning and reconcile them with contemporary structures and systems. The authors demonstrate how the approaches respond to students' needs, create opportunity for both learning and identity development, and invite young people to play active roles in their schools and communities. Notably, the authors argue that the partnerships and practices they examined are not unprecedented or new, but represent creative adaptations to a shifting global economy and to decreased investment in public goods.

In chapter 7, learning scientist Elizabeth Birr Moje provides research-based arguments supporting the need to protect and extend teaching and learning time. In a review of the growing body of research and meta-analyses on various expanded learning time designs, Moje highlights the benefits to both students and teachers. In particular, Moje shares that strategies designed to shift how time is distributed can have a positive impact on students' social and civic engagement and development. Further, youth development approaches that acknowledge the importance of learning beyond academic subject areas have a positive effect on engagement, motivation, positive school behaviors, and in levels of academic achievement. Given the compelling research that supports both the value of and the need for changing how much time is available and how it is used, Moje asks why expanded learning time is not implemented more widely. She concludes by outlining the structural and cultural barriers that stand in the way of such approaches, especially in large, urban school districts.

In chapter 8, Patricia Gándara explores the potential of expanded learning time approaches in meeting the learning needs of English language learners (ELLs) and immigrant students. Time is a critical variable for those students who must master the English language, the culture, and the expectations of school, while simultaneously attempting to learn academic material. Yet very little research has been conducted on the topic of time and learning specific to ELLs and immigrant students. Based on the available literature, Gándara concludes that time can be a powerful and positive variable for ELLs and immigrant students dependent on its use. Indeed, if more time in school reinforces negative self-perceptions that result from stigmatization, more time may be counterproductive. Gándara observes that the most effective expanded learning time strategies meet the diverse and individual needs of students, build social capital, strengthen a sense of identity, and pay close attention to children's culture and their prior "funds of knowledge."

In chapter 9, researchers Veronica Terriquez and John Rogers consider youth organizing as a promising site for expanded learning time. Youth organizing groups can provide students with purposeful and supportive time for learning after school, during weekends, and over the summer. Terriquez and Rogers found lasting implications for many students' developmental and educational trajectories, particularly for students who participate in these activities over a series of years. They discovered that expanded learning time, which members themselves help to shape, supports students' overall well-being and the development of a range of skills, capacities, and civic commitments that contribute to high school completion and postsecondary educational attainment. Based on their research on afterschool youth organizing programs, Terriquez and Rogers offer lessons about high-quality expanded learning time for educators and youth providers.

In chapter 10, Paul Ong and Elena Ong examine access to expanded learning time opportunities through the lens of urban spatial structures. Using Los Angeles as a case study, Ong and Ong focus on how spatial inequality and inadequate transportation options contribute to disparate access to expanded learning opportunities. They find that access to afterschool programming is insufficient for families living in poor neighborhoods. Families in these neighborhoods encounter similar challenges in accessing other types of enrichment activities that can contribute to students' learning and well-being. Ong and Ong conclude that the disparities in accessing expanded learning time opportunities are by-products of the larger urban landscape and both mirror and reinforce socioeconomic stratification.

The chapters in this section demonstrate how expanded learning time approaches can more accurately align with how students learn. Further, they demonstrate more equitable practices as they encompass learning across cultures and backgrounds (compared to the strategies focused on efficiency and measurable knowledge). Indeed, the authors find that expanding learning time approaches have the potential to produce effective and equitable outcomes by:

- leveraging the rich and sophisticated body of practice and knowledge experienced by students in their everyday lives
- providing opportunity for students to dig deep, explore, and create
- acknowledging that increasing access to learning requires meeting the needs of the whole child, the whole family, and the whole community as part of the learning process
- increasing adult interactions for students who serve as resources and enabling students to develop caring relationships with adults beyond classroom teachers

- giving students the chance to bridge institutional worlds (e.g., school, workplace settings) and to learn the skills and knowledge to participate in these different spheres
- providing opportunity for students to call upon a range of skills not bounded by traditional academic subjects
- creating authentic learning environments that enable students to solve real problems that matter to them
- developing positive identities that can challenge and transform stereotypes
- providing teachers with the opportunity to work collaboratively with colleagues (including external partners) to identify and meet the needs of their students
- offering teachers needed time to build their instructional capacity through professional engagement, continuous learning, and improvement cycles of inquiry

As the authors of these chapters elucidate, these emerging practices and reforms have the potential to cultivate the academic competence, essential skills, and commitment to meaningful, complex learning of all youth. It is not just that the traditional school schedule is out of sync with twenty-first-century life and work demands; it is out of sync with our fundamental insights about human learning. The authors make a strong case for how and why expanded learning time opportunities create the conditions for more complex, meaningful instruction, and personalized learning relationships with caring adults that lead to a wide range of positive school outcomes. The authors remind us that ensuring all students gain access to expanded learning and teaching opportunities, especially those students who are most marginalized by our current system, is essential if we are serious about disrupting social inequalities.

CHAPTER 6

INNOVATIVE USES OF LEARNING TIME

Perspectives from the Learning Sciences

BEN KIRSHNER AND REBECCA G. KAPLAN

EFFORTS BY SCHOOL districts and states to add time for learning have created an opportunity for structural changes that go deeper than merely adding more time to the school day or year. Basic assumptions about what we know as "school"—that is, as a physically bounded place governed by precise stop and start times—have been called into question.

For learning scientists such as ourselves, this opportunity to deconstruct school and reimagine the design of equitable learning ecologies is exciting. For too long, the systems built in the early part of the twentieth-century have not matched what research has found about how people learn. Programs described in this book, however, provide compelling evidence that quality changes can be made at the level of state or district systems. For example, we now see schools that *invite in* the community, in the form of community schools that leverage the resources of neighborhood adults, health providers, and community groups. We also see schools that *propel students out* to professions, in the form of Linked Learning systems that create apprenticeship opportunities for students in fields such as medicine and engineering. Community-based organizations, too, bring something essential to this new learning ecosystem: youth organizing groups show that when young people join together to ask critical questions about their school systems, and then participate in efforts to improve them, they learn, grow, and influence public institutions in generative ways.

These intentionally designed learning environments—community schools, Linked Learning, and youth organizing—integrate the latest evidence and theory from the learning sciences with practical models that show promise. Illustrative cases such as these are important because they show how our best science on how children learn can be realized and sustained in equity-oriented learning ecologies that weave together K–12 schools, community organizations, professional pathways, and postsecondary education.

PERSPECTIVES ON LEARNING AND SCHOOLING

Twentieth-Century Instructionism

Contemporary debates about the structure of schooling have origins in early twentieth-century deliberations about the nature of learning. As historian Ellen Lagemann described it, "Edward L. Thorndike won and John Dewey lost."[1] Thorndike, an educational psychologist, built a science of learning guided by behaviorist principles that valued efficiency and measurable knowledge. Behaviorist scholars emphasized the incremental acquisition of facts and procedures in response to rewards and feedback. This behaviorist view contrasted with Dewey's emphasis on the child's active construction of meaning and engagement in practical activity. Whereas Dewey articulated a vision of learning that emphasized open-ended inquiry, social relevance, and democratic goals, his vision was superseded by a new orthodoxy that treated school more as a sorting mechanism "for matching individuals to existing social and economic roles" rather than as a vehicle for social change.[2] Education scholars have described this approach as *instructionism* because of its assumption that experts should design instructional systems in the most efficient and logical way to transmit appropriate skills and knowledge, with little regard for how children learn.[3] Instructionism met the demands of a rapidly growing society for mass compulsory schooling and preparation for an industrial factory economy.

Despite its thin basis in scientific evidence, its poor match for today's fluid knowledge economy, and widespread dissatisfaction with reductionist forms of testing and assessment, instructionism continues to be the dominant organizing framework for mass public education.[4] The logic of instructionism even shows up in some of the new learning time reforms, such as those that focus only on adding time to the school day or year, without prescribing changes to how to spend that time. This is a particular concern when it comes to equitable access to learning for students in under-resourced schools or schools that have histories of low test performance. Rather than expand access to high-quality learning opportunities, such reforms serve to reinforce existing inequities among students and maintain the status quo around what counts as learning. Schools most affected by high-stakes testing serve neighborhoods whose residents often experience economic injustice. Since standardized tests focus on basic skills, these schools often find themselves trapped in a cycle of teaching basic skills in order to raise student test scores. A recent study found that teachers and schools that faced high-stakes consequences for their students' test performance often used extra time for test preparation rather than for students to cultivate and develop new interests and knowledge.[5]

New learning time reforms, however, create new opportunities to re-imagine the school day in ways more consistent with contemporary learning theory. How has the science of learning evolved since Thorndike and Dewey's time, and how might that inform new equitable learning time reforms?

The Turn Toward Sociocultural and Situated Learning

Developments in learning theory over the past three decades have contributed significantly to a new science of learning, one that has reclaimed "learning" from its narrow identification with knowledge acquisition. This approach has also advanced our understanding of learning toward a sociocultural perspective, in which learning is signified by increased participation within a community of practice.[6] Accordingly, learning means expanding one's repertoire of practices[7]—to know how to speak confidently in a writing workshop, for example, or how to participate as part of a team of scientists trying to test a theory about water quality in a local river. This view of learning is not at odds with improved academic performance. Knowing how to participate in discourse practices of academic communities leads to stronger performance in math, reading, and writing, but it is not reduced to those indicators.[8] Although a comprehensive review of learning theory is beyond the scope of this chapter, here we highlight a few broad principles that align with expanded forms of learning time discussed in this volume.

Belonging and identity. Children learn when they feel cared for and known. People are motivated to learn when they feel a sense of belonging in a school or youth organization—when who they are is celebrated and recognized by the educators in the building.[9] A learner's identity is also of central importance: Does the fifth grader see herself becoming a scientist like those she studies in class? Does the tenth grader feel as if he can be himself and pursue interests that reflect his goals for his future? Expanded learning time programs offer ways for students to strengthen their connections to subject matter, such as through field trips and interactions with professionals. They also strengthen connections to people, creating opportunities for community building with both peers and mentors.

Culture as resource. Students from nondominant backgrounds in American schools often confront a curriculum and school climate that discounts or ignores their culturally based funds of knowledge.[10] In contrast to a long-standing tendency to treat culture as a deficit, particularly for African American and Latino/a students, sociocultural theory calls for educators to treat culture as a resource in learning. Treating culture as a resource can take many forms, including bi-literacy programs that support students in learning new languages alongside their native languages, community school programs that invite families into the classroom to share their expertise and knowledge, and modes of instruction that encourage multiple ways for students to participate in activities and discussion.[11] For instance, Tara Yosso describes navigational capital as one form of community cultural wealth, referring to the knowledge and skills children gain when they translate for a parent at a parent-teacher conference or take younger siblings to a doctor's appointment. Children and youth develop cognitively sophisticated repertoires of practice in their everyday lives that they can leverage for school learning, particularly in learning environments that engage not just cognition but identity and affect. Kris Gutiérrez and colleagues, for example, foreground the kinds of ingenuity shown by Latino/a and working-class families in their use of digital media and technology in the home as a resource for learning.[12]

Access to mature practices. When people engage in an activity that is new to them, they typically look to those with more experience to see how to participate.[13] In activities that require complex tools, whether in a car mechanic's shop or digital media lab, it helps to see or be part of the settings and contexts where those tools are used in practice. And as learners interact with different communities of practice within the various social and institutional spheres they inhabit, they learn how to participate within each group. Initiatives that expand the boundaries of school and connect students to individuals and learning resources outside the classroom reflect an understanding of a sociocultural theory of learning. When learners have access to mature practices, and opportunities to connect their identities to the practices in which they participate, they can gain access to an inbound trajectory, becoming more central within a community of practice.[14] For instance, in the Linked Learning example we examine later in this chapter, students are able to access mature practices of medical professionals by being located on the same campus as a hospital and invited into observation rooms within the medical facilities.

Open-ended tasks. When young people engage in practical activities with more seasoned actors, the kinds of tasks they work on also shift, becoming more open ended, ill-defined, and authentic. In the youth organizing example we discuss later in this chapter, young people have to continually adjust their work to a shifting policy context and weigh pros and cons when deciding on various strategies. Engaging in these sorts of open-ended projects not only allows young people to see the work of mature policy activism, but also provides them opportunities to receive just-in-time feedback and coaching from experienced group members as they work toward a practical goal.[15]

Summary

Global economic changes—and attendant shifts in the kinds of skills and knowledge required for living-wage jobs and democratic citizenship—have been accompanied by theories of learning that prize diversity, ingenuity, and participation. Calls for youth participation in meaningful, practical activity alongside other community members echo Dewey's arguments about learning from the early part of the twentieth century. Learning scientists have diagnosed the problems with instructionism and provided persuasive evidence about its limitations. But too often we lack existence proofs showing how participatory, digitally connected, culturally responsive learning can be organized in US public schools. The majority of powerful examples have been shown in case studies of learning outside school: the challenge has been to scale what we know we need in public school systems, which are susceptible to mandates and historical practices that can be at odds with this vision. This book provides examples that suggest some ways forward for integrating these learning principles into systems rather than leaving them as isolated boutiques.

In the following section, we consider how several of the innovative uses of time described within this volume represent core principles from sociocultural learning theories and point the way toward greater equity in learning opportunities for youth in low-income communities of color.

CASE STUDIES

Community Schools

Efforts to bridge community and schools, discussed in chapter 3 by Fehrer and Leos-Urbel, reflect several insights from research on learning. First, community schools expand the focus on learning beyond cognition to consider how the whole body, whole family, and whole community need to be supported as a part of learning and schooling. Second, they increase the number of adults with whom students interact daily—individuals with a wide range of expertise and experiences. Third, they create potential for linking a culture-as-resource approach to the everyday practices and routines of schools.

Community schools work to make school a central resource within a neighborhood ecology. This involves connecting schools to a plethora of community-based organizations to support health and wellness for students and their families. Family resource centers housed on school campuses, for example, often provide health services, housing services, and adult education, including language classes. Community schools offer programming before school, after school, and throughout the summer. As Fehrer and Leos-Urbel point out, community schools diverge from the traditional "schools as sanctuaries" model that permeates the US school system and focuses on academic achievement as the primary engine for realizing income and racial equality. Community schools adopt a broader view, which argues that poverty negatively affects people's readiness or capacity to give their best to academic learning. Community schools, therefore, work to alleviate the damaging influence of poverty—its tertiary effects on physical health, mental health, and readiness for school—and to value and incorporate people's cultural repertoires of practice in local communities.

Supports for students, families, and communities. The community schools approach in Oakland, California, expands the focus on learning beyond the mind. It recognizes that students will be able to get so much more from an innovative curriculum or engaging instruction when they have stable housing, food, and health care. As learning theorist Carol Lee described, "The cognitive, social, physical, and biological dimensions of both individuals and contexts interact in important ways."[16] The community schools approach used in Oakland brings together academic, health, and community resources to support children's development in each of the aforementioned dimensions.

At the same time, the community schools approach uses creative strategies to free up classroom teachers to focus on what they are best trained to do, which is to cultivate the cognitive and academic development of learners. The model shifts the role of classroom teachers, and how classroom teachers are able to use their time, both inside the classroom and out. Classroom teachers often try valiantly to track down resources for whatever challenges arise for their students, but in the approach taken in Oakland, there is a wider support network available to meet the physical and psychosocial needs of students. This support network allows teachers to spend more time focusing on academic learning as they plan and teach. Additionally, the presence of adults outside the teaching profession also creates potential to cultivate students' learning.

Interactions with adults. The community schools approach increases adult interaction for students. In this approach, parents, health-care providers, and various mentors from community-based organizations have a presence within the school before, during, and after regular school hours. These adults act as resources to the students, each other, and classroom teachers. This effort to saturate a school community with caring adults is consistent with the literature on high-quality youth development programs, which identifies supportive relationships with adults as a core feature of positive developmental settings.[17] Students might connect with their classroom teacher for one type of support, but they may also bond with a track coach or community organizer in ways that foster a sense of belonging and connection to the school.[18] The presence of these adults creates increased opportunities for students to develop relationships with adults other than their classroom teachers.

Although students in traditional schools may also interact with a variety of adults, the community schools approach creates an opportunity for students to see adults from separate institutional and social spheres interact with one another. Human development scholars have discussed the advantages to students when they can bridge the different spheres they inhabit, and the key role adults can play as cultural brokers for young people.[19] When different social and institutional spheres are physically located in the same place, there is potential for this brokering to happen more often and in more comprehensive ways. The approach used by the Oakland community schools also blurs social and institutional lines by employing *push-ins*, in which adult mentors come into classrooms. The cohesion of programs and collaboration among adults within the Oakland community schools approach can be generative for students to observe and experience. School is not isolated from other institutions in the community schools model.

Leveraging culture as resource. Beyond bridging institutional worlds, the community schools approach opens the possibility to view culture as a resource within the everyday practices and routines of schools. In viewing parents and families as partners, and inviting them into the school for multiple purposes and roles, the community schools approach values familial and cultural practices and leverages them for student learning.[20]

The presence of adult mentors from community-based organizations may also support the norm of culture as a resource within the schools. The adult mentors get to know a different side of the students than the classroom teacher might know. In this way, the community schools model offers potential for students to be recognized by adults for their strengths and interests outside of what classroom teachers might be privy to. And because of the blurred boundaries created by the push-ins, this adult recognition could happen within classroom walls and time.

The community schools approach bridges community and schools in ways that support equitable access to learning. Such schools do, however, remain part of broader systems that can undermine these efforts. For instance, pressure to show increases in test performance can narrow classroom endeavors, and professional hierarchies can have an impact on how various adults are viewed or treated within the school.[21] Still, by looking beyond the individual and their academic achievement to consider how the whole student and whole community need to be supported, bringing adult mentors into the school, and linking culture as a resource for learning, the community schools approach represents a promising model of an equitable learning ecology.

Linked Learning: Bridging School to Professional Practice

Whereas community schools draw upon important insights about the role of everyday cultural practices of youth and their families, Linked Learning offers a different approach to the use of time to reorganize the school day: access to mature professional practices. Learning theorists sometimes describe the movement from novice to expert within a domain as an *inbound trajectory*. An inbound trajectory comprises opportunities for both learning and identity development, which support the newcomer in becoming a full participant in the community of practice.[22]

The Linked Learning approach of the Benjamin Carson High School of Science and Medicine (Ben Carson High School) discussed in chapter 5 by Gary Hoachlander and his colleagues illustrates an inbound trajectory of participation for careers in science and health professions. The approach makes the pathways to these professions visible to students and positions students for authentic participation in internships, which supports their development of *practice-linked identities* in the science and health fields.[23] Learning theorists Na'ilah Nasir and Jamal Cooks described three core resources that support students to develop practice-linked identities: material, relational, and ideational resources. The Linked Learning approach at Ben Carson High School provides resources in each of these categories.

Material resources connect individuals to a practice through artifacts or features of the physical environment.[24] Ben Carson High School is located on the campus of the Detroit Medical Center. The location of the school supports opportunities for internships, surgery observations, and other student experiences at the location where medical professions do their work. Since the school is situated within the medical center, students encounter professionals during their daily travel to and from classes. In traditional schools, students might only see other students and school personnel throughout the school week. The Linked Learning approach in Detroit makes the professional domain visible and positions students as members of that field.

Another example of a material resource that affords practice-linked identity development is the students' uniforms. Students wear scrubs to class. In wearing scrubs, students are marked as part of the medical field; professionals throughout medical campuses wear uniforms that signify their domain of work. The Linked Learning approach to uniforms helps establish that the students are doing the kind of everyday work that the field requires, rather than the work of traditional schooling.

Relational resources connect individuals to a practice through positive relationships within the context of the practice.[25] The students connect to professionals in hospitals, businesses, and community-based organizations. Additionally, the advisory board for the school, made up of medical professionals, works to create paid internship opportunities for students within the medical field. These kinds of connections to professional practices are rare in traditional schools.

Ideational resources connect individuals to a practice through ideas about one's place in the practice and how the practice is valued beyond the domain.[26] The competency-based assessment system used in this Linked Learning school serves as an ideational resource to ground both educators' and students' purpose, as well as their understanding of success. The idea that the students need to be not only college-ready but also career-ready shifts traditional conceptualizations of success in schooling—to include not only academic indicators but also practical, social, and emotional skill development. The Graduate Profile (a material resource) reinforces the ideational resource of the competency-based system.

The Linked Learning approach includes project-based learning challenges that integrate knowledge and skills from multiple content areas in order to create products for a real-world purpose. When students were asked to create a marketing campaign for a healthy beverage for the youth of Detroit, they integrated their learning from every class to investigate what it would take to create a successful campaign. History, math, and science classes each provided an angle for approaching the challenge, rather than separate knowledge in silos. Students described how they appreciated the cohesiveness of the challenge and the ways in which the challenge felt authentic.[27] They used authentic tools in their campaigns, including surveys, sampling methods, social media, and film; they presented their campaigns to an external audience; and they brought what they were learning home as well, aiming to change both their own and their family's health habits.

In addition to encouraging these inbound trajectories, Linked Learning shows great promise for cultivating a key twenty-first-century learning outcome: *adaptive expertise*.[28] Adaptive expertise refers to the ability to flexibly respond to unexpected contingencies or to apply one's knowledge to new situations. It depends principally on deep conceptual understanding rather than a superficial mastery of procedures. Consider, for example, the medical assistant who encounters symptoms that they had not yet seen in a textbook, or a doctor who must stabilize an injury when all the emergency room beds are taken. How does the expert call upon core knowledge to adapt when the typical resources and tools are unavailable or require new combinations?[29] Students can develop this adaptive type of expertise through encountering open-ended challenges that call for creativity and ingenuity. Learning theorists also note that individuals can build skills "through well-practiced routines" and fostering "a metacognitive awareness of the distinctive roles and trade-offs" of their actions.[30]

By engaging students in interdisciplinary challenges with authentic tools, products, and audiences, the Linked Learning approach creates the potential for the development of adaptive expertise. Schools commonly create *routine* problems for students to learn to solve that somewhat resemble and are loosely based on nonroutine problems that professionals encounter. When students are able to answer these kinds of routine problems, they are exhibiting routine expertise. However, "experts often need to go beyond [routine] schemas" when adapting to new information, environments, or challenges.[31]

The Linked Learning approach requires students to call upon a repertoire of skills that is not bounded by traditional academic subjects. Students had to integrate skills from each of their classes, for example, in order to create their marketing campaigns. They described their desire to do strong work because they felt that others were counting on them; the results of their work had an impact on other people. When students must apply knowledge from school in discussions and interactions with people outside the classroom, opportunities to go off script occur, such as when students presented their work to Dr. Reginald Eadie, head of Detroit's school board and three hospitals. The unpredictability of speaking with an outside audience and responding to questions contributes to the development of adaptive expertise.

Beyond the marketing campaign challenge, students engaged in internships and field-based experiences across the medical campus. Working in settings alongside professionals can create opportunities for students to encounter unexpected challenges that they must shift to meet. When learning environments present unscripted challenges that require students to innovate and solve problems, students can develop adaptive expertise, especially if they engage in metacognitive and reflective practices in which they consider their own actions and adaptations.[32] These kinds of opportunities promote the kind of creative and resourceful thinking that the professional domain requires.[33]

Youth Organizing: Young People Mobilizing to Create More Equitable Systems

Youth organizing groups engage young people, often African American, Asian American, and Latino/a youth in low-income neighborhoods, in collective action to improve their schools and communities. Organizers identify common interests, mobilize their peers, and work collectively to make their voices heard in the public square.[34] Contemporary youth organizing in the United States has its historical roots in the Civil Rights Movement, such as the lunch-counter sit-ins organized by African American college students of the Student Nonviolent Coordinating Committee and high school walkouts organized by Mexican Americans in Los Angeles.[35] Youth organizing gained renewed momentum in the 1990s as part of a broader shift toward community engagement among young people and in response to punitive policies toward youth of color, in particular. Unlike community schools and Linked Learning, youth organizing groups are typically based in community organizations outside school.

Because of their ambitious policy goals, such as to dismantle the school-to-jail track in Colorado or ensure quality college preparatory classes in Los Angeles, youth organizing groups are often perceived more as a vehicle for political activism than for learning and development.[36] But there is much evidence that youth organizing groups do, in fact, offer powerful developmental settings for young people experiencing structural dispossession. In chapter 9 of this volume, for example, Terriquez and Rogers draw on longitudinal data to show that alumni of youth organizing groups demonstrated greater civic engagement and four-year college enrollment than their non-organizing peers. Other scholars have reported similar evidence of higher academic aspirations and ongoing commitment to civic engagement among young organizers.[37] Recent findings from a multisite international study of organizing also document social and emotional learning among members of youth organizing groups.[38]

Youth organizing both embodies and expands on core principles from the learning sciences and positive youth development. As educators, activists, and policy makers consider new ways of using expanded learning time, lessons from research on youth organizing as a developmental setting deserve attention.

In certain ways, youth organizing groups embody qualities called for by learning and developmental scientists. For example, echoing learning scientists' emphasis on the benefits of authentic learning, organizing groups engage youth in open-ended tasks, collaboration, and mature community practices with meaningful goals.[39] Consider some of the complex cognitive and social tasks required in effective political action campaigns: participants develop long-term strategies, they construct and frame arguments for high-stakes audiences, and they respond to setbacks and unexpected contingencies. Organizing groups also reflect many of the features described in the National Research Council consensus report about community programs for youth development, including structure, supportive relationships, opportunities to belong, skill building, and support for efficacy and civic participation. Participants engage in cycles of practice, performance, and feedback as they work together on long-term campaigns.[40]

Where youth organizing groups tend to depart from the above-described learning environments is their explicit focus on young people as citizens in the present who turn their critical gaze to education systems and participate in efforts to improve them. The curriculum is based on struggles that youth experience in their everyday lives, such as substandard schools or xenophobic immigration policies.[41] Generally speaking, in the early stages of campaign development, young people share experiences in talking circles or check-ins. This can help participants become more aware that what they thought was a personal issue is experienced by others in the group. After identifying shared challenges or struggles, effective organizers invite youth to reflect on what they want to see improved or changed—in short, to articulate their interests.[42] This way of framing social problems can be significant in identity development because it contributes to feelings of empowerment and collective self-determination.[43] For example, Shawn Ginwright described the case of a young mother seeking her high school diploma who encountered barriers to finding childcare during school hours. Rather than interpret the situation as her own isolated problem, she organized other teenage parents to make their case to the district superintendent.[44]

A second feature of most youth organizing groups is that their relational practices affirm the dignity and humanity of oppressed youth and their communities. Such groups explicitly recognize youths' experience of racial oppression and make racial and ethnic identity development central to their work.[45] These opportunities enable youth of color and immigrant youth to forge identities that challenge and transform false narratives about their communities. This focus on youth's well-being and dignity is important for young people's readiness and willingness to play leadership roles in community coalitions.

Third, youth organizing groups invite participants to play mature and meaningful roles. Youth learn leadership by doing. A recent international study of youth organizing documented a range of ways that youth stepped into mature roles, including participating on hiring committees, recruiting peers to school chapters, speaking with elected officials in public settings, facilitating workshops for peers, handling logistics for youth summits, and planning strategic discussions about messaging and publicity.[46] The young people enacting these roles are typically those directly affected by the issues at hand. A young person who had been suspended several times from school, for example, was the same person who educated the school board about the school-to-prison pipeline. In this sense, youth organizing groups embody a key finding from learning sciences research about the importance of learner agency and meaningful roles in community practices.

DISCUSSION

The cases in this chapter—community schools, Linked Learning, and youth organizing—reflect compelling educational approaches that embody consensus findings emerging from learning sciences and youth development research.[47] One limitation of our review is that we did not conduct original research about the Oakland community schools, the Detroit Linked Learning program, or the California youth organizing sites, which would likely surface the nuances and challenges that face any initiative or program engaged in changing systems. But we see value in identifying core principles guiding their work and showing their relationship to learning theory.

The cases discussed here show people drawing on old and new ideas to transform educational experiences for young people. They represent hybrid innovations that draw on fundamental insights about human learning and reconcile them with contemporary structures and systems. Community schools, for example, respond to people's need for community, belonging, and well-being, and make use of school infrastructure and community resources to meet that need. Linked Learning draws on age-old apprenticeship traditions and updates them for our contemporary economy.[48] Youth organizing invites young people to play active roles in their schools and communities. It encourages them to not merely reproduce societal practices, but to renew and transform them, as young people have done throughout history.

The value of these innovations, therefore, is not that they are somehow unprecedented or new. Instead, they represent creative adaptations to a shifting global economy and decreased investment in public goods. In places where affordable health care is unavailable to low-income families, doctors and nurses are working within community schools where they can provide services to students. Recognition of the shifting nature of work—and the diminishment of manufacturing jobs—calls for Linked Learning approaches in Detroit that prepare young people for new forms of work. Youth organizers, too, are responding to a shifting context that offers a promise of educational opportunity but only delivers on that promise for some.[49] Changes to how educators and communities use existing resources, including time, reflect a creative response to contemporary challenges.

In addition to their hybridity, we also see in these educational models a commitment to addressing issues of equity for children and youth. All three of the cases represent quality learning environments situated in communities experiencing poverty and structural racism. Rather than offer a curriculum reduced to academic test preparation and the rudiments of math and literacy, these models affirm the dignity of young people while inviting them to participate in complex and challenging learning environments. For too long, deficit orientations have dominated American education discourse about people of color, particularly Black and Latino/a learners.[50] These assumptions, coupled with structural disparities in school resources and access to quality learning opportunities, add to an "education debt" that the United States owes to communities of color.[51]

Community schools, youth organizing, and other initiatives in this volume represent the kinds of educational practice that can strengthen efforts to address this debt. As activists and policy makers fight to bring more resources to public education, particularly in the most underserved areas, they will need models, programs, and designs that can be developed and sustained. These examples offer evidence of the kinds of learning environments that merit new public investment.

We conclude by pointing out that the cases discussed here do not merely *reflect* core principles of learning sciences research. They also *challenge* learning theorists to expand our assumptions and take issues of power and inequality more seriously.[52] Common in both the community schools and youth organizing cases is recognition of the issues of power, self-determination, and human agency. Many of the community schools forming now emerged from marginalized groups' efforts to reclaim some measure of local influence over their neighborhood schools. Youth organizing groups, too, demonstrate a sophisticated understanding of politics and power that is too often ignored in learning theory. Youth activists testify to the harms caused by police violence, zero tolerance discipline policies, and restrictions on immigrant rights. For young people facing such harms, merely offering new instructional strategies, such as inquiry-based learning or small-group work, is not adequate. We need a robust learning theory that takes into account the struggles many young people face, affirms their dignity and humanity, and cultivates their capacity to be thoughtful and engaged democratic actors. As educators, parents, and students develop and sustain these new education models, learning scientists need to be there alongside them—to listen, learn, and build together.

CHAPTER 7

DEEP AND MEANINGFUL LEARNING

Where Do We Find the Time?

ELIZABETH BIRR MOJE

WHAT DOES IT TAKE TO LEARN something really well? How do experts become experts? Most research—and even popular theories—suggests that learning to do something well takes time.[1] Why is time important? For one thing, becoming knowledgeable or skilled requires practice. Even the most prodigious musicians, for example, practice their art faithfully. In some cases, a musician will play a phrase repeatedly to "get it right." This skill becomes engrained in a way that carries a musician through multiple performances in a range of contexts and throughout a lifetime of playing music. Consider the elderly woman with Alzheimer's disease who can sit down at a piano and play song after song, despite being unable to recognize her own daughter. That long-lasting, deeply engrained skill is a result of regular practice over time. Similarly, dancers—whether soloists or members of the corps—practice relentlessly to perfect the extension of a leg, the shape of an arm, or the precision of a tap. In addition to perfecting the look of their moves, this repeated practice builds muscle memory, allowing the artist to perform proficiently even under duress. I have watched several dance teams able to complete a dance with perfect synchronicity and grace, even when recorded music malfunctions in a high-stakes performance. Such precision stems from repeated and focused practice over time.

The value of time for learning is not only about the practice that time affords. Time provides not just an opportunity to practice in routinized ways, but also a chance to dig deep and explore various ways of engaging in a particular riff, move, or phrase. Thus, the art or sport or task can be perfected in terms of both precision and artistry, or technique, also allowing for variation, improvisation, and creation.

Time also matters because it allows learners to focus, wonder, and concentrate. People who learn with the luxury of time can look at situations differently. In a recent study of research engineers, for example, the authors observed an engineer pull data output off a machine, look at it for a few seconds, and conclude that the machine was not properly calibrated.[2] That ability to see—or to read—data quickly did not happen overnight. People who learn a skill or a concept over time can reflect, discuss, analyze, and question. They can think. And thinking matters to learning.

This chapter presents research-based arguments about protecting and extending time to teach and learn. I offer a case of attempted reform as an exemplar of the structural and cultural barriers standing in the way of such reforms, especially in large, urban school districts. Finally, I propose four principles that can guide attempts to expand and better use time during and beyond the school day and year.

TIME AS A PRECIOUS RESOURCE FOR LEARNING

Time is a resource in the learning scenarios described above. And it is a privilege. For some students, this kind of thinking and practicing time is available in school and in the out-of-school opportunities they are able to access. For many others, however, the time they spend in school is wasted or deadly. Many students are denied the opportunity to learn because the time available in their schools is seriously compromised.

Time can be compromised in least three ways. One is the compromise that comes with constant interruptions. A second is the compromise evident when teachers are compelled to rush through instruction (often because of interruptions) or to march through pacing charts because time is a scarce resource monitored in artificial ways. In a recent intervention study, researchers noted that the three main barriers to enactment of the inquiry-based discussion curriculum were insufficient time for instruction, too many revolving programs, and time lost to testing and test preparation.[3] Protecting and using available time well is as important as making more time.[4] Finally, time can be compromised because the time spent together is painful or boring for students. Students who are, for example, routinely positioned as "struggling" or, worse, as "unengaged" or "behaviors" are not benefiting from the time they spend in school. For these students, learning time is demoralizing and even abusive.[5]

What's more, although these students learn valuable concepts and skills in their homes and communities, many have few opportunities to engage in meaningful academic learning activities outside the school day or year. They are not afforded opportunities to learn a wide range of skills and concepts that their more privileged peers take for granted (or assume are some kind of right they should have as a result of status or effort). These include opportunities in the arts (e.g., dance, instrumental music), in advanced science and mathematics applications (e.g., first robotics), public discourses (e.g., mock trial, debate, student government), and business and entrepreneurship (e.g., internships).

More time, however, is not always better. Adding time to the school day and year could be more of a problem for many students than leaving things as they are if the time is not well used or if additional time is dedicated to remedial drill and practice.[6] Far too many youth already experience poorly structured and routinely interrupted classes, monotonous and uninspired instruction, and negative relationships with adults. More of the same is not what we are calling for in this volume. Children and youth need more learning time, to be sure, but that time must be about real learning and it must be used with respect for the child. With that caveat in mind, I turn to the research on expanding and improving time to learn.

WHAT DO WE KNOW ABOUT EXPANDED TIME TO LEARN?

Research and practice on school models that extend the school day and year are in their infancy, especially for secondary (middle and high) schools.[7] However, a growing body of design and basic research studies and meta-analyses, together with research on schooling in other countries, suggests benefits to both students and teachers of extending the school day and year.[8] These studies must be read with some caution, however, because they typically group many different kinds of programs together, including out-of-school-time programs that may not connect in any sustained way to what happens in a child's school day. There are three types of programs that are often counted in the expanded learning time literature:

- *Extended-year programs designed to reduce summer learning loss.* Several studies generally find that extending time spent in school seems to make a difference most for students at risk of failing academically. However, many students who are deemed "at risk of failing" actually attend schools that are at risk of failing their students. Thus, if the failing schools fail to change their practices, then extending the students' time throughout the summer months is unlikely to stem summer learning loss; indeed, it might lead to greater student push-out rates.[9]

- *Extended-day models that shift how time is distributed throughout the year to acknowledge student needs.* Studies in neuroscience, education, sociology, and economics have explored the question of school start and end times, particularly for older youth (e.g., high-school-aged youth). These studies suggest that later school start times are better for adolescents' social and civic development and engagement.[10] Although some claim that few direct effects on academic achievement have been noted as a result of changed school start and end times, the American Academy of Pediatrics recommended change in start times as a policy lever for improving adolescent physical and mental health, safety, and academic performance.[11]
- *Youth development models: equitable access to the extracurricular.* Meaningful learning also depends on more than time spent in dedicated subject-matter settings where academic content, skills, and practices are emphasized. Numerous studies have shown that attending to non-academic barriers to success can have a positive—if small—effect on school engagement, motivation, positive social behaviors, reductions in problem behaviors, and increases in levels of academic achievement.[12] Programs most successful for long-term engagement and retention provide leadership opportunities for youth in the program, develop relationships with staff, and are community-based.[13] Research also suggests that students of color from under-resourced communities may particularly benefit from youth development with a service-learning focus.[14] Similarly, service-learning focused youth development programs can link to increased civic engagement and pro-social attitudes and behaviors when programs include strategic site selection related to youth interests, together with clear articulation of goals and vision.[15]

All this said, such programs take time, and many youth find it difficult to participate in such programs after school or in the summer. In some cases, lack of participation stems from youth working in the afterschool or summer hours to help their families make a living wage; in other cases, youth and their families simply cannot afford the program or related transportation costs. Perhaps most noteworthy, few programs are actually connected to school time in powerful ways.[16] That is, many out-of-school-time programs offer social and emotional benefits for youth, but their effects on school learning or achievement generally are small and/or difficult to measure, largely because they are not connected to the specific learning goals or learning standards that are the subject of classroom and other in-school activities. Or the converse may be true, insofar as school activities do not connect to, or meaningfully amplify, the social and emotional learning experienced in out-of-school programs. Expanding learning time can occur when children and youth are encouraged to attend afterschool and summer programming, but would likely benefit from the extension of the school day and year to include programs integrated with academic learning. This is not just a matter of adding more school to the day. Instead, programs should connect to, without replicating, academic experiences. Meta-analyses on expanded learning time demonstrate that increased academic achievement is more likely to occur in programs taught by certified teachers. For that reason, a strong argument can be made for expanding the school day and year to integrate afterschool and summer programs with school classes.[17]

USING EXPANDED OR PROTECTED TIME WELL: MORE THAN JUST A TIME CHANGE

In *Time Well Spent*, the authors outline four "interlocking gears of school success," all of which revolve around ensuring enough time in school for:[18]

- rigorous and well-rounded learning experiences, with a focus on college and career readiness
- teachers to develop their skills to use time more effectively
- teachers to engage in data-based formative assessments of students' learning so that they can intervene and foster increased leaning
- developing a culture of learning and high expectations, for both academic learning and social interaction

In what follows, I build on the gears offered in *Time Well Spent*, but I offer modifications that focus more on understanding learners and on developing meaningful, inquiry-based instructional approaches, which both demand and expand learning time. Of central importance is the question of which features of learning time promote meaningful learning.

Consideration of the Learner

As a principle, *consideration of the learner* puts the learner first, drawing from research on how children and youth learn, from research on young people's sleep patterns and effects on mental and physical health, and from research on engagement and persistence in learning.[19] This work considers the research on brain development, social and cognitive development, and differences in needs of populations as mediated by socioeconomic, cultural, and familial contexts. Specifically, if schools really considered the learner, then school leaders and teachers would immediately demand changes to the daily schedule. That is particularly true for adolescent students, based on what research tells us about how people learn and when they learn most effectively.

A number of models make central the idea that more time is needed or argue that time must be structured effectively and carefully monitored.[20] Although it makes sense to use time effectively, some of these approaches emphasize rigid time-on-task interventions that provide children and youth very little freedom to explore and create. Such models risk reproducing the factory model of education that persists in most middle and high schools today and are unlikely to sustain students' motivation to learn.[21] As developers engage in building expanded learning time that is tightly structured, they may want to balance such plans with models that make spaces for youth to create, to explore, and to try on new identities that may be better matched to their developmental needs.[22] Such initiatives should consider the demands of disciplinary learning in particular.[23] Furthermore, a model that fails to acknowledge the brain-based and other medical research on adolescents' best learning, socio-emotional health, and physical safety does not consider learners. A simple policy move is to shift middle and high school start times.

Planning for expanded learning time also requires planning for the context of learning. For example, in places where transportation is an issue, expanded learning time developers need to consider bus routes, parents' work schedules, the school or care schedules of other children in the families, and the safety of the neighborhood, in the event that walking to school or independent travel on mass transit is an option.[24]

Finally, expanding learning time demands a consideration of the family structure and the sociocultural values families hold. In several communities we studied, parents strongly valued education but simultaneously held strong values about commitments to family. In my own work, students admitted to missing school or neglecting homework because they had family obligations.[25] Expanded learning time models must find ways to support students in achieving both commitments. The models should not be subtractive; they must add to learners' options, which requires understanding the values and commitments held within families and social and cultural groups.[26] Attention to cultural values and practices might require adjusting how projects are assigned, where and when work gets done, and the provision of supports for students to carry out extended tasks. Making cultures, social groups, and homes a part of the instruction also holds power for extending learning beyond the regular school day, as families are invited to be part of youth learning, rather than outsiders to it.[27]

Integrated Youth Development Activities

Proposals to extend the school day and year often meet with resistance from parents, youth, and even community leaders because the proposals fail to attend to children and youth as whole beings who have lives outside school. This point is particularly salient for proposals that affect adolescents because as children age, they become more independent and ideally are engaged in structured activities outside of school. Extended-day and extended-year programs can threaten those activities unless they acknowledge that children and youth do things they value outside of school. At the same time, extended-day and extended-year models make it possible to provide those rich learning opportunities beyond schooling for those who families cannot afford to provide them. Schools can also *integrate youth development activities* that are typically relegated to the extracurriculum into the regular academic day. For example, starting the day with youth development activities might address findings about how adolescent brains function in the early-morning hours. Extended days also allow for opportunities to carry out long-term inquiry activities beyond limited classroom time periods.

Inquiry-Based Learning Experiences

The authors of *How People Learn* argue that learning is enabled when learners have a clear learning frame and when their prior learning (or knowledge) is engaged.[28] Specifically, the report identifies dimensions of well-formed opportunities to learn. One is that teachers need to engage, expand, and refine students' prior knowledge as they seek to help students construct complex foundational knowledge. Teachers also introduce new information within a conceptual framework. Finally, they help students organize knowledge in ways that facilitate retrieval and application, and they provide opportunities for students to monitor and control their own thinking. Drawing from these dimensions, a number of scholars have argued for the benefits of *inquiry-based learning experiences* for student achievement and engagement. In addition, re-searchers and curriculum developers have designed inquiry learning experiences in multiple subject areas.[29] Inquiry-based curricula, however, require extended time to launch and complete inquiry activities, as well as extensive teacher planning. The work of building a foundational factual knowledge, framing new learning, eliciting prior learning, discussing new ideas, connecting across a range of ideas, and coming to new understandings or conclusions takes time.

Imagine a group of twelve-year-olds designing the best living structure to withstand a range of weather conditions.[30] The kind of design thinking, science concept knowledge, and literacy skill necessary to produce such designs does not develop overnight. Nor do the designs themselves. That kind of meaningful and conceptual learning takes time. Similarly, a group of high school students examining the archives of a particular historical period need time to read documents carefully, cull the relevant data, and seek corroborating and disconfirming evidence.[31] Students learning to engineer new technologies also need time. As demonstrated by a number of studies, students learning to be engineers must develop the ability to "see" problems and solutions, what Reed Stevens and Rogers Hall refer to as "disciplined perception."[32] These also represent the kinds of skills practiced at Benjamin Carson High School of Science and Medicine in Detroit. As described by Gary Hoachlander and his colleagues in chapter 5, students within Linked Learning pathways use project-based learning to connect relevant, community-based learning experiences with academic, conceptual learning.[33]

Disciplined perception and deep engagement with concepts and ideas are developed over time, with engaged practice. They are not learned in bits and pieces while listening to lectures. These skills and habits of mind are not developed by following pacing charts that require teachers to march through curriculum standards day by day, hour by hour.[34] Yet, teachers in a number of studies I have conducted often report that they lack the time needed to engage fully in the inquiry-based curriculum units we designed, with a number of teachers skipping key lessons or cutting units short when faced with a time challenge.[35] Thoughtful expansions to the school day can allow for better uses of block scheduling and for opportunities to expand or link inquiry activities into courses at the end of the day and in intersession experiences.[36]

The case of Edwards Middle School in Charlestown, Massachusetts, featured on the Edutopia website, an online education magazine, makes a strong argument for adding time to the learning day.[37] With an increase of three hours a day and a dedicated half day on Fridays for whole-school teacher development, teachers and leaders at Edwards claim that they are better able to cover material in greater depth, connect concepts across disciplines, and discuss and reflect on lessons with other teachers. They claim growth in mathematics, reading, and science outcomes, together with a significant decrease in the school suspensions.[38] The end of the day at Edwards Middle School is dedicated to "Academic League" and enrichment electives. Academic League gives students opportunities to work on skills and practices they need to master or on extended inquiry. Teachers meet in grade-level teams during enrichment electives, a scheduling innovation that leads to the last principle for making the most of expanded learning time.

Regular and Common Planning and Development Time

Teachers and school leaders need *common planning time* to facilitate innovation, develop and implement new curriculum, and increase teacher skills and content knowledge through professional learning activities. Indeed, every review or meta-analysis I read cited teacher professional development and planning time as a key ingredient to effective time use in schools.[39] A strong school schedule not only allows teachers to plan individually and collaboratively, but also makes it possible for teachers to enact the curricula they plan without interruption and other management challenges.[40] Too often, teachers are asked to initiate new programs or models with very little additional time to learn those programs or models. In particular, teachers need time to participate in curriculum development with researchers and other curriculum developers rather than merely being handed prepackaged materials to implement. They also need classroom coaching and ongoing logistical support to encourage the enactment of inquiry-based learning.[41] All of this work also takes time, which certain kinds of expanded learning approaches can provide, if time is wisely used and professional development provided.

WHY IS CHANGE TAKING SO LONG? A CASE OF ONE ATTEMPT TO FIND MORE TIME

The research reviewed clearly supports both the value of and the need for changing how time is used as well as how much time is available for learning. With so much research available, why have schools around the country not changed? In this section I describe some social, cultural, and institutional constraints that my colleagues and I experienced as we worked with a range of schools to attempt these changes.

In two radically different school partnerships (one each in a suburban and an urban setting), my colleagues and our partners identified exciting scheduling possibilities that seemed to address the needs of children and youth. In one case, we worked with an arts-integrated high school in an urban setting. Several teachers and leaders collaborated to develop a proposal for a different kind of school day and year, one that achieved an expanded time model by distributing learning time across both day and year (they referred to it as a "balanced calendar" because it distributed time more evenly and eliminated the extended time away from school during summer, as found in traditional calendars). They simultaneously worked to use time more effectively. In particular, the model acknowledged the research on adolescent brain and social development, which, as noted previously, strongly suggests the value of later start times for older youth.

This scheduling innovation was intended to address a number of current problems in the typical public school schedule. Problems addressed included the lack of common teacher planning time, student tardiness and attendance (a problem exacerbated in cities where both school and city bus systems are either nonexistent or unreliable), the demands of adolescents' changing neurology and motivation, and teachers' and students' lack of opportunity to engage in real-world problem-solving activities. This model would have brought other adults into the school and into educating the community's children by engaging artists, university students, community program leaders, and elders. Finally, such a model could have provided a space for preservice teachers to interact with young people without the demand of teaching to standards or benchmarks. They are thus able to learn about students as whole beings before they begin to learn to teach content and skills.

Despite the enthusiasm the team brought to this proposal, we were unable to make these changes due to a host of structural barriers. Unlike the Massachusetts example described by Davis and Farbman in chapter 1, the communities in the cases I describe here were divided on expanded learning time approaches, citing any number of structural barriers to changing the school day and year.[42] In truth, however, most of the structural barriers existed not because they were immutable but, as I elaborate below, because they were held in place by social and cultural beliefs and traditions.

Students' Work Possibilities

A common challenge to the schedule we proposed was that school leaders and some teachers reported that students needed to work in the afterschool hours to help their families survive. It was certainly the case that a number of students' families lived in challenging economic circumstances, and yet many students stayed on the premises waiting for rides after school most days or regularly participating in afterschool choral, theater, dance, and art activities. Thus, the actual number of students who needed to work to support themselves or families would not have prohibited an expanded-day model, particularly if the model day built opportunities for paid internships into the morning and afternoon sessions.

Afterschool and Summer Activities

Another objection to the proposal was that extending the day and year would cut into opportunities for youth to participate in afterschool rehearsals and other activities, as well as forestall opportunities for summer camps. Again, our data challenged this argument. Our logic was that if the day were extended, students would not have to wait for rides outside the building. Moreover, our design placed arts and elective classes at the end of the day. Consequently, students who were in rehearsals or afterschool clubs could have participated in those activities as part of the school day, rather than beginning the day early and extending until after 5:00 p.m.

Transportation

School leaders also raised concerns that extending the day would conflict with parents' work schedules, given the lack of district-provided transportation or even reliable public transportation. Again, the observation that students waited as much as two hours for parents to arrive calls such an argument into question. Nevertheless, in an urban environment that lacks reliable and safe access to public transportation, the transportation issue is one that the school leaders and policy makers need to take seriously.[43] The logic of an extended day, however, suggests that running the day from 8:00 a.m. to 5:30 p.m. would accommodate most parents' work schedules. Expanded school time would engage young people in meaningful activity when their parents were finishing their workdays, rather than releasing them to paid caregivers or to unsupervised activity.

Teacher Time

Some teachers in our case objected to the proposed schedule, arguing that if their days were to extend, their existing contract would require higher salaries. This argument is sensible; why would one assume that any employee would put in more time for the same pay? There are ways, however, to avoid extending teachers' actual work time. Split-day schedules would have resulted in the same number of hours on the job and would have provided even more time for professional development and individual meetings with students and parents. Indeed, the model built in morning planning time for all teachers, and afternoon planning or student meeting time for the teachers of the non-arts-based and nonelective subject areas.

In addition, the extended-year model did not demand more time of teachers, but rather distributed learning time across the calendar year in an attempt to diminish summer learning loss and to provide deep, engaged, inquiry- and performance-based learning activities for youth. Still, the distributed-year model met with some resistance because teachers expressed the desire for "down time," perhaps because they did not understand that the model would distribute time throughout the year. In addition, a number of teachers expressed concern over the need to work for additional pay at other jobs in the summer months. The issue of teacher time and pay was the most challenging to surmount; it is difficult to argue the point with weary, and sometimes embattled, professionals who need to earn additional income to pay their bills.

We observed the same resistance to change in the suburban school district, although in that case, the access of affluent families to high-quality afterschool and summer programming motivated some parents to resist a distributed calendar option that was under consideration in that district. Again, the distributed calendar was brought to the board by teachers, school leaders, and university partners, and was designed to increase learning opportunities for all students. Less-affluent parents supported the distributed-year model, but were ultimately overruled because the majority of parents in the district considered the disruptions to their schedules to be overwhelming.

As noted previously, most of the structural barriers exist because they are held in place by social and cultural beliefs and traditions, rather than by any real barriers that could not be overcome. That is, the people who ran the school and who sent their children to the school believed that the school structures should not change, largely because they represented the known and, for those in power, served them well—or at least adequately. Those structures then became ways of doing school, or cultural practices for schooling. Culture—that is, ways of knowing, doing, believing, and acting—produces structures that underpin institutions such as schools.[44] As long as those structures serve people in power, then it is unlikely that they will change. And more important, even when people are not served by certain institutional structures, they may participate in them because they are taken for granted or simply comfortable.

Thus, to make more and better conceived learning time available in schools, policy makers, school leaders, teachers, and parents will have to consider not only the technical or pragmatic dimensions of structural change, but also the cultural changes required. Leaders who wish to extend, expand, increase, or better distribute and use learning time will need to help all stakeholders learn new ways of doing school. They will need to reveal the ways that such structures privilege some and disenfranchise others. They will have to make new cultural practices that help to develop different cultural and social beliefs about school schedules and about how time should be spent in school.

IT'S HIGH TIME TO MAKE MORE TIME: MOVING THE CLOCK FORWARD

What will it take to make more time in our nation's schools? The preponderance of evidence across a range of fields (education, medicine, psychology, to name just a few) suggests that changing the structures and uses of time in schools would be a wise move if we want children and youth to learn in deep and meaningful ways. Increased costs of extending the day and year are often named as an objection to making this change.[45] Yet, the studies cited in this chapter and throughout the volume show benefits to children and teachers alike of even modest changes to the schedule. What's more, the cost of failing to serve many children and youth is far higher than the assumed costs of increasing the day and year. With university and business partnerships, internships can be developed to expand the day in ways that do not increase costs dramatically. Existing expanded learning time programs—many of which are described in this volume—can be integrated into the school day, thus reducing the need to hire additional staff members. Integrating these programs with schools, as is done in Linked Learning and the community schools approach, can also make better use of school buildings, which sit empty for vast stretches of the week and year. Policy makers, school personnel, parents, researchers, and even students need to turn the clock forward, challenge taken-for-granted cultural beliefs and practices about how people learn, work together to enact new models, and study the effects of various models for expanding time to learn.[46] It's time to learn.

CHAPTER 8

ENGLISH LEARNERS, IMMIGRANT STUDENTS, AND THE CHALLENGE OF TIME

PATRICIA GÁNDARA

THERE IS NO LEVEL playing field when it comes to academic learning for English language learners (ELLs) and immigrant students. They must master the language, the culture, and the expectations of school while simultaneously attempting to learn the academic material that all other students are learning. Time is a critical variable. For most ELLs and immigrant students, it is mathematically impossible to accomplish all of this and stay apace with their English-speaking peers academically. And the older the student is when entering school in the United States, the greater the challenge, *unless he or she has had a strong education abroad* and has been able to learn in his or her own language.[1] But most ELLs and immigrant students are not so fortunate and arrive at school without this benefit. Thus, it is surprising that so little attention is given in either research or education policy to the need for more time for these students to catch up with their native English-speaking peers and to integrate successfully into a new environment. This chapter describes ELLs and immigrant students, the challenges these students bring with them to US schools, and the potential benefits of expanded learning time strategies.

ENGLISH LANGUAGE LEARNERS AND IMMIGRANT STUDENTS

What's the Difference Between ELLs and Immigrant Students?

Most immigrants—students who originate from another country—are ELLs, as most come from non-English-speaking families. But most ELLs are *not* immigrants. Common parlance uses the term "immigrant students" to refer to students who are either immigrants themselves or whose parents are immigrants, and often makes little distinction between the groups. Only 3.8 percent of young people under eighteen in the United States are actually foreign born, or immigrants, but in 2014 almost 22 percent of all youth under eighteen were the US-born children of immigrants.[2] Taken to-gether, foreign-born youth and the first-generation children of foreign-born immigrants make up one-quarter of the youth population in this country. Overwhelmingly, students in both of these demographic categories speak a language other than English at home and consequently start school as ELLs. Moreover, while most of these young people are Spanish speakers, an increas-ing percentage of immigrant youth come from Asia and speak a variety of Asian languages, most prominently Chinese, Vietnamese, Korean, and Taga-log.[3] Twenty-five percent of all immigrant youth in the United States in 2014 were from Asia.[4]

The distinction between native-born and foreign-born immigrant ELLs is important. As demographers have long emphasized, foreign-born ELLs—especially those who first enter US schools in the secondary grades—are in-creasingly likely to be poor, often have fewer transferable literacy skills in their native languages, are more likely to be undocumented or to live with undocumented parents, and are more likely to have experienced emotionally traumatic experiences than their native-born ELL counterparts.[5] All of these factors multiply the academic, social, and emotional learning challenges for youth and for the educators who must design programs that meet their needs and that engage their parents as partners.

Goals of Schooling for ELLs

The goals of schooling for ELL students, as for all students, are multiple and not limited to performance on academic tests. In a recent national poll, fewer than half of adult Americans chose academics as the primary purpose of public schooling. Respondents also thought preparation for citizenship and preparation to enter the world of work were important outcomes.[6] Parents of ELLs, like other parents, want schools to prepare their children to succeed in American society, and this necessarily means receiving a well-rounded educa-tion that includes opportunities to be successful in different domains.[7] ELLs perhaps need this even more than other students. In addition to learning a new language, and usually a new culture and set of expectations, they have to develop an identity that matches their new circumstances. Like all children, they want to fit in and have friends. They want to feel good about themselves and feel both accepted and efficacious.[8] However, it is especially difficult to develop a strong sense of self when time in school is almost exclusively devoted to trying to catch up academically, and opportunities to learn English through informal interactions with English-speaking peers are limited.

ELL Students Experience Many Challenges at School and in the Community

The very terms we use to refer to these students place them in a deficit "remedial" frame: they were formerly referred to in federal legislation as "Limited English Proficient" students and now more commonly called "English language learners" or simply "English learners." They are framed by what they do not know—English—rather than what they have: knowledge of another language. (Indeed, in the majority of cases, they know an important world language.) This label can have a negative effect on how schools and teachers see them and typically results in their placement in a separate track where it is difficult, if not impossible, to access the regular curriculum.[9] Even well-intentioned teachers often lower expectations for these students, believing them incapable of meeting grade-level demands.[10]

The literature has also pointed out a series of other challenges that these students often face: underprepared teachers, inadequate resources in their schools, intense segregation, assignment to the lowest-performing schools, and in some cases, overt discrimination and bullying. Researchers have shown the relationship between the rigor of teacher credentials required to serve ELL students in a state and the academic outcomes of the ELL students in that state.[11] A study of resources for ELL students in California found that ELLs were significantly more likely to be taught by teachers without even a basic credential, much less one that certified them to teach ELLs, and California is among the most stringent of states with respect to requirements for ELL teachers.[12] With respect to time, this study found that ELLs do not receive sufficient time to catch up with English-speaking peers. Also, due to the ways that instruction is organized, the amount of time these students have with support personnel in the schools was less for ELLs than for other students.

Segregated learning environments. Latino ELLs and children of immigrants are heavily segregated in low-performing schools and communities where English is not widely spoken. More than half of California's elementary-school ELLs in 2005 were concentrated in only one-fifth of the state's public schools, where they made up more than 50 percent of the student body.[13] In such a context, students may have difficulty making friends whose primary language is English. In addition, ELLs are significantly more likely to be found in the lowest-performing schools. According to 2014 data from the California Department of Education, two-thirds of the state's ELL students were clustered in schools that were in the five lowest school performance deciles on the state's former Academic Performance Index.[14]

Where ELLs are segregated for instruction and few attempts are made to integrate them into the mainstream of the school, students can experience severe marginalization and bullying. In one study of schools across Arizona, ELL students within schools implementing a segregated instructional program for ELLs were commonly referred to as "those kids" or the "ELLers" and were viewed as being separate from the school as a whole. In another study, teachers of ELLs in "specialized classes" recounted common experiences in which ELL students doubted their ability and talked about their inferiority to other students in the school. In cases where ELLs were reclassified as English proficient, they mocked students who remained in ESL classes.[15] These challenges are exacerbated in secondary schools, which tend not to be staffed or organized to provide both the language and *literacy* instruction that many late-entering secondary school students need to effectively tackle grade-level academic content.[16]

Time deficits and educational policies and practices. Lack of assistance with homework, especially in English, creates a significant disadvantage for many of these students. Homework is commonly assigned as a way to increase learning time and reinforce classroom lessons. Teachers may assume that students' parents will oversee homework assignments. However, parents who are unfamiliar with US schools and who do not speak English may find it impossible to help their children with homework or special projects that require knowledge they do not have, or access to materials they cannot get. This can create a time deficit. These students effectively receive less learning time than their English-speaking peers.

Likewise, progressive educators often like to assign projects that help students integrate what they are learning and make the learning active and engaging. This good pedagogical practice can provide ELL students with important opportunities to use language in a natural context with peers. However, when parts of the assignment include doing research at home and seeking out information outside of school, this can also disadvantage those students whose parents are unable to support the projects. Thus, it is important to plan homework assignments and similar forms of expanded learning time in ways that support ELLs, while also providing opportunities for active engagement with English-speaking peers.

Another policy that can shortchange ELL students' time for learning, while ostensibly supporting their educational progress, is an overemphasis on reclassification from ELL to English-proficient status. Both under NCLB and ESSA, as well as many state accountability systems, the primary education goal has been reclassification or movement out of the ELL category. Thus, schools and districts are rewarded for rapid reclassification on the belief that this represents the primary goal of instruction for ELLs. However, the emphasis on reclassification can actually impede the students' acquisition of strong English skills and disadvantage them in several ways. Research has shown that those students who are allowed to learn in their primary language and acquire English more slowly—while acquiring literacy in the primary language as well as English-—tend to outperform the ELLs exposed to English-only instruction by secondary school.[17]

Other research has also questioned the wisdom of rapid reclassification, as many students appear to stumble in school later when support for English acquisition is removed because they were prematurely considered "proficient."[18] We have learned that it is possible to speed up the acquisition of English, especially in the early grades where linguistic demands are lower, but it can come at a high cost as those early reclassifiers may ultimately have less of a grasp of academic English. Moreover, if the primary language skills are lost in the process, these ELL students will have lost a potentially important asset. Acquisition of academic English requires time, *at least* five to seven years, though teachers are frequently pressured to make this occur more rapidly, reducing the time needed to become truly proficient in English.[19]

Latino ELL children are less likely than any other subgroup to attend preschool, resulting in a time deficit dedicated to learning from the very beginning of schooling.[20] Studies show that most ELLs begin school significantly behind other children academically. They are less likely to have basic pre-reading and math skills, like recognizing the alphabet or being able to count to ten. Students of Mexican and Central American heritage, and those from homes where English is not spoken, have the lowest math and reading skill levels at kindergarten entry but show the greatest achievement gains in the early years of schooling.[21] Low initial achievement scores are due to low preschool attendance rates compounded by poverty and language difference.

ELLs are also more likely to lose ground over summer and vacation periods when school is not in session. A great deal of research has been dedicated to understanding the nature of "summer learning loss" for low-income students, and there is some debate over whether the phenomenon is primarily one of learning loss or the lack of learning reinforcements and amplification experienced by middle-class students.[22] When low-income children return to school after a long summer vacation, they tend to score lower on tests than they did at the end of the previous school year, and teachers routinely note the need to spend valuable time "refreshing" students' learning. While children in middle-class families may enjoy summer camps, travel, and other enrichment activities, many ELL families do not have the time or resources to partake in these activities, and summer becomes a time of scrambling for childcare. It also is a time when many ELLs are thrust back into a non-English-speaking environment. Summer presents very different opportunities for children depending on the resources of their parents, and it is also precious time that can be used to help children catch up and reinforce language learning rather than lose ground academically.

Many immigrant parents are much more transient than others, often needing to relocate their families in search of work and affordable housing.[23] Thus, their children move from school to school, which generally has a negative effect on learning outcomes.[24] Students lose learning time as a result of the transitions, as teachers need to repeatedly get to know new students, and the students need additional time to catch up with the rest of the class. Students' ability to learn can also be affected by trauma and stress, when children are separated from parents for prolonged periods of time—something experienced by many children of immigrants.[25]

WHAT IS KNOWN GENERALLY ABOUT TIME AND LEARNING?

Given the multiple time deficits these students experience, it is tempting to believe that simply adding more time to the day or to the year, or to the hours dedicated to studying English, will automatically result in better outcomes for ELL students. Yet surprisingly little research has been done on the topic of time and learning that is specific to ELLs, and the existing research should give us pause. If more time in school simply reinforces negative self-perceptions that result from stigmatization, it may be counterproductive. As the opening chapters in this book amply document, for time to be a powerful and positive variable in student learning, it depends on how the time is used. While there appears to be a general consensus among researchers that additional time *can* be productive for disadvantaged students, surprisingly few researchers have considered the special nature of time for ELLs and immigrant students.[26] In addition, common schooling practices appear to assume that given the same amount of time as other students, ELLs can acquire English in addition to the regular curriculum. Deborah Short and Shannon Fitzsimmons, for example, have called explicit attention to "double the work" these students have to do in order to catch up to grade level in English.[27] Their analysis, however, does not consider how the availability or lack of additional learning time might be a serious problem or a viable solution. Well-prepared teachers, specifically designed curriculum, and integration into rigorous courses with adequate support are recommended approaches for ELLs who struggle to balance learning English with their academic course load, but students' chances are considerably improved if more time can be provided for them to accomplish all they must do.[28] But how is additional time best deployed?

Research on Expanded Learning Time Strategies for ELLs

Expanded learning time can be organized in different ways. As described in chapters 1–5 of this volume, instructional time can be extended by adding more time to the existing school day or year, or by adding to the total number of years that students attend school, such as in the case of five-year high schools for students who enter secondary school significantly behind. Learning time can also be expanded through summer and afterschool programs, through out-of-classroom experiences offered through programs like Linked Learning, or by addressing the barriers that prevent students' learning as in the community school approach. And time for students to learn can also be conceptualized as time for teachers to hone their skills working with ELLs and children of immigrants. However, the literature on effective practices suggests that time must be both extended and reconceived around learning goals, both in school and in expanded learning time settings with afterschool and community-based partners and in family engagement activities.

Although the research on use of learning time for ELLS is scant, Aida Walqui and Leo van Lier sum up a broad body of evidence on model practices for ELLs.[29] Their report identifies at least three important overarching strategies that implicate the effective use of more time:

- engaging ELL youth in learning tasks that are relevant, meaningful, engaging, and varied
- developing and nurturing forms of student collaboration among ELLs that maximize learning opportunities to interact while making sense of language and content
- providing multiple opportunities for ELLs to extend their understanding and apply knowledge in both classroom and out-of-school-time settings

In discussing the application of these broad strategies, examples illustrate how schools use more time in collaborative relationships among teachers, families, community-based partners, and employers, who agree to shared learning goals and provide expanded learning opportunities across a reconceived day, year, and in school, family engagement, and community spaces.[30]

Other researchers consider how best to use out-of-school time for Latino immigrant students.[31] Taking into consideration that Latino immigrant families are typically very low income and face many social stresses, Sherylls Valladares and Maniaca Ramos, for example, note the importance of providing structure and supervision, emotional and cultural support in addition to academic assistance, and linking families to counseling services.

The foregoing recommendations speak to the importance of children's healthy development as well as academic achievement. In the following section, I consider these recommended interventions because they may find support in the expanded learning time models advanced in chapters 1–5.

EXTENDING THE EXISTING SCHOOL DAY AND YEAR

In a four-year experiment extending the length of the school year from the standard 180 days in California to 223 days in four public schools, participating schools agreed to restructure their curriculum into smaller units with built-in review and more careful monitoring of student progress.[32] These design features allowed educators to use the expanded time to engage in strategies such as team teaching, small group learning experiences, and mastery-learning techniques. Schools also had the opportunity to provide intersession instruction and enrichment for students with particular learning needs that were falling behind. One of the four experimental schools chose to focus on ELLs and provided these students with at least fifty hours of instructional activities during intersession periods through the year. The school calendar was also reconfigured in favor of several short breaks during the year rather than a long summer break. The targeted ELL students showed a significant gain in reading scores over the two-year evaluation period, and both parents and teachers registered extremely high satisfaction with the program. As successful as the experiment was, it was complex to implement and swam against the current of what most people considered to be a "normal" school schedule.

In many ways, the Massachusetts experiment, as recounted by Davis and Farbman in chapter 1, confirms key findings from our earlier 1994 study. In particular, their review confirms that students with prior low-performing experiences could benefit most from an extended year, but only insofar as that additional time and the interventions included were guided by a set of clear and coherent learning goals. These findings suggest that learning can be accelerated when more time is used to give ELLs the opportunity to apply emergent language and content learning skills.

Extended Time for Teachers of ELL Students

Davis and Farbman also discuss how schools use additional time for teachers to collaborate and focus on professional learning. Here, Walqui and van Lier's work suggests that learning conditions for ELLs can be enhanced if additional school time can be devoted to helping teachers—including content-area teachers—build their language development skills and capacities.[33] Indeed, there is a growing literature on the importance of extended, protected time for teachers to meet, share perspectives and methods, and plan instruction for students, in particular, those with special needs. Traditionally, professional development for teachers has consisted of onetime whole-group presentations and workshops for teachers to learn new skills or sharpen the ones they already have. However, a consistent criticism of this type of professional development is that there tends to be little follow-through and it does not address the specific needs of teachers of ELL students.[34] In ongoing professional learning communities, teachers can focus on their greatest needs and use the additional dedicated time to build their instructional capacity through professional engagement, for example, in continuous learning and improvement cycles of inquiry.[35]

Expanded Learning in Out-of-School Time

Popular strategies for increasing learning time are afterschool and summer programs that partner with community-based providers to offer such programs. Out-of-school-time (OST) programs generally cost less than extending the regular school hours or days, making them more attractive to districts.[36] LA's Best program, described briefly in chapter 2, provides three hours of afterschool academic support and enrichment daily to about twenty-five hundred children in low-income areas of the city. The program has been evaluated extensively, and researchers have found that students who attended the program for at least a hundred days performed significantly better on tests of mathematics than those who either did not attend the program or attended for fewer days. Students did not, however, increase their achievement in English language arts (ELA) beyond the comparison students. The researchers concluded that this was likely related to the fact that two-thirds of the students in the program were ELLs and that other factors related to this status likely impeded their achievement in ELA. Researchers suggested that this may have been due to limited opportunities to read and speak in English at home. But it is also critical to consider the nature of the instruction, the preparation of the adults providing services, and whether programs like these adequately consider the special learning needs of ELLs.

In a review of the literature on OST for ELL students, Julie Maxwell-Jolly found program evaluations that involved analyses of outcomes for ELLs to be "scarce."[37] However, she did find one study of OST programs that served fifty-three hundred students, half ELL and half non-ELL, at five sites in California. According to the evaluators, "ELs made literacy gains similar to those of their non-EL peers after the Communities Organizing Resources to Advance Learning (CORAL) program increased its focus on literacy strategies including primary language reading and one-on-one primary language support."[38] This research suggests that superior outcomes for ELL students were associated with the provision of instruction in their primary language. This should challenge educators to examine the nature of their instructional programs for ELL students in the context of opportunities for primary language instruction provided by expanded learning time programs.

The extensive research on summer school explores its potential to extend learning time and, at the secondary level, to assist students in recovering credits to make high school graduation on time possible. A recent review of the research on summer learning and academic outcomes, conducted by Jennifer

McCombs and colleagues, found that both mandatory and voluntary summer school programs, as well as at-home reading programs, could be effective in both reducing summer learning loss and increasing academic scores. That happened under conditions where students attended consistently and are engaged in the instruction, and high-quality instruction was provided.[39] However, only one of the studies cited in their extensive review considered the effects on ELLs. While most students participating in an at-home reading program appeared to benefit, ELLs did not. As in the LA's Best study, researchers hypothesized that out-of-school conditions were impeding program effects. Lack of alignment of instruction with the special needs of ELL students (e.g., teachers specially prepared for ELL instruction) would seem to be a candidate for explaining this finding.

One OST option not often considered in the extant literature is the implementation of supplemental schools like those that have a rich history in US Asian communities.[40] In a study of expanded learning time, researchers examined the community-based social web of nonprofit and for-profit ethnic supplemental schools that provide bilingual language development, tutoring, and college preparation programs to Chinese and Korean children and youth in the Los Angeles area. These schools serve many thousands of students in weekend classes focused on Asian language and culture, but also reinforce the importance of learning beyond the regular classroom and in the community. Min Zhou and Susan Kim argue that these supplemental schools provide critical social capital that helps to explain the extraordinary success of many Asian students.[41] Supplemental schools, however, have not been adopted in the Latino immigrant community in the same way. However, such schools do exist, and this author was deeply involved in operating and sustaining such a school in Sacramento, California. *Escuela Arco Iris* met every Saturday during the school year for about two decades and provided Spanish language and cultural immersion classes for three and a half hours. At its peak, it served about seventy-five children aged three to twelve, charged a very modest fee, and offered scholarships for low-income children to try to increase economic diversity. Although no formal evaluation was ever conducted, the students clearly developed a strong appreciation for their cultural and linguistic heritage as well as literacy skills. All students who stayed with the school into the elementary grades learned to read and write in Spanish, something that was unavailable in their public schools and that served them well later on in high school, college, and career. Perhaps, however, the greatest advantage came from building a strong and supportive community that offered the kinds of social capital provided by the Asian supplemental schools described by Zhou and Kim. Such out-of-school learning opportunities can be enormously enriching for students, but finding the resources to operate them, especially in low-income communities, can be difficult.

Expanded Learning Options in Secondary School Settings

Linked Learning approaches, as discussed by Hoachlander et al. in chapter 5, constitute another way to reconceptualize time for ELL and immigrant students in secondary schools. I have argued elsewhere that the Linked Learning approach—high school programs that combine career and technical education with purely academic elements—can be structured in such a way to provide more learning time, with more options for students who are still learning the language and the culture.[42] For example, many ELLs and immigrant students find themselves in secondary schools where there are few, if any, teachers who can communicate with them or have time to focus on their particular needs. The opportunity to learn in off-site settings, such as internships, can provide important adult connections and support that would be unavailable on their campus. Opportunities to engage in project-based activities in a work or community-based setting, when carefully supervised and tied to specific learning objectives, can provide important avenues for academic learning and for building language skills through task-embedded social interactions. Opportunities for participating in performance assessments where ELLs might better demonstrate and model what they are learning can help them to demonstrate efficacy. Linked Learning can open up both the calendar and the clock to allow students who need more time to take advantage of settings and times that are less restricted than the typical school can offer.

Another strategy that can be employed for ELL and immigrant students in particular is the extension of high school by an additional year for those students who need extra time to meet the requirements for high school graduation and college preparation. With my colleague Rebecca Callahan, we demonstrated how ELLs are routinely channeled into less rigorous course work, and often into courses that do not even provide credit toward graduation, which makes it challenging if not impossible for ELLs to graduate on time or to pursue postsecondary studies.[43] Norm Gold, who has had thirty years of experience working in California high schools serving immigrant students and ELLs, and his coauthor Julie Maxwell-Jolly laid out a plan to re-organize high schools to better serve these students' needs. They argued that extending high school to five years can increase graduation and college go-ing for those students who choose to take advantage of the option. They ex-plain that,

> Designing proactive programs to allow students greater time to com-plete their studies could replace the stigma and attrition of failure with success. There should be multiple opportunities and encouragement for acceleration, but no label of failure for a student who sets a five-year goal and works diligently to meet it. With appropriate initial diagnostic assessment, and individual counseling and monitoring, such extended programs, including opportunities for internships and career and com-munity engagement, may be exactly what is needed both for newer im-migrants and for many long-term English learners whose earlier school experience was colored by frustration and failure.[44]

Of course, more learning time must consist of better learning time. A fifth year of high school is only beneficial when systemic issues and barriers to students' learning are removed (e.g., tracking into less rigorous and/or non-credit courses).

Expanded Time for Parent and Community Engagement to Advance ELL and Immigrant Student Learning

Most parents of ELLs have had no personal contact with public schools in the United States and know little about how to guide their children through the system. They do not know the expectations of the system either for them-selves or for their children, and they do not know their rights. They may also lack strategies for supporting their children's education, believing incorrectly that they have little to offer in this regard.[45] Luis Moll and colleagues have shown, however, how teachers can create assignments that draw on the skills and abilities of immigrant parents, allowing them to engage with student learning effectively in both in-school and nonschool settings.[46] The potential for these kinds of programs is great, as they can not only provide critical in-struction in culturally consonant contexts, but also reinforce students' sense of self-worth and efficacy, working alongside skilled parents and commu-nity members.[47] As noted by Jessica Gunderson et al. in chapter 2, teachers and school partners need training in how to bridge the chasm between home and school that too often exists for many ELL students and to identify the strengths in students' homes and communities.

A program called Parent Institute for Quality Education (www.PIQE. org), with a thirty-year track record, illustrates how community-based partners can engage Latino parents in their children's education. The program consists of nine weekly parent training sessions focused on learning about the US education system. Parents learn how to advocate for their children, access opportunities such as postsecondary education, and find practical information on, for example, how to check homework when they don't really understand it. The program has been evaluated very positively. Researchers found that parents who attended PIQE sessions continued to engage in supportive educational practices at home long after they completed the training.[48] PIQE stands as a model program to engage Latino parents in their own language. It recognizes parents' funds of knowledge and is based on a respect for parents and their often underutilized skills to help their children succeed in school.

Likewise, the broader community schools and Promise Neighborhood strategies described in this volume, chapters 3 and 4 respectively, offer opportunities for community-based organizations and school staff to engage in culturally relevant efforts to engage families as partners in their children's education. The Promise Neighborhoods examples in Chula Vista (chapter 4) demonstrate how a direct focus on parent engagement and the promotion of family economic security can contribute to school readiness and instructional capacity in schools. In San Francisco, where a Promise Neighborhoods initiative has focused on supports for immigrant families and students, researchers found that wellness services as well as standards-aligned tutoring improved immigrant and ELL students' readiness to learn. Additionally, culturally relevant support services allowed teachers to focus more on direct instruction as they had assistance in addressing student's other needs. Several teachers also reported that the presence of more caring adults who can work directly with youth across an expanded day allowed teachers more time to plan and reflect on their own practice and to collaborate with colleagues.[49]

If Expanded Time Is So Successful, Why Isn't It Implemented More Often?

A primary reason that these strategies are not routinely incorporated in school or in out-of-school programs is cost. And good programs do cost money. Qualified people must be paid, and effective programs require reasonable student-to-adult ratios so that they can build caring relationships. Critics can always use cost as a way of undermining programs they do not support. Daniela Di-Giacomo and her colleagues describe the efforts in Colorado to extend learning time for students in that state as an equity measure that would target the students in greatest need.[50] While the reform started out with significant support, it was "hijacked" by initiatives that were "sexier" (e.g., using digital resources) and less costly and that promised to provide benefits for all students, not just those students with the greatest need. Of course, this meant that the students with the greatest needs actually received less support, and efforts were not targeted to their particular needs.

Another challenge to sustaining these programs is the narrow way in which their outcomes are measured. Programs that set out to provide safe afterschool spaces where children can engage in a variety of activities that support personal development are too often evaluated only on whether they raise math or reading scores. Falling short on this, they can be defunded. A meta-analysis of twenty-one federally funded afterschool programs found that the programs, while criticized for not meeting academic achievement goals, actually did increase students' self-perceptions as learners, positive social behaviors, and bonding to school, as well as supporting other things, such as completing homework, which can have a longer-term impact than a minor test score increase.[51] Setting goals that are too narrow can set up OST programs to fail.

CONCLUSIONS

The research is clear and consistent that additional instructional time can be an important benefit for many students who struggle in school. Beyond the narrow measures of success based on test scores or grades, results such as staying in school, graduating, developing positive and supportive friendships, and increasing one's sense of efficacy and self-worth can pay enormous dividends over a lifetime. While these goals are found among many expanded learning time approaches, in the case of ELLs in particular, more learning time is needed to simply achieve the goals of schooling that most parents appear to want: academics, preparation for citizenship, and preparation for a satisfying work life. Like all students, ELLs arrive at school with different needs depending on their age and their own histories. Some ELLs will thrive if just given more school time. Other students will need a reconceptualization of learning time, as exemplified by programs like *Escuela Arco Iris*, where they can build social capital and strengthen a sense of identity; others will need the wraparound services provided by a community school; and still others may be best served in programs like Linked Learning that offer off-site learning experiences, such as internships.

We can assume that the findings on the importance of *how* time is used to advance the academic, social, emotional, and language learning of students holds for ELLs as well, but this is by no means certain. Very little research has been conducted on these outcomes for ELLs or immigrant students, even though a common characteristic of the two groups is that they have "double the work" to accomplish in the same or less time as other students. There are also indications in the literature that the language of instruction provided during expanded learning time, as well as the specialized preparation of the adults serving in these programs, may be critical variables for ELLs' success. Paying attention to a student's culture as well as providing content instruction in a native language that the student understands and can build on may also be important elements in achieving desired effects. All these dimensions of expanded learning time deserve to be researched much more carefully in diverse settings.

A final note of caution is in order. While additional time spent in productive activities may increase learning and be beneficial to students in many ways, the enrichment activities provided to "disadvantaged" students in school or in OST programs, even when similar in content to those that middle-class students are exposed to, do not provide the critical social networks that middle-class students profit from. In other words, while both groups of students may be enrolled in a ballet class, to the extent that these occur in separate spaces, the advantages that accrue to the students are different. Zhou and Kim argue that social capital sharing in the Saturday programs is a critical factor for the Asian students, and Alejandro Portes and Min Zhou have argued powerfully that the social group into which immigrants integrate can determine student outcomes.[52] Achievement gaps as well as gaps in self-efficacy will likely persist if ELL and immigrant students are not provided the same experiences—*alongside their more advantaged peers*—in ways that foster friendships and informal flows of information about how opportunity exists in the broader society and how to access it.

CHAPTER 9

TIME FOR SOCIAL CHANGE

The Youth Development and Educational
Outcomes of Youth Organizing

VERONICA TERRIQUEZ AND JOHN ROGERS

*Without the SCYEA it's very likely that I wouldn't have graduated
from high school—and I can only speculate as to what would have
happened. I could have ended up working a dead-end job. I could be
out on the streets, I could be in jail, I could be dead. I don't know.*

—FELIPE, age twenty-three

FELIPE, QUOTED ABOVE, was majoring in urban studies and planning at
a four-year university at the time of our interview with him. In the early
2000s, he attended Fremont High School, a predominantly Latino and African American school in South Los Angeles, which then had a graduation
rate under 50 percent. By his own account, he and his friends weren't up to
much good when he started high school. Things began to change in tenth
grade, however, when another student invited him to a South Central Youth
Empowered thru Action (SCYEA) meeting. SCYEA is a youth organizing
group run by the Community Coalition, a South Los Angeles nonprofit
501(c)(3) organization. Like other youth organizing groups across the United
States, SCYEA combines elements of youth development with the strategies
of grassroots organizing to engage young people in addressing local community concerns.

Felipe participated in a variety of SCYEA's activities—attending weekly
lunchtime gatherings at school and afterschool meetings at the Community
Coalition. He enjoyed the activities and established friendships with other
members. But there was more to this participation than camaraderie. Much
of Felipe's time with SCYEA centered around a campaign to expand access

to college preparatory courses across Los Angeles schools. As part of the campaign, he discussed education policy, examined data, planned and led meetings, conducted outreach to his peers, made public presentations, wrote op-eds, and met with elected officials. In the process, Felipe acquired skills that contributed to his academic success. All the while, he was mentored by young adults from his own community who had gone to college and encouraged him to do the same. Felipe believed his experience in SCYEA was transformative. "It really kind of shaped who I am as a person, my values, my work ethic," he explained, "and developed a lot of leadership skills, my potential to think critically and to write, speak, and to articulate goals and solutions." These attributes, Felipe argued, not only helped him get into college, they prepared him to succeed.

In this chapter, we demonstrate that Felipe's case is not unique. We show that low-income high school students of color report developing a range of skills and capacities as a result of their spending additional time engaged in California youth organizing groups. The members of the groups also attend college, especially four-year institutions, at far higher rates than their peers with similar backgrounds. Our research suggests that youth organizing serves as an important model of quality expanded learning time for low-income students of color. The groups offer purposeful, structured, and supportive time for learning after school, during weekends, and over the summer. And many students participate in the activities over years, entering as novices and leaving as leaders. Time spent out of the classroom in organizing groups promotes the development of valuable knowledge and skills, motivates academic achievement and a college-going identity, expands social networks, and advances collective action for positive change.

Our chapter proceeds in five sections. Section one highlights the rationale for considering youth organizing as *high-quality* expanded learning time with lasting implications for youths developmental and educational trajectories. Section two discusses the data and methods we used to investigate how youth organizing groups develop students' skills and promote their educational attainment. The third section draws on survey data to provide a demographic description of youth organizing members, their reasons for participating and the nature of their involvement, as well as their reflections on how they benefited from their participation. The fourth section leverages both survey and semistructured interview data to demonstrate how youth organizing can contribute to high rates of postsecondary enrollment. Our concluding section points to implications of the study for expanding high-quality learning time inside and outside the classroom.

YOUTH ORGANIZING AND ITS IMPLICATIONS FOR YOUTH DEVELOPMENT AND EDUCATIONAL OUTCOMES

Youth organizing groups began forming in urban centers during the late 1980s and early 1990s against the backdrop of growing economic inequality, a declining welfare state, and dramatic increases in incarceration rates.[1] In contrast to community service efforts that focus on helping others in need through short-term and largely apolitical solutions (e.g., cleaning parks, tutoring children, serving food to the homeless), youth organizing groups have sought to bring about systemic change.[2] Over the years, some of the groups' campaigns have resulted in a broad range of concrete policy wins that address social inequality and injustice. The groups have prompted public officials to build new schools, establish less punitive and more supportive school discipline policies, create equity-based education funding formulas, and much more. Their campaigns also stretch beyond education to include issues such as hazardous environmental conditions, immigration policies, health disparities, LGBTQ rights, juvenile justice, and police-community relations.

Like others who participate in voluntary associations, students who join organizing groups expect to get something in return.[3] Youth organizing groups tend to offer a welcoming and safe environment, food, and academic and social supports, all while maintaining a focus on training their members to lead grassroots campaigns.[4] Recruitment generally occurs through peer networks that often attract new members by validating and celebrating youth culture, using hip hop or other cultural arts in their outreach and campaign efforts. Importantly, the groups do not simply appeal to high-achieving students, but tend to draw students with varying levels of academic achievement who can relate to the issues and concerns that the groups aim to resolve.[5] As such, some students' motivations for joining may have to do more with the pressing need to effect change in their community than short- or long-term personal gains.

Youth organizing groups commonly maximize member participation by scheduling activities during weekly lunchtime meetings, during afterschool meetings, and through intensive political education workshops on weekends or over the summer. The democratic and developmental nature of youth organizing means that student members shape their meetings as they take on increasing levels of responsibility. The time young people spend in the groups varies. While most spend about three to five hours per week in their groups, more established leaders spend up to ten hours or more. Students play leadership roles during regular meetings: setting agendas, facilitating discussions, identifying problems, and collectively determining strategic actions. Regular meetings combine time for campaign activities with time for academic and social supports. Many groups provide tutoring, college counseling, legal advice, and referrals to an array of counseling services.[6]

Whether students realize it or not, youth organizing groups produce similar developmental outcomes as other adolescent civic groups, such as community service clubs or student leadership. In creating a safe space to collectively tackle public issues and concerns, organizing groups provide student members with a range of opportunities for meaningful learning through practice.[7] Students enhance their capacities to communicate with others, speak in public, plan activities and events, and work collaboratively around shared goals.[8] They can also develop social networks that cultivate healthy behaviors and promote well-being.[9] Moreover, students can bond with caring adult staff in ways that are often impossible in classrooms where teachers must attend to many more students. In addition, whereas time in classrooms is often driven by a standards-based curriculum, time in youth organizing groups is structured around collective problem solving. This problems-based approach requires time for informal exchange among novice students and their more experienced peers, as well as opportunities for students to share *their* questions and concerns with caring and supportive adults. As discussed by Ben Kirshner and Rebecca Kaplan in chapter 6, youth organizing staff tend to play an important role in fostering feelings of safety and belonging, while also scaffolding learning and leadership development.

Youth organizing groups also develop students' capacities in ways that differ from other adolescent civic groups that simply focus on service or leadership.[10] Students sometimes report acquiring a broader set of leadership skills and receiving a stronger orientation to college than do young people in civic groups that do not focus on effecting policy change.[11] In particular, youth organizing encourages critical thinking through political education workshops that equip their members with the analytical tools to understand how larger economic, political, and social structures contribute to their community's problems.[12] Many groups also employ ethnic studies workshops that instill ethnic pride and/or multiracial solidarity.[13] Through the course of campaign efforts, students undergo intensive civics training as they learn to mobilize their peers, plan protests, lobby politicians and other decision makers, and/or participate in electoral work.[14] Additionally, grassroots campaign efforts require students to apply academic skills to real-world problems. For example, students often conduct surveys, analyze quantitative data, make sense of school and government policies, write about their campaigns, or produce art or public media to spread a message.[15]

The skills and capacities developed through youth organizing can affect students' educational outcomes both directly and indirectly. Youth organizing enables students to forge civic identities that are committed to improving their communities and addressing broader social inequalities.[16] The civic identities can have an impact on students' own academic achievement and postsecondary educational attainment. For example, as students learn to use academic tools to challenge discrimination or inequality, they can better understand the relevance of, and an investment in, classroom learning.[17] They may also come to understand their own academic achievement and attainment as a form of resistance that challenges broader educational disparities. Moreover, some students may view higher education as a resource for helping their own communities, rather than simply viewing a college degree as a ticket out of their communities.[18] This sort of identity formation (as empowered and knowledgeable civic agents) is made possible by participation beyond a single school year. New members join as novices, interacting with more experienced members for several months before gradually taking on leadership roles themselves. Retention rates in youth organizing groups afford participants the opportunity to reflect on their current circumstances and their aspirations for themselves, their families, and their communities.

DATA AND METHODS

Our research relies on data from California, a state in which children from immigrant families outnumber those from non-immigrant families, and young people of color outnumber white youth.[19] The state is home to established youth organizing groups that have been engaging low-income youth of color in a range of civic efforts since the 1990s, as well as groups that have more recently adapted this strategy for youth development.

Our analyses rely on two waves of data collection from youth organizing groups. The first and more recent wave comes from paper surveys administered as part of the larger Youth Leadership and Health Study. The survey data analyzed here were collected from 2013 to 2015 from 452 high-school-aged students who participated regularly in any of twenty-three separate youth organizing groups. Some of the groups included members who were no longer in high school, but our analysis is limited to those who were in high school at the time of the study. Located in high-poverty urban and semirural communities across the state, these groups typically convened students as a group one or two times a week, and often gave them assignments to work on independently or in small groups. The groups were all part of Building Healthy Communities, a ten-year initiative funded by the California Endowment that includes youth leadership development as part of its strategy to improve health and well-being in fourteen very low-income communities throughout the state.[20] We compare the demographics of youth organizing members to the demographics of the general population of adolescents ages thirteen to seventeen (produced through an analysis of data from the California Health Interview Survey [CHIS]).[21] We then report on the reasons why high school students join the groups; our analysis offers evidence of the importance of leveraging students' social and extracurricular interests in order to support learning outside the classroom. Next, we show the varying extent to which members develop a range of skills and civic capacities as a result of their participation.

The second wave of data comes from telephone surveys and in-person interviews conducted in 2011–2012 as part of the California Young Adult Study. Telephone surveys were conducted with 410 alumni, ages eighteen to twenty-six, who had participated in one of eight established youth organizing groups while they were still in high school.[22] Our comparison group comes from a representative sample survey of 2,200 young adults who completed at least some portion of their K–12 schooling in California. To complement survey findings, we draw on in-person interviews with eighty-four alumni who participated in the survey, along with interviews with staff.

YOUTH DEVELOPMENT OUTCOMES

The California youth organizing groups we studied engage youth of color from low-income backgrounds. Table 9.1 presents survey results for members of youth organizing groups and for the general population of adolescents in California. Our findings show that members of youth organizing groups disproportionately come from lower socioeconomic backgrounds. Specifically,

TABLE 9.1.   Demographics of youth organizing participants and California adolescents

	Youth organizing sample (N = 452)	CHIS sample (N = 786)
Socioeconomic background		
• Raised by parent(s) with a BA	9%	41%
• Low-income	85%	44%
Race/Ethnicity		
• Latino	60%	46%
• White	<1%	31%
• Black	12%	7%
• Asian-Pacific Islander	25%	14%
• Native	1%	1%
• Other	1%	2%
Immigrant family	78%	55%
Gender		
• Male	38%	53%
• Female	62%	47%
Average age	16.2	15.5
Time involved in youth organizing group		
• Less than 1 year	51%	
• 1 year or longer	49%	NA
Reasons for joining youth organizing group		
• It seemed like fun	52%	
• Wanted to make a difference	43%	
• Invited by friends	42%	
• Liked what the group focused on	40%	
• Wanted to develop new skills	33%	
• Looks good on my résumé	23%	
• Had free time to get involved	21%	
• Free food	21%	NA

*Results may not add up to 100% because of rounding error.

youth organizing members are less likely than the general population to have been raised by a parent with a bachelor's degree (9 percent compared to 41 percent). At the same time, 85 percent of youth organizing members come from low-income families—as measured by free and reduced lunch eligibility—compared to 44 percent of the general population.

Nearly all youth organizing members (99 percent) identify as nonwhite. Statewide, 70 percent of the adolescent population is nonwhite, with Latinos making up the plurality (46 percent). Accordingly, Latinos, African Americans, and Asian Americans (many of Southeast Asian descent) are well represented among youth organizing participants.

Girls outnumber boys in youth organizing groups. However, concerted efforts to increase the proportion of boys involved in youth organizing in California have met with some success, at least between 2014 and 2016.[23] Our youth organizing sample is somewhat older than the general population because of the significant representation of high school seniors among groups' memberships.

Students can remain involved in their youth organizing groups for multiple years, creating opportunities for students to take on new roles as they gain more experience. In our sample, just under half of students (49 percent) were "veteran" members who had been involved a year or longer, while the remaining 51 percent were newer members who had joined their group within a year of taking our survey.[24] Overall, youth averaged 1.25 years of membership. It is fairly common for veteran members in youth organizing groups to provide orientation and training for newer members.

To understand how to make extracurricular interventions appealing to racially diverse low-income students, it may be useful to learn what attracts adolescents to youth organizing groups. We therefore asked participants to report the main reasons why they joined their organization. As shown in table 9.1, the top reason is social—52 percent of respondents joined because the group seemed like fun. Youth organizing groups' missions and programming were also important, as were peer invitations. Some students were also motivated by personal benefits, such as developing new skills or because they thought it would look good on their résumé. It is worth noting that just over a fifth joined because of the free food, while the same proportion joined because they had the free time. This latter finding signals the limited opportunities for meaningful extracurricular participation available to low-income youth.

We asked respondents if, through their organization, they had participated in any of a list of activities. The list was based on activities commonly reported among youth civic groups across the state. Figure 9.1 illustrates the most common activities reported by veteran members who had been involved for a year or longer (dark gray bars) and by newer members who had been involved in their group for less than a year (light gray bars). Interestingly, both newer and veteran members reported participating in college preparatory or college success activities more than any other activity, even though the

FIGURE 9.1   How students participated in their youth organizing group

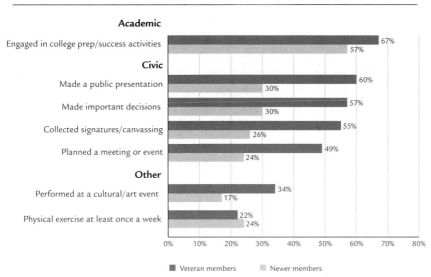

primary mission of most groups was to engage members in addressing local school and community concerns. For many groups, these college preparatory activities are part of the regular afterschool routine, while for others, such activities occur during specific times of the year, such as the fall or summer.

Students also participated in civic activities connected to their local campaign efforts, with veteran members significantly more likely to report engagement in such activities than newer members. For example, 60 percent of veteran members made a public presentation compared to 30 percent of newer members. Meanwhile, 57 percent of veteran members (compared to 30 percent of newer members) felt that they made important decisions as part of their group. Such experience can be empowering to students who have limited opportunities to exercise power and influence. Fifty-five percent of veteran members, compared to 26 percent of newer members, also went door-to-door or engaged in some other form of canvassing for a campaign. Veteran members were also more likely than newer members to have planned a meeting or event. This was also true of performing in a cultural event or showcasing artwork. These findings suggest that students expand their roles within youth organizing groups as they obtain more training and familiarity with campaign activities.

As part of our study, we asked respondents to rate how their youth organizing involvement affected their personal development—did it have *no impact, very little impact,* some impact, or *a lot of impact?* Such self-reports are, of course, subjective and could be favorably biased. However, the range of responses indicate that participants acknowledged no or very little impact, when appropriate. To be conservative, figure 9.2 only accounts for the percentage of students who reported "a lot" of impact. Presented separately for veteran and newer members, the findings suggest that students felt empowered by their participation, especially if they remained involved in their group for over a year. Results indicate that 77 percent of veteran members and 62 percent of newer members learned "a lot" about how to stand up for their beliefs, while 74 percent of veteran members and 59 percent of newer members improved their ability to communicate with others. Meanwhile,

FIGURE 9.2   How students benefited from youth organizing: percent responding "a lot"

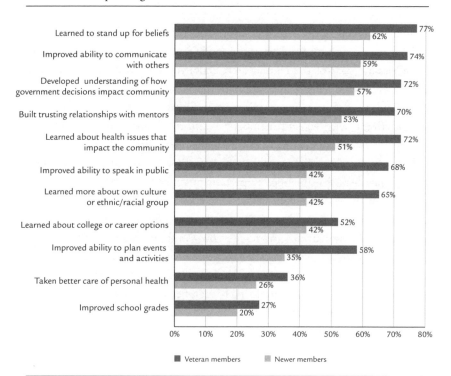

Veteran members   Newer members

72 percent of veteran members and 57 percent of newer members learned "a lot" about how government decisions have an impact on their community. This finding may have implications for students' lasting interest in civic affairs. Also important are the findings indicating that the overwhelming majority of veteran members, along with somewhat smaller percentages of newer members, reported "a lot" of impact in terms of building or strengthening trusting relationships with mentors, learning about health issues or other issues that affect their community, improving their ability to speak in public, learning about their ethnic group or culture, and improving their ability to plan events and activities. Meanwhile, 52 percent of veteran members and 42 percent of newer members learned "a lot" about college and career options. Smaller percentages of members reported taking better care of their health or significantly improving their school grades. Taken together, these findings reveal the varying degrees to which students developed skills and capacities relevant to their academic achievement, personal development, and future civic participation.

POSTSECONDARY EDUCATIONAL ATTAINMENT

In addition to developing students' skills and capacities in the short term, our research suggests that youth organizing can promote four-year college attendance. To make this case, we draw on data from the California Young Adult Study, which includes surveys and interview data from youth organizing alumni and the general population.[25] Similar to the youth organizing members described above, those in the 2011 survey disproportionately came from low-income families and almost all were students of color. As such, they belong to demographic groups with fairly low levels of enrollment in four-year colleges. Moreover, most attended under-resourced high schools with fairly low college-going rates.

To examine postsecondary educational enrollment, we distinguish among three groups: (1) youth organizing alumni who never enrolled in college (but may have enrolled in a general educational development program, adult school, or vocational program); (2) youth organizing alumni who enrolled in a community college, but never enrolled in a four-year college; and (3) youth organizing alumni who enrolled in a four-year college or university.

Figure 9.3 shows the postsecondary enrollment of survey respondents from the youth organizing alumni and general population.[26] Results indicate that 8 percent of youth organizing alumni did not enroll in college, compared

FIGURE 9.3   Postsecondary enrollment among youth organizing alumni
and the general population

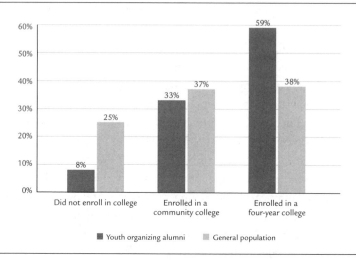

to 25 percent of the general population. Although somewhat similar percentages of both groups enrolled in a community college, the percentage of youth organizing alumni who enrolled in a four-year institution is quite striking. While 59 percent of youth organizing alumni enrolled in a four-year college, 38 percent of the state's young adults did so overall. This comparison does not account for the fact that, on average, youth organizing alumni come from more modest socioeconomic backgrounds than do youth in the general population. The four-year college attendance rates among youth organizing alumni are even more remarkable when compared to those of young people from similar socioeconomic backgrounds (results not shown).

Of course, the students' high rates of postsecondary educational attainment cannot be completely attributed to youth organizing. Personality characteristics and other factors that lead youth organizing alumni to join and remain in these groups likely contribute to their postsecondary educational attainment. Regardless, there is a clear correlation between youth organizing participation in high school and enrollment in four-year colleges.

Our interviews with staff and alumni indicate that youth organizing groups promote college enrollment, especially in four-year colleges, in at least a few ways. First, the groups offer direct academic support and college guidance. Second, campaign efforts enhance students' skills and develop their intellectual interests. Third, the groups encourage members to see a connection between college attendance and a broader community empowerment agenda.

As the groups in our study work to advance social change, they also devote time to setting students on a pathway to college. This concern with academics is related to a more general interest in the welfare and development of members. Groups create structured time for homework, offer tutoring, or connect members to other academic services in their communities when needed.

Some groups paid special attention to students who were not very academically oriented. This meant tracking students' academic progress, confirming that they went to class, reminding them to complete their homework, and helping them develop plans for life after high school. This was the case for Emmanuel, who was more focused on what was going on in the streets than at school when he first got involved in youth organizing. Thanks to staff, he managed to stay on track to graduate on time. "They want to make sure you do your homework," he explained. "If they caught wind you were doing bad, then they make you give progress reports." Emmanuel, like many other students, felt accountable to the youth organizing staff who, he believed, authentically cared about his future.

In line with the survey findings above (see figure 9.1), many study participants reported receiving direct guidance on how to apply for college. Through their youth organizing groups, many learned about the importance of enrolling in and completing the classes required for admission to California's public four-year colleges. Such college counseling guidance was a critical supplement during the period of our study, when California had the highest student-to-counselor ratio in the nation.[27] Adelina, an immigrant student from Mexico, was one of many who benefited from the youth organizing staff's college guidance. "They would tell you, 'These are the classes you need to take, and this is what you need to do [to get into a four-year college],'" she recalled. Without her youth organizing group, Adelina believed that she would have failed to complete the course requirements for admission to the University of California.

In addition to acting as conduits of information, staff and others connected to campaign efforts served as role models who had already navigated a path to college. Vanessa, a former member of an immigrant rights group, remembers feeling a deep connection to one staff member who had "gotten out from that community that I came from and gone off to Berkeley."

Meanwhile, Patricia, who had been an active member of a group in the East-side of Los Angeles, remembers being impressed by all the people she met through the organizing efforts who had gone to UCLA and USC. "Being in those spaces kind of made you realize that maybe college was a possibility," she explained, "and even though you had a 60 percent dropout rate at your high school, there were still kids making it out."

Time spent in youth organizing groups enabled students to develop skills relevant to their academic success. Mandy, a twenty-two-year-old college student, noted that she learned to think creatively about difficult problems in her organizing group. Youth organizing staff encouraged members to "brainstorm different solutions," a strategy she still used in college when she approached a research paper. Meanwhile, Lily, the daughter of Southeast Asian refugees, remembers learning communication, leadership, and public speaking skills. She said, "All of those skills I could apply when it comes to dealing with people at school and dealing with my own classmates when it comes to group projects." Students also reported developing their critical thinking skills, while a few reported developing a stronger work ethic through their youth organizing groups.

Campaign-related activities also fostered students' investment in developing their academic skills. Gordon, an Oakland graduate and son of a single mother, appreciated the ways in which his organizing group taught him to analyze community problems and develop potential solutions. "It opened my eyes to what is in front of my face," he explained. "It is the root of my writing. It makes me want to write." It is significant that Gordon's grades improved in his English class after he joined his youth organizing group. Others, like Jocelyn, daughter of Filipina immigrants, deepened her interest in social studies, thanks to workshops that linked local issues to larger global developments. "We learn things that we don't learn from the school," she reported. "It opens us to a different dimension. Like, 'Wow! There's another world that we don't know that exists.'" Meanwhile, Robbie, who grew up in a polluted Bay Area neighborhood, developed a new appreciation for math and statistics through his work on an environmental justice campaign. For Robbie, data collection and statistics proved critical in understanding how "toxic waste factories are affecting our community and other low-income communities of color."

Finally, youth organizing groups inspire young people to view their own academic achievement as both a personal project and one that benefits their entire communities. Groups often educate their members about the educational and resource inequalities that contribute to poverty, crime, and other problems in their community. Staff often teach students about the "power of an education" to transform their lives, but also make a difference in their communities. Jermaine, an Oakland graduate, heard this message. As part of a youth organizing group that inculcated in its members the legacy of the local civil rights movement, he was motivated to make a lasting difference in his community. "It's not really about you," he explained. "You're doing something for the people that come after you." Similarly, Raymond, a South Los Angeles native, claimed that his organization gave him a "new frame of thinking" about access to higher education. He understood that because of under-resourced schools and poverty-related challenges, very few people like him completed their bachelor's degrees. This awareness motivated him to beat the odds and attend a four-year college. As a four-year college student at the time of the interview, he wanted to open the doors of opportunity for others in his community and was "focusing on how to create access for kids to come to college and how to keep them in college."

Not surprisingly, many former youth organizing participants reported pursuing degrees so that they could obtain jobs that helped their community. These young people disproportionately aspired to careers as teachers, social workers, urban planners, and other fields that allowed them to serve their community. Youth organizing instilled in many a sense of community responsibility and an understanding that a college degree would enhance their capacity to give back and serve as role models for younger cohorts.

SUMMARY AND IMPLICATIONS FOR EXPANDED QUALITY LEARNING TIME

Youth organizing groups engage high school students in collective efforts to have an impact on educational and other social policies. Our research shows that these organizations afford their members high-quality expanded learning time during regular meetings at school and at community-based sites, as well as in the context of extended campaigns. This time, which members themselves help to shape, supports students' overall well-being and the development of a range of skills, capacities, and civic commitments that contribute to high school completion and postsecondary educational attainment.

As voluntary civic organizations, youth organizing groups achieve these positive outcomes by offering an array of developmental opportunities. While students may elect to spend their time in the groups because they find the atmosphere to be fun and sociable, youth organizing prompts students to learn about, critically analyze, and collectively address issues and concerns that affect their lives. The groups also offer students links to college guidance and other forms of support. As a result of their participation, students forge civic understanding and skills, become empowered to stand up for their beliefs, learn about their culture, develop caring relationships with mentors from their communities, enhance their academic skills, and enroll in college (especially four-year institutions) at fairly high rates. Those who remain involved in their groups for a year or longer especially reap the development benefits of participation.

Our findings about the positive benefits that accrue to youth who spend time after school in youth organizing groups builds on a broader literature about political socialization. McIntosh and Youniss have shown that when young people collaborate, resolve conflicts, and address meaningful problems in voluntary groups, they are more likely to become civically engaged adults.[28] Similarly, McFarland and Thomas find an association between youth participation in "politically salient" groups (which afford opportunities for service, public speaking, and deliberation) and later patterns of community service, voting, and participation in electoral campaigns.[29] This association is particularly strong for youth growing up in low-income families and immigrant youth.

Youth organizing groups represent a *promising site* for expanded learning time. By facilitating civic participation and college enrollment among low-income youth of color and immigrant youth, the groups advance equity and social inclusion. Accordingly, the 501(c)(3) nonprofit organizations seeking to offer comprehensive programs, like the ones studied here, merit ongoing investment from philanthropic organizations, government agencies, and individual donors.

Youth organizing also offers a *promising set of lessons* about high-quality expanded learning time for other educators and youth service providers. Certainly, not all of what the groups do can or should be transposed into other settings. After all, youth organizing is a voluntary activity that appeals to a subset of young people. It represents an intensive intervention that most benefits core members who participate regularly. Not everyone has the interest, commitment, or time for such participation. Nonetheless, elements of youth organizing can be incorporated into other types of out-of-school programs. These include:

- *Offering students the choice of whether or not to participate.* Optional or voluntary inclusionary programs allow students to pursue their own interests and develop an investment in their own extracurricular participation.
- *Inviting students to determine how they spend their time.* Precisely because time is structured by adults during the school day, young people appreciate the opportunity to shape after school time—what activities they participate in and the purpose to which these activities are addressed.
- *Meeting students' interests and immediate needs in the course of offering other structured learning opportunities.* Safe afterschool spaces that enable students to socialize and enjoy themselves have the potential to attract participants with different levels of academic preparation. When possible, afterschool programming in high-poverty communities should also aim to provide a range of other services or provisions that tend to students' overall health and well-being.
- *Devoting time to guided, critical, and interactive approaches to learning about students' own neighborhoods and/or racial or ethnic communities.* This localized approach to learning can enhance students' critical thinking skills and investment in academic subjects.
- *Providing ample time for youth to tackle complex problems that they care about with one another, with more experienced peers, and with supportive adults.* In developing their civic skills, students also learn how to apply academic skills to real-world problems.
- *Encouraging a trajectory of development over a sustained period of time, such that students can enter as novices and move toward positions of leadership.* Regular, ongoing, and sustained time affords students the opportunities to broaden their participation and deepen their learning.
- *Presenting opportunities for students to connect with and receive mentorship from caring adults, including those from their communities who have accessed higher education.* Such social networks can inspire students to pursue higher education and obtain culturally relevant guidance in preparing for and applying to college.

Finally, youth organizing represents a *promising strategy* for building the political will necessary to expand learning time. Research we have conducted in California shows that youth organizing groups can play an important role in focusing the public and policy makers on investments for low-income youth of color and immigrant youth.[30] The groups in California have used new participatory structures created by the state's recent education finance law to influence educational budget decisions. As part of these groups, high school students have been responsible for conducting research on their community's needs, mobilizing other youth to attend rallies and government meetings, meeting with school board members and other elected officials, and serving on advisory committees. Their efforts insert the voices and ideas of low-income youth and youth of color into the political process. This participatory approach introduces new ideas and understandings, fosters legitimacy, and builds broad-based public support for equity-focused policies.

CHAPTER 10

SPATIAL INEQUALITY AND GAPS IN EXPANDED LEARNING TIME OPPORTUNITIES

PAUL ONG AND ELENA ONG

INTRODUCTION

This chapter examines the expanded learning time (ELT) gap—the difference in access to educationally enhancing opportunities beyond the school bell—through the lens of urban spatial structures.[1] These structures are societally constructed through highly complex and interacting social, economic, and political dynamics. To better understand the link between spatial educational inequality and the ELT gap, we analyze the phenomenon through the case study of the Los Angeles metropolitan area. The chapter is organized into three parts. Part one describes the Los Angeles region, including its demographic and socioeconomic characteristics, patterns of racial and economic residential segregation, and the stratified landscape. Part two examines spatial inequality experienced by elementary school students due to place-based disparities in educational achievement, differences in physical access to out-of-neighborhood resources, and transportation disparities. Part three examines how spatial inequality contributes to disparities in ELT opportunities, focusing on the availability of nearby afterschool programs and constraints on travel to educationally enhancing activities beyond the neighborhood. The chapter concludes with a discussion of how urban structures and dynamics reproduce socioeconomic stratification with recommendations to offset the ELT gap.[2]

The starting point in this analysis is to define three key elements of spatial inequality in the urban landscape—place, space, and transportation accessibility. These interlocking spatial inequalities affect every aspect of urban society.

Place refers to a specific area, a particular neighborhood and to its people and institutions. Place inequality is produced by clustering privileged and disadvantaged populations, mirroring larger socioeconomic hierarchies. It is further accentuated because of inequitable distribution of resources allocated externally and produced internally.

Space refers to relational location, geographic positions, and distances to natural, human, and economic resources and opportunities. Space inequality is produced when a population is significantly separated physically from positive amenities and goods, and when less desirable activities (e.g., the placement of manufacturing using toxic materials) are disproportionately concentrated within and near disadvantaged communities. The last element comprises the networks that enable people in one place to participate in activities in other locations beyond their neighborhood.

Transportation is the mechanism that links workers to jobs, and shoppers to stores. Inequality within a network is produced when there is a systematic disparity of transportation resources across places. Where accessible public transportation is a scarce commodity, as in the Los Angeles region, the lack of access to reliable private vehicles is a central concern. While transportation inequality is generally associated with income inequality, those in disadvantaged communities also face higher car prices, loan rates, and insurance rates. Disadvantaged neighborhoods must depend on less reliable, less flexible, and less effective modes of travel that amplify the barriers created by geographic distances, further isolating them into unequal places.

Existing literature indicates that educational inequality is embedded in segregated residential patterns and other dimensions of geographic inequality. At the metropolitan level, the level of ethno-racial (the complex overlap and intersection of ethnicity and race) student segregation across schools is highly correlated with the level of housing segregation. This is not surprising because school and district boundaries often coincide with neighborhood boundaries.[3] Student segregation is further accentuated through a gerrymandering of school attendance zones.[4] After *Brown v. Board of Education*, the United States experienced a slow and partial decline in school segregation, but recent decades have witnessed a trend toward resegregation, with predominantly minority and low-income schools suffering from poor educational outcomes.[5] Even alternatives to traditional schools, such as magnet schools that are specifically proposed to address resegregation, have been unable to attenuate the problem.[6] Spatial educational inequality is a product of broader forms of stratification and is also a contributor to the reproduction of an unequal society. K–12 educational disparities both in and out of the school setting can perpetuate the production of inequality, now and in the future. This can be seen through an exploration of the Los Angeles landscape.

LOS ANGELES AS A CASE STUDY

Los Angeles is a "global city" with a very diverse population, representative of modern metropolitan areas shaped by the automobile. Table 10.1 provides information on its key demographic and socioeconomic characteristics relative to the nation as a whole.

Over the last half century, the Los Angeles region has gone from being predominantly white to being "majority minority," a transformation that is

TABLE 10.1   US and Los Angeles statistics, 2015

	United States	Los Angeles
Total Population	321.4 million	10.2 million
Race/Ethnicity		
• Non-Hispanic whites (alone)	73.1%	26.4%
• Blacks (alone)	12.7%	8.2%
• Asian Americans (alone)	5.4%	14.5%
• Hispanics	17.6%	48.4%
Nativity		
• Immigrants	13.5%	34.6%
• Noncitizen among immigrants	52.2%	48.8%
Economic		
• Mean household income	$78,378	$86,156
• Median household income	$55,775	$59,134
• Poverty rate	14.7%	16.6%
Housing		
• Renters	37.0%	54.9%
• Median gross rent	$959	$1,279
• Renters paying 50% or more of income toward rent	23.5%	29.6%
Transportation/mobility		
• Households with no vehicles	8.9%	9.1%
• Automobile commuters	85.6%	83.2%
• Mean commute time (minutes)	25.7	29.6

Source: US Bureau of the Census; 2015 American Community Survey 1-Year Estimates.

projected to happen at the national level in the early 2040s. In 1970, non-Hispanic whites made up 71 percent of the population, and by 2015, they made up 26 percent of the population. While the absolute number of African Americans remains the same, the group's share of the total population declined from 11 percent to 8 percent. Immigration has driven the demographic transformation of Los Angeles during this time. Immigrants make up more than a third of Los Angeles's population, a proportion that is about two-and-a-half times that for the United States as a whole. Nearly half of the immigrants are noncitizens, and a substantial number are undocumented.[7]

Income inequality in the Los Angeles region has grown over time and is more severe than that for the nation. Despite having a higher average household income, Los Angeles has a higher poverty rate than the rest of the nation (17 percent versus 15 percent, respectively), and a larger share of households at the top end (14 percent have an annual income of $150,000 or more, versus 11 percent for the United States overall). Economic inequality is also manifested in differences across ethno-racial groups. Average (median) household income for people of color is lower than for non-Hispanic white Americans (9 percent lower for Asian Americans, 39 percent lower for Hispanic Americans, and 44 percent lower for African Americans).

Average income statistics, however, can be misleading, because an Angeleno's higher income is offset by the higher cost of living in Los Angeles. The net result is a lower standard of living for residents of the region. This is clearly evident in the housing sector, where Los Angeles is among the most expensive housing markets in the United States, absolutely and relative to income.[8] The problem is particularly burdensome for low-income Angeleno households (those with an annual income of less than $35,000), where 64 percent spend at least half of their income on rent, compared to 45 percent for the nation.

One of the consequences of the higher cost of living is that less money is available for transportation, which is a basic need in Los Angeles. The region is auto-centric and has a less robust public transit system than many other major metropolitan areas. With the combination of urban sprawl and limited transportation resources, the average commute time to work in Los Angeles is longer than the national average. The travel burden is particularly heavy for those using public transportation.[9] The implication is that Angelenos, especially low-income populations, are more time constrained. The problem is compounded with the commute to school and ELT opportunities, particularly for a zero-vehicle or one-vehicle household, and one or more working parents.

One of the unmistakable features of the Los Angeles landscape is residential segregation along ethno-racial lines (see figure 10.1), which has increased over time.[10] In 1970, only 1 percent of Asian Americans lived in Asian majority neighborhoods, but by 2010–2014, that increased to nearly a fifth.[11] Similarly, in 1970, more than a quarter (28 percent) of Hispanic Americans lived in Hispanic majority neighborhoods, but in 2010–2014, over half, 59 percent, lived in Hispanic majority neighborhoods. The proportion of African Americans in African American majority neighborhoods, on the other hand, experienced a decline, from about 79 percent to less than 30 percent in 2010–2014. Whites still remain the most residentially segregated (67 percent live in majority non-Hispanic white neighborhoods in 2010–2014).

Los Angeles's urban landscape is also fragmented along economic lines. With increasing overall economic inequality and a widening divide between the haves and have-nots, the number of households in middle-income

FIGURE 10.1   Map of Los Angeles by ethno-racial areas

Source: 2010 TIGER/Line; US Census American Community Survey 2010–2014 5-Year Estimates.

neighborhoods has declined, with a corresponding increase in the number in richer and poorer neighborhoods. In 1980, 15 percent and 17 percent of households were in affluent and poor neighborhoods, respectively. By 2010–2014, the corresponding rates were 19 percent at both ends.[12] Overall, the rich and poor live in different parts of the city, with the former concentrated along the coast and hills, and the poor concentrated in the older urban core and older working-class suburbs.

SPATIALIZED EDUCATIONAL INEQUALITY IN LOS ANGELES

The spatial inequality that shapes Los Angeles's residential landscape also shapes educational outcomes and opportunities for children. We start by examining the pattern and magnitude of place inequality among elementary schools because they are most likely to be tied to neighborhoods, and then discuss access and transportation disparities. Neighborhood types are defined by poverty levels (very poor, poor, not poor, and least poor) of zip code areas.[13] These categories are not identical to those used in the previous section.

FIGURE 10.2   Map of zip code areas by poverty categories

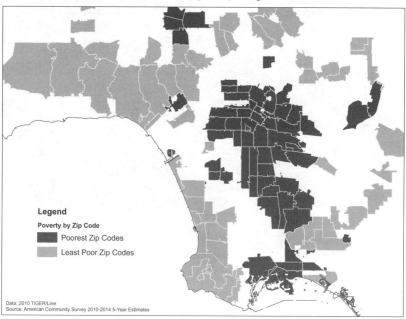

Source: 2010 TIGER/Line; Census American Community Survey 2010–2014 5-Year Estimates.

Figure 10.2 maps the distribution of the poorest and least poor zip code areas. The urban landscape can be described as having a concentric pattern, with the poorest neighborhoods concentrated in geographic cores (flatlands) and the more affluent neighborhoods located along the urban edge, along the coast, and in the hills.

Table 10.2 reports the demographic and socioeconomic characteristics of students and schools by the four neighborhood categories. There are relatively more elementary schools and students in the poorest zip code areas because these are more densely populated (partly to keep housing costs down), have more families with children, and have more children per household. The number of Hispanic, African American, low-income and English language learner (ELL) students is positively correlated with the level of neighborhood poverty, with very large differences between the two extremes.[14] For example, the number of ELL students as a proportion of all students is more than

TABLE 10.2   Characteristics of Los Angeles elementary school students

	Least poor	Not poor	Poor	Poorest
Schools and students				
• Number of schools	251	218	385	426
• Enrolled students (in thousands)	143.5	111.5	220.5	266.3
Race and ethnicity				
• Non-Hispanic white	37.8%	23.1%	7.3%	3.0%
• Hispanic	31.4%	51.8%	75.3%	82.3%
• Asian and Pacific Islander	20.4%	14.4%	9.0%	3.6%
• African American	5.5%	8.1%	7.2%	10.2%
• Other	4.9%	2.6%	1.2%	0.9%
English language learners				
• English language learners	12.3%	20.5%	34.9%	45.5%
Free or Reduced Price Meals (FRPM)				
• Students receiving FRPM	28.4%	54.8%	79.6%	88.3%
Charter and magnet schools				
• Students in charter schools	10.3%	9.3%	5.9%	7.6%
• Students in magnet schools	5.7%	9.7%	9.5%	5.9%

Source: California Department of Education, "Enrollment by School," Student & School Data Files, California Department of Education, 2016, http://www.cde.ca.gov/ds/sd/sd/filesenr.asp; "Student Poverty FRPM Data," Student & School Data Files, California Department of Education, 2014, http://www.cde.ca.gov/ds/sd/sd/filessp.asp; Census ACS 2010–2014 5-Year Estimates.

three times higher in the poorest neighborhoods than in the most affluent areas. Attendance in charter schools is negatively correlated, although differences are not extreme, and attendance in magnet schools is highest in the two middle categories.

One indicator of place inequality in Los Angeles's educational system can be seen in the academic performance of schools as measured by the now defunct Academic Performance Index (API).[15] (See table 10.3.) Although California has recently moved away from the API and its almost exclusive reliance on test scores to measure a school's academic progress, we have used API results because these scores were available at the time of our analysis. The problem of low academic performance, as measured by the API, is compounded by higher truancy rates and lower attendance rates. At the two extremes (poorest and least poor), the rates are about twice as high. These latter indicators suggest additional disruption to the educational process.

Nontraditional public schools, such as magnet schools and charter schools, have been touted as a partial solution to the low academic performance in poor neighborhoods by increasing school choice options. The evidence, however, is mixed.[16] Despite their promise, these alternatives produce only limited results. For analytical purposes, given the relatively smaller numbers of nontraditional public alternative schools, we collapse the neighborhood types into two brackets, one with the two lowest poverty categories and the other with the two highest poverty categories. Within each category, the nontraditional public alternative schools tend to perform better in

TABLE 10.3   Indicators of place disparity: School performance indicators

	Least poor	Not poor	Poor	Poorest
API score				
Mean API score	896	850	804	766
• Scores of less than 750	1.2%	3.2%	15.5%	39.9%
• Scores from 750 to 850	17.3%	47.0%	65.5%	53.9%
• Scores of 850+	81.5%	49.9%	19.0%	6.2%
Attendance indicators				
• Truancy rate	14.3%	20.6%	23.8%	26%
• Low attendance rate	11.0%	19.5%	23.8%	28.3%

Source: California Department of Education, "API Data Files," Academic Performance Index, 2016, http://www.cde.ca.gov/ta/ac/ap/apidatafiles.asp; "Public Schools and Districts Data Files," Schools & Districts, California Department of Education, 2016, http://www.cde.ca.gov/ds/si/ds/pubschls.asp.

standardized tests, although this may be due to creaming—the biased selection of those more likely to succeed academically. (See figure 10.3.) What is surprising is that for each type of school, schools in poorer neighborhoods have lower academic performance scores than their counterparts. In fact, magnet and charter schools in poorer neighborhoods perform worse than traditional nonalternative schools in nonpoor neighborhoods; consequently, these alternatives have had only a marginal impact on closing the achievement gap.

To address these disparities in educational outcomes (and sometimes the parents' commute to work), some students and their families want to attend schools outside the neighborhood. Assuming they are able to register out of area, students in low-income communities face geographic disparity in accessing schools with higher test scores located outside their neighborhood. This is seen when measuring the minimum distance to the nearest high-performing school (schools with average API test scores in the top quarter among all public schools in Los Angeles). On average, students from poorer areas would have to travel nearly a mile more to get to the nearest high-performing school.

FIGURE 10.3   Indicators of place disparity: Academic Performance Index (API)
scores for alternative nontraditional public schools

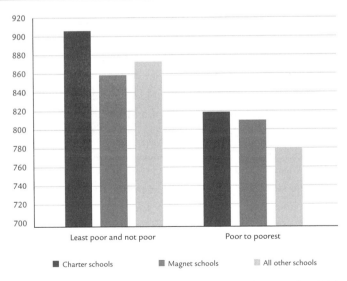

Source: California Department of Education, "API Data Files," Academic Performance Index, 2014, http://www
.cde.ca.gov/ds/si/ds/pubschls.asp.

While 46 percent of those from the poorest neighborhoods would have to travel more than 1.5 miles to get to a high-performing school, only 23 percent of those in the least poor neighborhoods would have to do so.

Clearly, geographic distance is not the only barrier. Social distance compounds the problem when disadvantaged students and their parents decide to attend out-of-area schools. For example, Palisades Charter High School is located in an affluent neighborhood and enrolls out-of-area students. Monica Iannessa, assistant principal of the school, explains that "[w]hen the kid gets to Pacific Palisades, it's 'Do I fit in? Is this for me?' Kids go out to lunch in Pacific Palisades and get resistance from shop owners who believe some of them are shoplifting."[17]

Although the statement refers to high school students, similar geographic and social barriers affect elementary school students. This is compounded by the fact that younger students may need to be supervised en route to and from school. They also have fewer options and flexibility for travel when it comes to the commute to and from school, and/or the commute to and from ELT opportunities.

A relative lack of transportation resources for students in poorer neighborhoods exacerbates the lack of geographic accessibility. Table 10.4 reports statistics based on elementary school students in Los Angeles from the California Household Travel Survey (CHTS). Those in the poorest neighborhoods are more likely to reside in a household with no private vehicle, lower vehicle-to-person ratio, and an older vehicle. This translates into lower odds of being driven to school by a family member, and greater likelihood of relying on mass transit and alternative modes. While there are positive aspects to using active transportation (e.g., exercise from walking and biking) in the commute to and from school, students who live in disadvantaged neighborhoods also experience higher safety risks associated with traffic and unsafe passages to and from school.[18]

For those students and families who choose to attend their neighborhood school, there are still travel issues with reference to the commute home, both to and from school, and the commute to and from ELT. According to Dee Ann Rivera, director of operations, and Regino Chavez, director of evaluation, at LA's BEST, which serves 193 schools in Los Angeles Unified School District: "There's the issue of winter and night safety. So many students live locally, and if they don't have a car, they walk [unless there's a safety issue]. We don't have a lot of yellow school buses because LA's BEST programs are

TABLE 10.4 Indicators of mobility disparity: Transportation resources

	Least poor	Not poor	Poor	Poorest
No-vehicle households	0.0%	3.0%	8.8%	14.6%
Vehicle per person	0.52	0.47	0.36	0.29
Vehicle age 15+ years	9.1%	14.7%	25.3%	30.1%
Driven to school	69.5%	80.3%	50.8%	47.1%

Source: Tabulated by authors from California Household Travel Survey, 2010–2012.

located in community schools, where most walk to school. Picking up children is an issue because of other little ones at home, and parents [have to] rely on finding an adult who can sign out their child."[19]

The lack of adequate transportation resources, along with other spatial challenges, means that those in the poorest communities face multiple barriers to accessing regular classes and afterschool programs.

SPATIAL INEQUALITY IN EXPANDED LEARNING TIME IN LOS ANGELES

A strategy to offset the educational disparities described in the previous section is to increase participation in learning opportunities beyond the traditional school day. Spatial inequality, however, also affects opportunities for expanded learning beyond formal schooling, including those opportunities within the neighborhood and educationally enhancing activities outside the neighborhood. While there is a lack of systematic data on the latter, it is possible to examine reasonable proxies and indicators related to place inequality, disparities in geographic access, and differences in transportation mobility. We also draw on insights provided by practitioners involved in providing ELT services, who have a grounded knowledge of the issues.

Place inequality can be seen in the uneven distribution of expanded learning time opportunities. Our analysis focused on afterschool programs (public and private). These programs are important because they can provide tutorial help, educational programming, social-emotional learning, and a range of enrichment activities (see chapter 2). The programs can provide safe and caring spaces where students can connect with adults other than their classroom teachers and families and friends, and learn from additional role models in the community.[20]

Nationally, existing studies show that federal and state policies prioritize elementary schools with a disproportionate number of minority or low-income students to receive funding for afterschool programs.[21] A study of Los Angeles shows the differences in the availability of private-sector and public-sector resources. An analysis of the availability of the two types of expanded learning services where a value of one means parity with the region's average, a lower value indicates less availability, and a higher value indicates more availability is shown in figure 10.4. Not surprisingly, private tutorial establishments are relatively more prevalent in more affluent areas, driven by markets responding to the greater ability of parents to pay for services. The parity pattern for publicly funded afterschool programs is just the opposite, because of an allocation formula that is based on the number of disadvantaged students. Prior research finds that these programs can have a positive impact on improving the academic performance for those students at risk of not graduating, but only if they are content-specific and provide more than just childcare.[22] However, there is roughly only one slot available for every seven students enrolled in public schools in poor neighborhoods.

FIGURE 10.4   Availability of afterschool tutoring

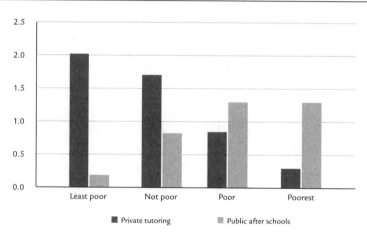

Source: California Department of Education, 2016; Census ACS 2010–2014 5-Year Estimates.

While the discussion above focuses on access to programs that offer after-school tutoring within or near one's neighborhood, access to more distant enrichment activities follows a similar pattern. Disparities in geographic access can be seen in the distribution of museums, nature centers, and art and music programming.[23] These are regional resources that cannot be easily deconcentrated because of economies of scale; utilization depends in part on the ability to reach the facilities. From an educational attainment perspective, attendance and participation in these institutions are associated with higher educational achievement.[24] The positive impact of arts experiences is particularly significant among students from low-socioeconomic groups. Among low-socioeconomic-status (SES) students, the difference in science and writing test scores was, and is, greater between those who did and did not participate in arts activities when compared to the same difference among high-SES students.[25] Although this correlation is due in part to self-selection, exposure to the arts can have an independent effect in increasing knowledge and learning skills.

Unfortunately, many students in disadvantaged neighborhoods encounter challenges to attendance and engagement in science- and arts-related institutions. One previous study found that Angelenos in disadvantaged neighborhoods are less likely to visit art and cultural museums because of financial, cultural, and spatial barriers.[26]

The importance of these extracurricular activities is not lost on practitioners. According to Pam Martinez, a founding member of Padres & Jóvenes Unidos, a community organization in Denver, Colorado, "We really believe that sports, arts, dance, theater, and more are critical for students to develop as little human beings, to learn critical thinking. These things really enrich their lives and give them a broader vision of the world, and perhaps tap into talents they didn't know they had."[27]

Exposure to performing arts can have other benefits. According to Robin Manzer of LA's BEST, "It's important to look at the desired outcomes—the socio-emotional as well as academic. We want to produce solid academic outcomes, and to do so we need also focus on socio-emotional outcomes. For example, funders are interested in cultivating new classical musicians. For us, we hope that happens too, but we want children to experience confidence building that comes with learning a new instrument, and performing on the . . . stage."[28]

There is also a desire to promote engagement with nature-oriented experiences to broaden a child's world view beyond what she and her parents know. According to Katya Bozzi, executive director of the STAR, Inc., Enrichment Program, "There were meetings with parents, [where we made suggestions for extended learning] opportunities with environmentalists and oceanographers, but we were met with 'the ocean is not for us.' Our job was to break down those barriers, and affirm that 'everything is for you, including the ocean.'"[29]

Increasing parental interest in broadening their children's horizon may not be sufficient. Many of the important sites for these enriching arts and cultural experiences are not geographically accessible.

The spatial barriers to science- and arts-related institutions in Los Angeles can be seen in figure 10.5, which maps major art and cultural museums and educational nature centers in Los Angeles. There are a few located in the poorest areas, but their location is more related to being in or near

FIGURE 10.5 Cultural or art museums and nature centers

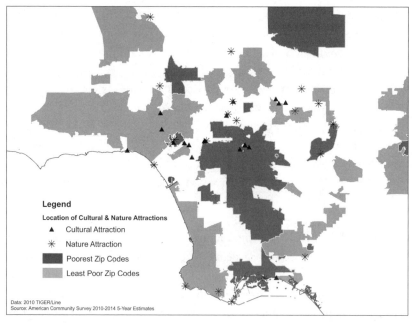

Source: 2010 TIGER/line; Census American Community Survey 2010–2014 5-Year Estimates; Los Angeles County GIS Portal, "Locations/Points of Interest (LMS Data)," Los Angeles County GIS Data Portal, January 2016, http://egis3.lacounty.gov/dataportal/2016/01/14/locationspoints-of-interest-lms-data/; Los Angeles Almanac, "Zoos, Gardens & Nature Centers," *Zoos, Gardens & Nature Centers*, http://www.laalmanac.com/environment /ev13.htm; County of Los Angeles, Department of Parks and Recreation, "Los Angeles County Department of Parks and Recreation—Nature Centers," Los Angeles County Department of Parks and Recreation, http://parks .lacounty.gov/wps/portal/dpr/?1dmy.

downtown than to purposefully serving disadvantaged communities. While this provides geographic accessibility to some disadvantaged students, these mainstream science and arts institutions are far away for most disadvantaged students. The majority of the other institutions are far from the poorest areas and thus are spatially less accessible.

The inequality in mobility discussed earlier for the region and elementary school students also applies to ELT activities. This inequality can be seen for the children living in poorer neighborhoods and engaging in some form of expanded educational activity before and after the school bell. They live in households that have few private transportation assets; consequently, they are more reliant on getting to and from science and arts experiences during non-school hours via public transportation or nonmotorized modes such as biking and walking. (See figure 10.6.) Fewer than half of those in the poorest neighborhoods access expanded learning opportunities by private vehicle, while an overwhelming majority of children in nonpoor neighborhoods do so. Biking and walking are the most common alternative when cars are unavailable, while use of mass transit is limited because of cost, inconvenience, and slow speed. The net impact is that poor students have a constrained range of choices and are limited to using local ELT resources, which are less available nearby. Seven in ten children in the poorest neighborhoods travel less than 1.5 miles to an ELT activity, while only a third of those in nonpoor neighborhoods do so. Interestingly, over half of those in the most affluent areas stay

FIGURE 10.6   Transportation mode to ELT activities

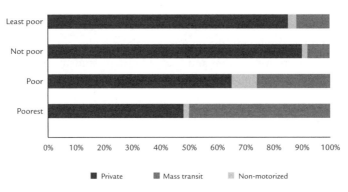

Source: California Household Travel Survey, 2010–2012.

within this range, due perhaps to having a richer set of local ELT opportunities nearby or within walking distance.

Lack of mobility and transportation resources are evident among those who provide afterschool ELT services to students in Los Angeles's disadvantaged neighborhoods. According to Dee Ann Rivera of LA's BEST:

> [F]amilies have one car, usually with a dad who is at work, and a mom who doesn't have a car or know how to use public transportation. There's also a safety issue re: public transportation with gunfire risks, and public transit is not even an option. Families struggle—kids say, "We don't have transportation/car because of financial situations." Many parents have unreliable transportation, transportation [cars] that can get them from point A to point B, but not from point A to point Z. Many have no luxury of having a vehicle, and couple up with neighbors to jump a ride.[30]

The lack of transportation also has a negative impact on attending non-local art programming, as evident in the experiences of ELT providers.

> We often get invitations to museums, shows, park spaces, and then, transportation is a big problem. Money is the solution if we want to take advantage of every opportunity availed to us outside of the neighborhood . . . If we were to get 200 tickets to the Pantages [a major performing arts theater in Los Angeles] to distribute, we know by experience that we would be lucky to give [out] one-half or one-quarter of the tickets because of the lack of transportation . . . If we offered the transportation, parents would come.[31]

The mobility barriers severely narrow the world of ELT opportunities to these and other children in the poorest neighborhoods.

Because of transportation and spatial barriers, students and parents are often forced into making difficult decisions, trading one set of opportunities for another. Those who do opt to attend a distant magnet school often have a travel schedule that limits their ELT options, as evident in comments by Rivera:

> If a magnet school is four miles away, the child would be picked up at the LA's BEST school, so transportation getting to school is not the problem, but receiving the child might be. The child often loses at both ends. A child at a magnet . . . can't stay in ELT at the magnet school, because

they have to get on the 2:30 p.m. bus to the home school. [The situation is compounded because] if they aren't enrolled in the home school, they can't sign up for ELT. However, if a parent is able to drive the student to/from the magnet school, then the child can go to ELT [at the magnet school].[32]

Even those who opt to participate locally encounter challenges, Rivera says.

During the winter, we have an early release policy, as many places are not safe to walk home in the dark, so parents can pick up their child early from ELT. That's our accommodation. We have to balance the child's safety with the child's [ELT] experiences. We don't have a lot of yellow school buses because [LA's BEST programs] are located in community schools, where most walk to school.[33]

Overcoming the geographic hurdles and other forms of spatial inequalities will require greater attention to policies promoting social and spatial justice.

CONCLUDING REMARKS—BEYOND LOS ANGELES

Our analysis finds significant spatial inequality in place outcomes, geographic access, and transportation mobility in Los Angeles. Students in poor neighborhoods attend lower-performing schools (based on test scores) within their communities, are more geographically isolated from better-resourced schools beyond their neighborhood, and have fewer transportation resources. Similar problems and barriers exist in the expanded learning arena. These educational disparities are not surprising because they are by-products of the larger urban landscape, which mirrors and reinforces socioeconomic stratification. One of the key findings from the case study is that different forms of inequality interact and reinforce each other, forming a pernicious systemic cycle that produces and reproduces socioeconomic stratification. Spatial inequality is an integral component of the ELT gap, which, in turn, contributes to the educational achievement gap. Over the long run, these factors and dynamics perpetuate disparities across generations.

Are the findings generalizable? After all, Los Angeles is unique in terms of demographic composition, with a disproportionate number of Latinos and Asians, a large majority of whom are either immigrants or children of immigrants. Consequently, the observed outcomes are influenced by factors and dynamics specific to immigrants, such as selective migration, linguistic and cultural differences, and a protracted and potentially segmented assimilation process. Moreover, Los Angeles's urban structure and weather are dramatically different from other regions, particularly in the Midwest and East Coast. Los Angeles's economy is also unique: it was formerly the center of Cold War aerospace production and is currently the global center for film and the nation's most important port for international trade. Taken together, these factors suggest that Los Angeles is not representative of other parts of the United States.

On the other hand, a case can be made that Los Angeles shares common underlying economic and social superstructures. Los Angeles's level of economic inequality is more similar than different from the country as a whole. Our imperfect capitalist market system generates winners and losers, in both fair and unfair ways, regardless of location. Like other parts of the United States, Los Angeles is stratified along ethno-racial lines, a societally constructed system to maintain power and privilege. All regions experience social and class segregation, with each town, city, and metropolis producing desirable and undesirable neighborhoods. In each location, there is a political debate about the role of government to address these inequalities. Despite significant variations in ideological philosophy and levels of support for fairness, there is at least an opening to push pro-equality educational policies in our democratic system, as imperfect as it might be. In this broader sense, Los Angeles differs from other regions in the details and scale but not the larger structural form. Different specific populations may occupy societal positions within the urban landscape, but the more fundamental socioeconomic niches are nonetheless common to Los Angeles and other parts of the United States.

The underlying commonalities also apply to how the unequal urban landscape and transportation resources conspire to stratify educational and ELT opportunities. This is evident in Denver, for example. According to Martinez of Padres & Jóvenes Unidos, "School buses are privatized; it's very select. It's not the norm that buses take you home, you have to walk . . . [I]f the kids don't have parents to come to get them, they can't participate in activities that require personal transportation or aren't walkable."[34]

The Denver experience also shows the importance of holding government accountable to address the spatial and transportation disparities, "to keep the pressure on for equity."[35] While Denver, like Los Angeles, has unique challenges and specific locational conditions, the statements also reveal overlapping concerns, which are the foundation for common remedies.

Many of the recommendations practitioners offer focus on transportation as a means of increasing spatial accessibility to ELT opportunities. This means that school districts should adequately fund buses without placing the burden on parents.[36] Supporting travel also applies to outside donors and sponsors. For example, "the entity donating the tickets to a performance [or] program could also support transportation costs."[37] Improving the connection to a broader world can be further enhanced by encouraging parents to accompany their children to ELT events and activities.[38] Because many students use public transit, there is a need to design better routes and schedules to minimize time and travel burden.[39]

An alternative or complementary strategy is to close the geographic-accessibility gap by bringing the world to disadvantaged children. Or as one interviewee stated, "[I]f [we] can't bring the kids to the Santa Barbara Zoo, we bring the theme park/zoo to the students."[40] This would require forming partnerships with major art, cultural, and nature-oriented museums and institutions, many of which have an obligation to serve the public. Modern technology can also help to bridge the spatial gap, with the caveat that virtual interaction can only complement rather than substitute for real-world experiences.[41]

The above recommendations are important and broaden ELT opportunities, but they are not a panacea. While pursing feasible and actionable solutions in the short run, it is just as important to push for more fundamental changes to attack underlying structural stratification. As we have seen, educational spatial inequality runs deep, taking on multiple forms that mutually reinforce each other. Place inequality and disparities in geographic access are two sides of the same coin. Both are linked with mobility barriers, which, in turn, are linked to the spatial inequality experienced by their parents in the form of spatial-transportation mismatch. Taken together, these interlocking phenomena form a web of institutionalized urban inequality.

Tackling educational inequality, in our opinion, is one of the most critical because of the role of schools in the intergenerational reproduction of class and ethno-racial disparities. Closing the ELT gap is a move forward in addressing educational inequality and is necessary to breaking the cycle of spatial and societal inequality.

BEYOND THE TECHNICAL CHALLENGES

The three chapters in this concluding section tackle the cultural and political dynamics that can both create inequalities and reduce barriers to learning. If the nation addresses the widening gap in educational opportunity between children from low-income families and high-income families, it can help preserve the notion of equitable life chances—a notion that has long held our pluralistic democracy and ideals together. These final chapters take a hard look at the social and political dynamics that maintain inequality and explore political strategies necessary to build the public will to address them. Relying on the approaches and findings presented in the previous chapters, the authors stress the importance of changing fundamental beliefs to avoid replicating existing inequalities under a new guise.

In chapter 11, Fred Frelow and Barnett Berry, both former teachers, take a close look at the power of teachers in shaping the learning experiences and outcomes of our nation's most vulnerable students. Frelow and Berry emphasize the indelible links between powerful learning, powerful partnerships, and powerful teaching. They argue that creating rich and engaging learning opportunities for students does not rest on a technical fix, but rather demands a political solution. Redesigned schools and systems require dedicated resources that enable teachers to lead their own learning—time to learn from other teachers and to build the skills to lead transformation efforts. Schools and systems require a knowledge base that describes how expanded learning time schools are developed and to what end. Finally, transforming teaching and learning requires creating a demand for transformative learning experiences. If the successes of these schools and systems are made more visible—through collective stories—policy makers, educators, and parents will demand more and better learning time.

In chapter 12, educational researchers Michelle Renée Valladares and Kevin Welner use a political lens to explore how expanded learning time approaches move forward within an ever-shifting *zone of mediation* to improve the practice of teaching and learning. Valladares and Welner describe how this zone encompasses the collection of forces, structures, policies, history, economics, people, and resources that surround an effort and that is mediated by schools and districts. Working for expanded learning time requires actively shaping the zone through careful attention to technical solutions accompanied by normative change, and important political shifts. As ideas and beliefs about teaching and learning shift, reformers can overcome resistance to change and advance equity-minded reform.

In chapter 13, Jeannie Oakes reminds us of education's pivotal position in the struggle for social justice. She carefully makes the case for a commitment to a set of principles and pragmatics that can guide efforts to change policies and systems in ways that bring more equitable schooling to marginalized students. These principles must follow from our recognition of the contextual realities in which our struggle for social justice is waged: a reality wherein education and life chances are more tightly connected than ever before; where individuals without high-quality schooling face dim prospects for decent work and dignified lives; and where it seems normal for young people from materially and culturally advantaged groups to succeed at higher rates than others.

Oakes explains why expanded learning time approaches matter in our struggle for social justice. As highlighted in other chapters in this book, these approaches go beyond the technical. The core focus of expanded learning time strategies uses pragmatically accessible ideas and available tools to drive systemic, policy-driven improvements in the learning resources, opportunities, and relationships provided to young people who suffer most from larger social and economic inequalities. Oakes reminds us that expanded learning time, as a strategy, must never waver from this principled focus. The most essential and toughest work continues to be sustaining policies and practices that reflect these deep and powerful principles despite the hard realities of implementing reform in a system and society committed to an unequal status quo. Oakes shares that now, more than ever, advocates, educators, and researchers must redouble efforts to be loud and clear about a commitment to high-quality, equitable public schools in every neighborhood as the bedrock of a healthy, diverse democracy.

CHAPTER 11

MORE AND BETTER LEARNING TIME

Strategies for Improving Teaching

FRED FRELOW AND BARNETT BERRY

The purpose of education, finally, is to create in a person the ability to look at the world for himself, to make his own decisions, to say to himself is this black or is this white, to decide for himself whether there is a God in heaven or not. To ask questions of the universe, and then learn to live with those questions, is the way he achieves his own identity . . . The obligation of anyone who thinks of himself as responsible is to examine society and try to change it and fight it—at no matter the risk. This is the only hope society has. This is the only way societies change.

—JAMES BALDWIN, "Talk to Teachers"[1]

INTRODUCTION

James Baldwin's impassioned talk to New York City teachers in 1963 reminds us that there remain many challenges facing public education, teaching, and learning, particularly for children of color. His words serve as a clarion call for what teachers need to be able to do to engage and educate students, while also reminding us of long-standing social inequities that undermine efforts to improve learning and, ultimately, the human condition.

In our chapter, we keep Baldwin's poignant words in mind as we surface the lessons learned about strategies for improving teaching and advancing the profession in ways that promote meaningful and powerful learning for our nation's more vulnerable students. A recent research report commissioned by the Wallace Foundation suggests that expanded learning time can make a difference for student achievement, but only if done thoughtfully and well.[2] Promising models for expanding learning time suggest that more time in the school day and year should be utilized to think creatively about teaching and learning. However, taking advantage of those opportunities requires that we go beyond merely asking teachers and schools to do a bit more of the same. The problem with teaching is not that there are insufficient numbers of talented and dedicated teachers; rather, the problem lies in the system within which teachers work. We are certain that promoting both equitable and excellent education for all will not be fully realized unless students are able to take charge of their learning. Doing so requires that teachers be empowered to do the same.

Over the last several years, the Ford Foundation developed partnerships with local foundations, school districts, teacher unions, community-based organizations, nonprofits, and local businesses to explore ways to provide More and Better Learning Time (MBLT) opportunities for students in urban communities. With our partners in seven cities (Chicago, Denver, Detroit, Los Angeles, Newark, New York City, and Rochester, New York), we learned that the most powerful learning for students embraces a more humanistic approach grounded in their lived experiences. Our partners designed expanded learning opportunities within a reconceptualized day and year to help students meet new academic standards, and to reexamine who they are and the communities in which they live. These efforts have surfaced the indelible links among powerful learning rooted in communities, powerful partnerships driven by equity and excellence, and powerful teaching led by teachers.

POWERFUL LEARNING ROOTED IN COMMUNITIES

Powerful learning often begins by organizing the curriculum so students can learn more than just basic skills but also investigate important questions relevant to them. For students in communities such as Brooklyn, New York, for example, this kind of powerful learning includes attention to major environmental hazards affecting the neighborhood, including oil spills, incinerators, accumulation of toxic waste from improper storage of dangerous materials, and air pollution. In Los Angeles, this learning effort focuses on the underinvestment of public funds in communities of color, private development plans that do not value local culture, and the immense challenges of being an immigrant in the United States. In Detroit, this type of program revolves around what to do about the city's eighty thousand abandoned homes and the undemocratic policies that have snatched decision making from the local community and privileged state power. Students also confront institutional racism across communities nationwide.

We know from recent research that student learning in reorganized schools has resulted in student achievement gains on measures of math and reading.[3] These empirical findings are important. But student learning is not just about an increase in test scores in math and reading. And it is not just about engaging students in critical thinking and problem-solving skills demanded by the global economy. It is also about their personal growth and development that is inextricably connected to community and the broader world. As Robert Halpern and colleagues note:

> Research confirms that learning works best when young people can focus in depth on a few things at a time; when they see a clear purpose in learning activities; and when they have an active role—co-constructing, interpreting, applying, making sense of, making connections. Research also confirms that, though sometimes fragile, motivation is a powerful engine for learning, and that it can be fostered under the right conditions. Motivation to learn is stronger when driven by a young person's prior knowledge and interests; when it is located, not in rewards and punishments, but in the task itself; when it is driven by a desire for mastery and by identification with mentors and teachers.
>
> Not least, research findings emphasize that learning is often most effective when it is social; when it occurs as a shared activity within meaningful relationships; and when it allows for increasingly responsible participation—within a tradition, a community of fellow learners, in one's culture at large.[4]

Granted, calls for better learning focused on the lived experiences of children in American public schools are nothing new. As far back as 1916, John Dewey's *Democracy and Education* argued that children, not the curriculum or teacher, should be at the center of the classroom experience.[5] Historians such as David Tyack and Larry Cuban have noted that our nation's public schools have had the ideal of building a better society by enriching students with the skills to learn deeply, yet they have not come close to doing so.[6] A recent report of the Annie E. Casey Foundation estimated that almost 6.5 million teens are disconnected from school as well as the workplace, with the percentages especially troubling among Latino and African American teens.[7] While there has recently been a spike in high school graduation rates, this can mean very little for a young person's engagement in or readiness for college and career.[8] And while some school reform efforts of late have generated higher student test scores and better accountability ratings, they do not necessarily prepare students for examining, as Baldwin says, questions of the universe or gaining economic independence.

The latest National Commission on Teaching & America's Future (NCTAF) report made it clear through this example: "We have squeezed all we can out of the hard rind of econometric formulas. Now it is time to activate the human-factor—the motivation and intelligence of students and educators—to reorganize schools around what drives learning."[9]

At the National Commission's most recent meeting, Genevieve DuBose, NCTAF commissioner and a National Board certified teacher at the Bronx Studio School for Writers and Artists, shared a touching story:

> I'll never forget one of my proudest moments as a teacher. It happened this spring in my seventh-grade English class in the South Bronx in New York City. My students and I were at the end of a unit on scholar activism, and the culminating project asked them to identify a problem in our school community—our local Hunts Point community and the larger New York City community—that needed to be solved. They had to research, to identify root causes, share ways the community could be involved and interview people affected by the issue among other things. One of my seventh graders, let's just call him Hope, was standing in front of the room with a set of Google slides giving a presentation on transphobia in New York City. Hope was born female and in the middle of his seventh-grade year he let us know that he identified as a boy and asked us to use the pronouns "his," "he," and "him" in referring to him. Hope stood up there on a June afternoon and gave us tips on how to end transphobia in New York.
>
> He said, if you hear a transphobic person call them out. Be open minded when you engage with someone who is transgender. And to quote him directly, he said, "talk to trans people. Me and a lot of people in this school and in Hunts Point are trans. If you know someone and they are comfortable with you asking, ask about what it's like."

DuBose continued,

> Watching Hope standing in front of his adolescent peers speaking truth gave me goosebumps. I was proud of his bravery and academic scholarship. I was proud we had created a community and culture in the class-

room where my students felt safe enough to be their full selves—a hard feat at any point in life, but especially for a seventh grader. And I was proud that my students were using reading, writing, and research skills.

We know that the purposes of public schooling have long been buffeted by competing political, social, and economic forces whereby the least advantaged students may, at best, be trained to pass an achievement test or get ready for a job (that may or may not exist for them upon graduation or college). At the same time, their more privileged peers may be prepared for their future.

In America, too few students experience schools as democratic institutions—as Dewey envisioned—as teachers and administrators have too few models and tools to use in changing both the structures and process of teaching and learning.[10] And there is evidence that students in high-poverty schools are less likely to experience a broad curriculum in which they can take charge of their learning.[11]

Today, there is still insufficient demand for the kinds of learning that recognize that personal development (including academic development) is integral to family and community development. But the need could not be greater. Organizing learning through the lens of self and community could not be more important, given that US schools are now serving almost 19 million children under the age of eighteen who have an immigrant parent.[12]

These children, who constitute major proportions of the students served in MBLT partner schools, must negotiate "the here and now" and the "there and then," which filters the ways in which they view themselves and their new lives.[13] We believe, especially in light of the 2016 presidential election and the deepening divide over the importance of embracing racial, ethnic, linguistic, and religious identity, that schools can show us what to do and how. These are places where the "social welcome mat" of the right kind of teaching and learning can profoundly determine the academic and social development of immigrant children.[14] They also can tell us how schools can be organized differently, and they can help us explore how teachers, working in collaboration with community leaders and institutions, can take the lead in determining what is in the best interests of young people and their personal development.

We highlight here the stories of several urban schools and the students they serve. Our descriptions and analyses are grounded in the understanding that powerful learning cannot be achieved without a focus on collective teaching practice and with teachers serving as leaders in their schools. As far back as 1996, the NCTAF (which we both worked for), in its landmark report *What*

Mattters Most: Teaching for America's Future, advocated for teachers to work collectively to develop practice and solve problems in professional communities.

POWERFUL PARTNERSHIPS DRIVEN BY EQUITY AND EXCELLENCE

Building on the agenda of the NCTAF, the Ford Foundation organized a portion of its grant making around the promotion of powerful ideas driven by partnerships with a laser-like focus on both equity and excellence. The partnerships, and their growing visibility, offer a powerful tool for reframing public discourse and refocusing the actions of practitioners and policy makers on improving teaching. To advance powerful partners and system change, grantees worked along two fronts. First, they focused on strengthening alliances among school system leaders, teachers, nonprofit partners, and community organizations, blending expert and local knowledge to ensure that teaching policy and practices changes were effectively implemented and sustained. In addition, they worked to redefine the workday for educators using labor management agreements to provide flexibility and support for teachers and administrators.

Each of the schools described in the stories that follow have been part of, and have inspired, the Ford Foundation's MBLT initiative. As a result, the schools received new resources to support innovations in teaching and learning. They also received support for rethinking school design and evaluation in an effort to reorganize the ways teachers work and liberate their collective expertise.

El Puente provides an example of collective/collaborative teaching practice promoting powerful learning. The stories of InnerCity Struggle and Linked Learning Detroit illustrate how community-based organizations forged alliances to advance powerful learning and professionally empowered collaborative teaching at scale in multiple school settings. And, finally, the story of Social Justice Humanitas Academy illustrates how a school took advantage of local policy in Los Angeles to spur powerful teaching inspired by the leadership of teachers.

Williamsburg, Brooklyn: El Puente

Surfacing a powerful idea—personal growth and development that is inextricably connected to the community and the broader world

El Puente was established in 1982 by local church leaders, artists, educators, health providers, and community activists to address the outbreak of violence in the Williamsburg neighborhood in Brooklyn. From July 1979 to June 1980, of a population of little over thirty thousand, forty-eight young people—effectively one adolescent every week—were murdered in what the mass media termed the "teenage gang capital of New York City." To combat this problem, El Puente leaders believed they had to contest the prevalent treatment paradigm in social work at the time that fostered a sense of hopelessness in their community—to create not just a new school, but a movement. Jackie Ancess, codirector of the National Center for Restructuring Education, Schools, and Teaching, described the school's philosophy by noting that "[t]his understanding of education as a larger task of human development springs directly from the schools' roots as a community-based organization and the practices honed there for supporting and honoring young people [because] spirits and souls are important for this journey we take together."[15]

In this context, El Puente adopted twelve principles to guide its work with young people. Prominent among these principles were collective self-help and the use of human relationships to build, thrive, and "boldly go where no one had before." Another important principle was unity through diversity. That meant embracing and affirming the many differences that strengthen and make our common humanity powerful. From these principles, the El Puente Academy for Social Justice (a community school in New York) was created. In their case study, developed for the Kettering Foundation twenty years ago, Sharon Ramirez and Tom Dewar stated: "El Puente is Spanish for 'the bridge' and symbolizes a commitment to helping young people make connections. Through the program, staff [at El Puente] helped young people make the transition into adulthood and understand their [students'] personal development is integral to that of their family and community."[16]

At El Puente schools, teams of teachers, administrators, members of community, cultural organizations, and students regularly come together to organize learning for students. This team (where teachers play significant roles) identifies a central theme to develop integrated arts lessons. Those efforts focus on mastery through sequential skill building, one-on-one mentoring, and community-driven projects. In their study of El Puente, Jacqueline Ancess and Bethany Rogers state, "We found that the arts provide a safe space for young people to go within themselves to create a rich 'inner life' that nurtures a powerful sense of self, the world, and themselves in the world. During a time of life when 'safe passage' is so essential, the arts becomes the portal for young people to celebrate their creative power as human beings—to have an affair with their souls."[17]

A major goal is to extend learning beyond the traditional curriculum into students' homes and community. A yearlong investigation, the Garment Project, focused on Dominican and Brooklyn-based sweatshop workers. Students investigated working conditions in sweatshops locally and globally and the impact of fashion advertising on unhealthy perceptions of body image. This example of the humanistic approach advocated by El Puente, linking students' personal development to their family and community, could not have been realized without a longer school day and year.

El Puente's approach to learning helps students develop their identity and, in doing so, motivates and empowers them to apply and take ownership of their learning. In *Altered Destinies*, Gene Maeroff writes about El Puente and how school communities can simulantaneously develop academic skills while creating a sense of well-being, knowing, and civic responsibility. He describes how students were able to help win a court battle over the sandblasting of the Williamsburg Bridge and the dangers of filling the air with lead paint fragments. Individual student success, even when related to the core curriculum, is directly tied to community development.[18]

East LA and Detroit: Powerful Partners

Community-based organizations, teachers, and business partners joining forces to advance powerful learning

InnerCity Struggle (ICS). In East Los Angeles, ICS, a community center focused on social justice, has a history similar to El Puente. In 1994, leaders from East Los Angeles created ICS to promote safe, healthy, and nonviolent communities in the area. ICS organized youth and families, especially mothers, to end gang violence. Today, ICS, which works on several issues including education, immigration, and welfare reform, emphasizes empowerment and collective civic action. Maria Brenes, the executive director of ICS, stated:

> One of the core problems and issues that ICS identified early in its history was that there was a lack of opportunity and investment in young Latinos in our community. And [with] the Eastside being one of the oldest and largest *barrios* in the nation, ICS recognized that this was an important place to elevate the issues, expose the injustice, and build a case for solutions—build a case for why it is important to create opportunity for young Latinos . . . The most effective way to do that was to build

capacity, and agency, and voice at a collective level among those that are most impacted by the issues of lack of opportunity and that for ICS [this meant a focus] on young people, parents, and families.[19]

Students and their families have fought for and won concessions from policy leaders to invest in their community, including construction of the first new high school built in East Los Angeles in eighty years. In 2002, ICS, along with other community organizations, joined the fight to improve conditions at the Garfield High School (home of well-known teacher Jaime Escalante). ICS organized students and community leaders and collected over five thousand signatures in support of construction of a new high school. Former student Maria Salcedo, now a UCLA alumna, noted: "I fought for the new school to make change for future students because one year I was forced to sit on the edge of a science laboratory counter because there were just not enough desks for all the 63 students in my physiology class."[20]

But that was not enough. In a 2014 interview, Maria Leon, a parent and community member for over thirty years, asserted: "We had to fight with LAUSD [Los Angeles Unified School District] to get a new school. Then after it was built, we had to fight with the district to change what education should look like."[21]

After winning the fight to reduce overcrowding at Garfield, ICS parents and community members, as well as teachers and students, took action to redesign schools, rethinking how learning would be organized. In 2010, Esteban Torres High School was built and opened so that students' personal development would be linked to family and community.

The Esteban Torres complex—which is open from 7 a.m. to 7 p.m.—is home to five small schools serving approximately twenty-three hundred students from East Los Angeles. The East Los Angeles Performing Arts Academy (ELAPA) is one of the small academies on the campus. With additional time beyond the school day, teachers and administrators formed relationships with community partners to enhance and expand learning time. ELAPA's learning partners include LA Opera, the city's Repertory Theater, a local poetry performance group, a Brazilian capoeira instructor, and the Huntington Library. For example, in the partnership with Huntington Library, students were engaged in a major project in which they developed skills in portrait photography, lighting, storyboarding, graphic design, and project scheduling.

The Humanitas Academy of Art and Technology, another one of the small schools, uses a block schedule, which means that classes do not meet every day; this allows for in-depth simulations as well as more substantive and extended debates and Socratic seminars. Students receive traditional grades, but they are expected to communicate what they know through some sort of performance. Internships, in their junior and senior years, provide students with the opportunity to apply their passions in real-life settings, such as area museums, film studios, and community agencies. With additional resources, the school has been able to extend these learning opportunities beyond the school day.

Teaching includes a focus on interdisciplinary lessons guided by teacher teams and centered around themes relevant to students. These efforts are paying off with far higher achievement results and graduation rates than comparable city schools. These teacher-designed schools have served their surrounding community—predominately Hispanic and poor—and in 2015–2016, attained a graduation rate of 91 percent among students who often are the first in their families to finish high school and go to college. By comparison, in the same year, California's statewide graduation rate was 83 percent, while in Los Angeles, it was 77 percent.[22]

Excellent Schools Detroit. Detroit, a city of almost seven hundred thousand, has become well known for its serious challenges. According to a New York Times article, it is a city with "emptying neighborhoods, crime, insufficient city services and immense blight."[23] By 2015, one in three Detroit properties had been foreclosed due to mortgage defaults or unpaid taxes.[24] The multitude of abandoned buildings in Detroit is evident to all who visit, posing a serious hazard for those who live in the city. It was at this time that the Ford Foundation made a a major financial commitment ($100 million) to help Detroit exit bankruptcy. This important moment in the revitalization of the city was a way to begin helping its beleaguered schools.

Working in partnership with Excellent Schools Detroit, ConnectEd (a California-based nonprofit), and the Skillman Foundation created the Linked Learning Detroit family of eleven collaborating schools. The schools redesigned their programming so students could work on solving problems in their community. This effort has been so promising that JPMorgan Chase made a $4 million commitment to expand the project from eleven to twenty schools, with the support of Detroit's mayor.

Last year, teacher leaders at West Side Academy planned a community project that cuts across the curriculum. At the Benjamin Carson High School of Science and Medicine (Ben Carson High), a cadre of students worked with the Detroit Food Policy Council. Many of the students, who would like to become pediatricians, competed in a healthy beverages marketing campaign for the youth of their city. Located on the campus of the Detroit Medical Center, Ben Carson students can easily access internships, where they experience what health care is like daily. Interning students are able to watch open-heart surgery, shadow doctors, or spend time in the emergency room.[25] Now over 90 percent of Ben Carson students, who have taken advantage of a longer school day and twenty days each summer for enrichment and academic support, attend a two- or four-year college (see Hoachlander et al., chapter 5, for more information on the Linked Learning approach).

Another learning pathway has taken on a very pressing issue in the city. Detroit, with its eighty thousand abandoned buildings, has been besieged by arson. An award-winning documentary film, *BURN*, released several years ago, explored why anyone would risk their life in a fire in an effort to save an abandoned building. The movie, which offers a powerful portrait of bravery and commitment to the city, illustrates the devotion so many residents and others have for Detroit. Notably, one of the learning pathways in Detroit is the fire academy. What could be more relevant to the lives of students growing up there?

Cody Medicine and Community Health Academy, in partnership with the Detroit Fire Department, created opportunities for high school juniors and seniors to learn the skills of firefighters or emergency medical technicians (or both) and earn college credits as well. Students participate in the real world of the fire deparment two afternoons a week. As evidenced by student outcomes and their engagement, learning by doing is powerful for students.[26]

In each of these examples, teacher leadership played important roles in leveraging innovations focused on equity and excellence, notably because those who teach work most closely with students. There is growing empirical evidence of the power of *collaborative expertise* among teachers as a primary driver of school improvements.[27] Indeed, a plethora of research reports point to the importance of teachers leading school reforms, not just being the targets of them. One set of studies found that teachers learn to teach more effectively when they are supported in regulating their own teaching strategies, serve as resources for one another, and activate ownership of their own learning.[28] Other researchers found that teacher learning as well as leadership is more about *peer influence* and is rarely "vested in one person who is high up in the hierarchy."[29] Finally, another recent investigation found that teachers are more likely to make instructional shifts when, coupled with formal professional development, they have indirect exposure to new ideas through collegial interactions.[30] Andy Hargreaves and Michael Fullan have written extensively about *professional capital*, which is created by recruiting and developing teachers, as well as by cultivating their collaborative power to develop and use their expertise to make sound judgments about students. For Hargreaves and Fullan, professional capital is the additive qualities of human, social, and decisional capital.[31]

There is no better example of the power of collaborative expertise than Social Justice Humanitas Academy.

Powerful Teaching Led by Teachers

Shining a bright light on how teacher-powered schools spur student-centered teaching and learning

The Social Justice Humanitas Academy (SJHA), one of fifty pilot schools in Los Angeles approved in 2007 by the district and union, is a powerful example of how more and better learning time can establish the indelible links between students' personal development, school reform, and teacher leadership. SJHA, a Los Angeles high school serving a high-poverty neighborhood dominated by two competing rival gangs, makes it clear that relationships between students and teachers and between school and community are paramount. SJHA also demonstrates how schools can be organized very differently so that everyone's leadership can be cultivated and sustained.[32]

SJHA yields powerful student outcomes, including a 94 percent graduation rate, an astonishingly low suspension rate (0.2 percent last year), and reports from students (more than 93 percent) and parents (95 percent) that school grounds are safe.

Co-lead teacher Jeff Austin reports that alumni—many of whom are now college graduates, with some in graduate school or en route to the Peace Corps—remain engaged with the school: "I mean, that's the challenge . . . A lot of communities like this have kids that find their way out but don't want to come back. Ours are coming back." Current SJHA students speak with pride of their network of older peers who have beat the odds to thrive throughout the University of California system and who offer them advice and support. Austin tells us that alumni like Danny Rojo, now a UCLA student, are active in a range of campus and community activities to encourage justice, equity, and youth leadership.[33]

SJHA relies explicitly on teacher learning and leadership to serve students and to develop their capacity to lead themselves. Five key organizational structures are central to reorganizing teachers' time and their work in order to liberate their collective expertise as professionals.

First, SJHA is a teacher-powered school in which classroom practitioners have secured autonomy to make decisions often assumed to be the province of administrators.[34] Teachers set the school's vision, determine the curriculum and assessments, approve the annual budget, select and evaluate the principal, and hold one another accountable for student learning through peer review. And they intentionally rethink school schedules and leadership roles so that they can do so. SJHA teachers collectively and annually write an election-to-work agreement that outlines the school's teaching and learning conditions, which are very different from those found in the district's collective bargaining agreement with its unions. For example, faculty members teach in teams and draw on Japanese lesson study to assess one another's practice. Teachers require themselves to achieve National Board Certification or start the process by their fifth year of teaching, setting a very high bar for teacher quality and professional development. SJHA principal José Navarro, a National Board certified teacher and former California Teacher of the Year, teaches several classes a week and proudly describes himself as a servant leader. And while SJHA is dramatically underfunded, with less than $6,000 to spend per pupil, it is strategic with regard to how it utilizes teachers in hybrid teaching-leading roles.

Second, every student at SJHA has a personalized education plan. Every five weeks, teachers review a wide range of data—not just test scores—to craft strategies to support their students. To help teachers better align instruction to students' strengths, faculty members assess young learners' multiple intelligences and developmental assets. Austin says, "Working with students in this way . . . we know them. We know their story, and the horrible circumstances they've overcome, with our help, to get that diploma." In addition, every staff member steps in to "adopt" three students who need additional support in achieving their learning plans.[35]

Teachers' personalization of learning cultivates self-advocacy, which these young people recognize they will need for future success, particularly as first-generation college students. As one student put it, "It teaches you to be vulnerable and to let people in. Don't be too prideful and say, 'Oh yeah, I can handle my stuff, I'm good by myself.' No. Now you realize you need help and you shouldn't feel bad about that . . . Don't be self-defeating but do something about it by asking."[36]

Third, SJHA teachers work in horizontal, grade-level teams to design thematic units across disciplines so students see subjects as a unified and organic whole rather than compartmentalized pursuits. For example, students learn about the original thirteen colonies in American history class while simultaneously reading Thomas Paine's *Common Sense* in their literature course. In a recent visit to SJHA, we watched the entire eleventh grade prepare a project-based learning event around *The Great Gatsby,* with debates, readings, drama, dancing, and more—all representative of their classroom investigations of the "Roaring Twenties." This interdisciplinary curriculum, designed by teachers, means that the school does not have to offer an array of isolated courses in English, social studies, science, and math. As a result, teachers have about eighty students a day, including the all-important advisory period in which they work with the same group for four years.

Fourth, professional learning at the school focuses on teachers' collaboration to fine-tune their instructional practices. Teachers spend at least 2.5 hours a week in team-based professional learning, creating and refining interdisciplinary units, lessons, and assessments. When math scores dropped by 5 percent, teachers worked together to integrate math subjects for students in every grade. Thanks to the teacher-powered model, they had the curricular authority to make a quick shift in policy and practice. SJHA students responded better to this concept-focused approach than to taking algebra and geometry one course at a time. The school expects each teacher to conduct a peer review of a colleague's teaching for at least four hours over the course of a year. In addition, teachers frequently and voluntarily sit in on one another's classes to improve their practice. The reorganization of the school day makes it possible for teachers to devote time together on matters of teaching and learning.

Finally, fueled by the nontraditional leadership of the principal and teachers, SJHA partners with a number of organizations. For example, the Los Angeles Education Partnership supports the school's professional development efforts by helping its busy teachers lead subject-focused retreats, action research, and visits to other school sites that utilize the Humanitas interdisciplinary strategy. In addition, the school partners with the EduCare Foundation, which supports teachers in building close relationships with students (and which currently employs three SJHA alumni to work with students at their alma mater). SJHA also works with Youth Speak Collective, which helps ensure all students have opportunities to improve their communities and develop leadership skills.

CONCLUSION

Important lessons emerge for ways to ensure quality teaching and learning from the Ford Foundation's MBLT initiative. We learned that schools, which successfully provide students with powerful learning opportunities, use more learning time to better organize curriculum around the needs of students and their communities. And with expanded time, they empower their teachers to have more agency and the opportunity to lead; deploy an adaptive curriculum developed with community-based organizations; and embrace their teaching colleagues as leaders themselves to spread their expertise.

Stories from Los Angeles, New York, and Detroit are not the only ones to tell. Unfortunately, redesigned schools utilizing more time for students to advance powerful learning opportunities are all too often the exception, not the norm, especially in schools serving our most vulnerable students. In too many cases, our public schools, serving our most vulnerable children, remain desparately under-resourced. With these stories, and the evidence at hand, we offer the following final reflections.

First, there must be *dedicated resources* for teachers leading their own learning. The Learning Policy Institute has released a toolkit to guide school districts in California on how to best utilize $500 million for professional learning to implement new state academic standards, with a comprehensive set of strategies and resources.[37] The National Center on Time & Learning offers useful resources for system leaders to rethink time, roles, and school design to advance professional learning.[38] The Center for Teaching Quality and its partner Education Evolving are supporting a network of student-centered, teacher-powered schools like SJHA. This network will help classroom experts develop and spread the skills among their colleagues to design and lead schools to support learning for students (and for teachers).

Too many schools operate with inadequate financial resources. More money and new policies will be required to expand learning and redesign school days to give teachers the time to plan together and lead more, as well as to build school-community partnerships. New compensation systems are also needed for classroom experts to serve in the innovative roles as curriculum developers, assessment experts, and school-community liaisons so critical to powerful learning.

Second, we must continue to build *the knowledge base* that describes how expanded learning time schools are developed. Most educators and community members teach in traditionally organized schools because they do not know how to redesign and lead them. There are many organizations like El Puente, InnerCity Struggle, and Linked Learning Detroit (now housed at the United Way of Southeastern Michigan), which have successfully worked with schools and districts to use more learning time to co-construct meaningful and powerful learning with educators (teachers and principals). Armed with the knowledge to execute these strategies, many more teachers, administrators, and community leaders would pursue them.

Finally, we must recognize and celebrate *the collective stories* of teachers, community organizations, and their students—creating more demand for what is working well and why. We do not see the problem of expanding powerful learning—and student-centered, teacher-powered schools—as a technical one. It is a political one that can be addressed if the successes of these schools are made more visible to educators and parents as well as policy leaders who remain committed to improving public education.

We do know that the vast majority of the US public—about 80 percent—believe the effectiveness of their local public schools should be measured by how engaged the students are with classwork and by their level of hope for the future.[39] Nationwide, two in three public school parents have "trust and confidence" in teachers.[40]

In addition, with social media, teachers as well as students and their parents can now connect with policy leaders in an almost infinite numbers of ways—Twitter, YouTube, Facebook, and much more. They can put a spotlight on what makes for more and better learning time and reach millions of people. And opinion polls reveal that voters are willing to pay higher taxes for more services, including public education.[41]

We believe that if the American people, particularly parents, knew more about El Puente and Esteban Torres as well as Cody Medicine and Community Health Academy, Ben Carson, and SJHA, they would press our politicians to invest more, not less, in these exemplary schools and their community partners. Because, as we have stated in many ways in this chapter, the purpose of schooling goes beyond the narrow technical targets of tests and grades. The purpose of schooling is, as Baldwin says, "To ask questions of the universe, and then learn to live with those questions." In doing so, students develop who they are as human beings and create a better world to live in.

CHAPTER 12

EXPANDING LEARNING TIME WITHIN THE ZONE OF MEDIATION

MICHELLE RENÉE VALLADARES AND KEVIN WELNER

THE PERSISTENCE OF INEQUALITY

At their core, expanded learning time approaches endeavor to alter the structure of teaching and learning. They change when and how we teach and learn, who has access to high-quality teaching and learning, and even how we think about teaching and learning. As the chapters in this book make clear, such meaningful changes must overcome daunting obstacles. Transforming learning time can be highly beneficial, but it requires altering the content and structure of the curriculum and of public policies. Further, it requires changing the hearts and minds of policy makers, district leaders, administrators, teachers, and students.

Our goal in this chapter is to use theory—particularly the idea of a zone of mediation—to develop an understanding of some of the patterns that exist across all of these efforts. The zone of mediation is a term that describes the many different forces that "set the parameters of policy, behavior, beliefs, and actions" in schools and districts.[1] This zone can be thought of as an ever-changing context that shapes a reform's direction and viability. Like any significant institutional change, expanded learning time reforms are necessarily implemented within such interacting local, state, and national contexts. Every school change effort takes place within a zone that can be thought of as creating a favorable or hostile environment within which the reform occurs. This zone is constantly being shaped and reshaped by this connection of forces, structures, and the like.

The persistence of educational inequality is a significant result of the forces that shape the zone of mediation. Students coming from white and wealthier families have more access to resources and to engaging opportunities to learn, in school as well as outside school, as compared to their peers from lower-income families of color.[2] As a society, we have grown accustomed to these enduring opportunity gaps. Acknowledging these gaps, however, requires that we also accept the staggering achievement gaps that they predictably and invariably create.[3]

The chapters in this book describe learning time reforms that attempt to close both types of gaps by deliberately increasing opportunities to learn in communities that are under-resourced. The approaches presented here did not sail through unchallenged. To better understand why, we must first recognize that education reforms do not proceed in a vacuum. A reform transpires within a place—a physical school and its surrounding district, state, and nation. While the reform is being developed, initiated, and implemented, the school carries on; the existing curriculum is taught, professional development programs play out, books are ordered and distributed, lunch is served, children with special needs are identified, and so much more. Surrounding the school or district is a larger community in which people are housed or are homeless, families have variable access to health care and healthy food, people gain and lose jobs, and transportation systems shuttle those who can access the system from place to place. These gaps, like the opportunity gaps experienced within schools, have intergenerational consequences. The long-lasting nature of these inequalities leads to what Gloria Ladson-Billings refers to as an "education debt."[4] To this debt are added ongoing structural inequalities tied to racism, classism, and sexism that influence schools and their surrounding communities. The resulting patterns of inequality significantly affect who has political power and the resources to acquire opportunities to learn. It is within this multilayered context that the expanded learning time reforms discussed in this volume are taking hold.

In the following pages, we describe how expanded learning time reforms move forward within a shifting zone of mediation to improve the practice of teaching and learning. We begin by exploring the Linked Learning approach, using that example to illustrate how dimensions of the zone can be addressed in ways that move this particular learning time approach toward equity. We then flesh out the importance of the reforms' contexts by drawing on the previous chapters of the book to illustrate lessons with further examples of challenges and strategies for moving forward.

UNDERSTANDING THE ZONE OF MEDIATION
AND EXPANDED LEARNING TIME

The zone of mediation includes the entire context within a school, and it stretches to encompass the full landscape beyond the school and community and into surrounding federal and state policies, practices, and resources. The larger forces that have an impact on each school and community are mediated by local institutions such as schools and their districts, and they are then felt by teachers and students in homes and classrooms.[5] Sometimes these larger forces advance equitable goals, as is the case with civil rights laws or with Title I funding for schools serving high numbers of low-income students. Other forces, however, can lead to disinvestment, pollution, segregation, deficit approaches, and other elements of inequity.

The true measure of equity is the "treatment of less powerful people and groups in ways that confer benefits equal to those obtained by more powerful people and groups."[6] Shifting schools and school systems toward equity requires more than just good intentions; it requires intention and action.[7] Concrete initial steps, for instance, may involve acknowledging that inequities exist and matter, and identifying systemic oppression as a major cause of education inequity.[8]

As intuitive as this approach may be, many education policies and reforms underestimate or ignore the existence of educational inequity and instead focus on the efficiency of education systems.[9] From this perspective, reformers naively trust that better technology or tests or school size will somehow remedy deeply rooted injustices. But inequity is not a mere by-product of inefficiency. Instead, equity must be deliberately addressed and reformed in its own right, or it will be quickly pushed to the margins of any reform effort.[10] Inequitable policies are maintained in large part because of inequitable zones of mediation; if the reform context is not changed, it is highly unlikely that an equity-minded reform can take root.[11]

Shifting the zone of mediation requires locating responsibility for inequities in history, macro-social structures, and cultural patterns, rather than suggesting that the students, teachers, and families most affected by these inequalities are somehow responsible. This does not mean that a policy or reform effort must directly name racism or classism in its text. Instead, it means that the intent and implementation must be crafted in a way that acknowledges and counters deeply held deficit beliefs about students, families, and schools.[12] In a larger sense, it also means shifting the distribution of power and resources across the education system.[13]

More specifically, shifting the zone toward equity requires addressing four major dimensions of the zone: (1) fundamental *normative* ideas and beliefs about teaching and learning; (2) *inertial* resistance derived "from the comfortable and set ways of schooling . . . the habits, routines, customs and practices that . . . take on a life of their own";[14] (3) the specific *technical* solutions being proposed; and (4) the balance of *political* power between the different people involved in creating and implementing the reform.

In chapter 5 on Linked Learning, Hoachlander et al. provide a compelling illustration of how attention to these components moves this particular learning time approach toward equity. They describe four primary objectives to the Linked Learning approach: (1) identifying what students need to know and do; (2) a focus on teaching and learning; (3) high-quality design and implementation; and (4) systemic implementation. As explained below, these objectives illustrate the normative, inertial, technical, and political dimensions of a reform. The first objective implicates the normative, the second raises both technical and inertial issues, the third is primarily technical, and the fourth objective is political. Accordingly, we begin by applying the zone framework to Linked Learning.

The Zone of Mediation and Linked Learning

Equitable change must begin with truly understanding, and often challenging, the values and beliefs people hold about education—what we call the normative dimension of change. In describing the first objective of Linked Learning, the authors point out that Linked Learning requires a "paradigm shift" from the idea that there are two separate learning tracks—career or college—to the idea that succeeding in both college and career actually requires all students learning from a curriculum that is rigorous and is also related to the world around them. As Hoachlander et al. share, "Our own experiences, our memories of what worked and what did not, and the ways we encountered privilege and inequity all too often reinforce a traditional mind-set of what school should be." Indeed, this mind-set perpetuates resistance to changes such as new ways of learning and teaching, assessments of more than just content knowledge, or a reorganized school day and year that considers both in-school and out-of-school activities. Linked Learning and the other expanded learning time approaches described challenge our thinking about how schools should work, who should have access to what kinds of curriculum, and even the purpose of schooling.

Predictably, direct challenges like this are often met with correspondingly direct resistance, as Hoachlander et al. make clear. The Linked Learning field is meeting this challenge by sharing counter-beliefs. In their policy and implementation work, the reform's implementers shared stories and data demonstrating that all young people are capable of meeting the rigorous academic content of the curriculum. They explained how real-world experiences increased students' engagement in learning. And the stories of students—specifically those underrepresented in the medical field—are told through videos in which they share how they are viewed differently in their community when they head to school dressed in medical scrubs.[15] These multiple points of evidence are designed to directly challenge normative beliefs about education and schooling.

The Linked Learning approach is also extremely attentive to providing powerful technical solutions to educational problems. The reform's designers engaged researchers, educators, and school leaders in developing and testing out curriculum, assessment, planning, and scheduling guidelines. As described by Hoachlander et al., implementation begins with school and district leaders designing a Graduate Profile—what students should achieve by the time of their graduation for success in college, career, and community life. Leaders then map content, policies, and practices back to that goal. While such technical dimensions of reform are often the most immediately apparent, solutions are often far from simple or basic. Rather, equitable reforms blend evidence from research and practice into strong models that can be implemented with fidelity.

Hoachlander et al. are also clear that, as much as a reform may begin with proposed technical solutions, there are always unanticipated problems encountered along the way. Some of these obstacles are best understood as inertia within the larger system. For example, schools and districts implementing Linked Learning ran into significant challenges described as, "The inertia of the status quo [that] hampers designing and implementing new approaches to teacher preparation and certification." Other inertial obstacles can arise from within schools themselves, with students, teachers, and others showing an unwillingness to adapt to new ways.[16]

Hoachlander et al. also illustrate the insufficiency of only addressing beliefs and solutions; they raise the question of political influence. We think of the political dimension of an equitable reform as the role of power in developing and implementing education policy. The authors are clear that good ideas and even strong leadership at the top are not enough to ensure successful implementation: "While district leadership play a pivotal role in establishing and sustaining the conditions for high-quality, equitable Linked Learning pathways to grow and thrive, deep, lasting success depends on crafting a larger community-based commitment to Linked Learning."

Along with strong models being tested and developed in real schools within California and across the nation, powerful advocacy organizations like ConnectEd were formed. These organizations did not just offer technical assistance; they also worked to build the political power needed across sectors and communities. The result is both strong support from private foundations and, in California, policy and funding that expanded the reform to other schools in the state.[17]

While it is important to consider each of the four dimensions of an equitable reform independently, it is also important to realize that they are interdependent. Political power is most effective when advancing a solution that is based on resonant ideas. These policies and ideas are most effectively implemented if they speak to our beliefs and have sustained community and political support. The normative, inertial, technical, and political dimensions of a reform interact in ways that can shift the zone of mediation either toward or away from equity. In the case of Linked Learning in California, Hoachlander et al. report that an independent longitudinal evaluation of the initiative in California showed increased graduation rates, decreased time for students to reach graduation, decreased need for remediation in college, and increased student confidence in life and career skills. The initiative also reduced achievement and equity gaps within high schools. Such positive results were not achieved immediately or simply, but rather by sustained work and a deep commitment to equity throughout the entire initiative.

Davis and Farbman's chapter on the National Center on Time & Learning (NCTL) provides an example of how the zone of mediation in a local school system or state interacts with an expanded federal zone of mediation. They report that NCTL was working to create federal and state policy and resources for expanded learning time at a moment when there was a national economic crisis, as well as a new presidential administration with specific education policy goals. Expanded learning time was one idea among several—the Common Core, school turnaround, expanding privatization of public schools, and teacher evaluation linked to student outcomes, to name a few—that have competed in recent years for federal, state, and local attention and resources. NCTL, as well as other organizations referenced here, worked within these moments of crisis, transition, and competing priorities to shift attention toward equity and toward the expansion of learning time. Davis and Farbman explain that in several places, this was successful; places where expanded learning time became part of a school turnaround program or other federally funded efforts, and where governors and states created local expanded learning time initiatives. But as both Gándara and Moje describe in their respective chapters, other places saw expanded learning time efforts become watered down and stifled; the inertia, particularly at the local school level, proved to be too much for full implementation to be possible. The reformers were unable to move forward within the inhospitable zone of mediation created by these forces.[18]

LESSONS LEARNED THROUGH
THE ZONE OF MEDIATION

As the chapters in this volume demonstrate, the zone of mediation surrounding expanded learning time reforms is complex and dynamic. Together, these chapters discuss the deficit ideas that expanded learning time advocates are trying to counter and overcome, and they discuss the new paradigms they hope to create. They communicate the challenge of building a reform strong enough to surmount inertia across several different systems and structures. In doing so, these chapters also communicate a wealth of research-based and refined solutions for expanding when, where, and how students learn, while also outlining real-world implementation problems. They illuminate the complexity in building shared and sustained ownership of expanded learning at the school, district, state, and federal levels.

Although each chapter shares these lessons independently, the lens of the zone of mediation allows us to identify patterns across these chapters. While some of the lessons fit nicely into just one dimension of the zone, others touch on multiple dimensions. Below, then, we draw on the chapters of this book to illustrate each lesson with examples of challenges and strategies for moving forward.

Lesson 1: The education opportunity gap is long-standing, and closing it requires a deep and long-term commitment to schools and school systems

Normative, inertial, technical, and political dimensions. Throughout this volume, authors detail the challenge of creating a sustainable reform that produces a measurable closing of the opportunity gap. Writing about Promise Neighborhoods, McAfee and Pizarek recognize that in order to address the disparities that have been built over decades, their work in communities is viewed as a long-term commitment. To be certain, overcoming centuries of inequality both inside and outside school takes more time than quick political cycles allow. Systemic inequality did not suddenly appear in one year, and it takes much longer than a year to counter it. McAfee and Pizarek add,

> Like many under-invested neighborhoods, North Minneapolis and Chula Vista residents continue to experience the disparate effects of historically racist and elitist policy making that has shaped how infrastructure, public education, and economic development have inequitably developed in their communities . . . Each Promise Neighborhood is catalyzing the local energy of its community and a rich network of partners to reverse the egregious disparities experienced by its students, fundamentally reshaping the ecosystems in which they live.

This lesson encompasses all dimensions of the zone of mediation. As the authors of this volume detail, reducing the opportunity gap requires building enough momentum to overcome the *inertia* of several established institutions and systems. It also requires directly and repeatedly challenging the hopeful *normative* belief that there is a silver-bullet program or model that can solve educational inequality. Finally, closing opportunity gaps requires designing *technically* strong, sustainable reform models that are *politically* powerful because they are collectively owned within a school and between the school and community.

Lesson 2: Systemic inequality and opportunity gaps outside school significantly affect student learning

Normative, inertial, and political dimensions. Education opportunity gaps are connected to opportunity gaps outside school. For example, access to basic resources such as health care; safe, affordable housing; and transportation also shape students' learning experiences. While each model addresses this inequality in a variety of ways, the community schools and Promise Neighborhoods models confront it head-on. Writing about the former, Kirshner and Kaplan explain,

> Community schools adopt a broader view, which argues that poverty negatively affects people's readiness or capacity to give their best to academic learning. Community schools, therefore, work to alleviate the damaging influence of poverty—its tertiary effects on physical health, mental health, and readiness for school—and to value and incorporate people's cultural repertoires of practice in local communities.

If school inequality is connected to broader social inequality, then it follows that schools cannot work in isolation to address education opportunity gaps; the success of an effort is predicated on a commitment to addressing inequities across several systems. An example is provided by McAfee and Pizarek, who offer the following description of the relationship between Promise Neighborhood efforts and systemic inequality:

> To truly understand how we will build equity back into public education, we have to be comfortable with the complicated nuances of systemic inequity that affect students. The Promise Neighborhoods approach on its own will not achieve educational equity. However, Promise Neighborhoods as a strategy is a significant pathway to it.

Building support for programs that are "comfortable with the complicated nuances of systemic inequality that affect students" is much more challenging than building support for programs that promise quick and immediate test score gains. The examples provided in the previous chapters provide a convincing argument that this is a worthy and possible goal.

Lesson 3: Expanded learning time reforms confront the inadequacy of the traditional school day

Normative and technical dimensions. All authors in this volume agree that the existing school day is flawed. Davis and Farbman summarize it in this way: "Still operating on the century-old calendar of 180 6.5-hour days, the vast majority of schools are trapped in a structure that is inflexible and often unable to adequately meet the needs of today's learners." By accepting the inadequacy of what currently exists, each author reimagines how we can transform when, where, and how students learn. From Davis and Farbman's explanation of the NCTL's expansion of time across public school systems, to Terriquez and Rogers's rich explanation of learning that takes place in youth organizing groups, each chapter reimagines teaching and learning.

These authors explain how expanded learning time is essential for preparing students to succeed in college, careers, and civic life. As Gunderson et al. explain, "the research is clear that the way kids spend their out-of-school hours is essential to . . . improving their educational and social outcomes." An important nuance to this argument is that expanded learning time is not about simply adding minutes or hours to the existing school day; it is also about re-envisioning the existing school day. Moje explains that this includes reducing the daily interruptions and distractions, and reducing the number of "revolving programs" that put teachers, students, and parents through the constant churn of new curricula or teaching techniques. This reality is well documented by a survey of California school leaders, which highlights significant losses in learning time in schools serving high numbers of low-income children.[19]

Fully expanding learning time as described in this volume is comprehensive. It requires a combination of better use of existing time, adding and reorganizing learning time in school, and developing out-of-school learning places.

Lesson 4: In order to advance equity, expanded learning time reforms must push past the existing routines, practices, and complacency that create inequities

Normative, inertial, and political dimensions. As discussed above, research documents that school systems are resistant to change, and part of this resistance comes from the people inside the system who want to maintain the status quo. Expanded learning time efforts are no exception. Moje points this out in her chapter: "most of the structural barriers existed not because they were immutable but . . . because they were held in place by social and cultural beliefs and traditions." The existing structures are comfortable and established.

Pushing through this resistance is not simple or quick. Creating and successfully implementing expanded learning time reforms requires building public demand for the programs. As Frelow and Berry explain, "We do not see the problem . . . as a technical one. It is a political one that can be addressed if the successes of these schools are made more visible to educators and parents as well as policy leaders who remain committed to improving public education."

Gándara's chapter also explains that evidence alone is not enough to push past the inertia and make successful models possible. Although one of the expanded learning reforms discussed in her chapter improved reading scores of English language learners and also improved the satisfaction of their parents and teachers, "it was complex to implement and swam against the current of what most people considered to be a 'normal' school schedule." Rather, confronting inertia takes sustained political pressure and strong proven ideas. As such, the technical and political strategies outlined in the lessons below are critical.

Lesson 5: Technical challenges to expanding learning time often overlap with political challenges

Technical and political dimensions. Many of the authors in this volume document combined technical and political challenges to implementing expanded learning time reforms. While, at first glance, many issues such as inadequate funding for programs appear to be pragmatic and technical, the authors are quick to note the political dimension of resource issues. Education funding as a whole is inadequate, and the funding that does exist is not equitably distributed between schools and communities. Schools serving low-income communities have greater needs yet continue to suffer from fewer resources than schools serving high-income communities.

Using Los Angeles as an example, Ong and Ong detail the spatial challenges of providing equal access to educational opportunities outside school. They explain that private out-of-school programs are clustered in higher-income neighborhoods. And while recent years have seen more publicly funded out-of-school programs located within poor neighborhoods, opportunity to access these programs remains insufficient. For every seven students enrolled in public schools in poor neighborhoods, there is roughly only one slot available for public out-of-school programs. Access to more distant enrichment activities follows a similar pattern. Disparities in geographic access can be seen in the distribution of museums, nature centers, and art and music programming. Exacerbating this problem is the lack of affordable and reliable transportation between low-income families and learning opportunities—a problem discussed in several of the cases shared in this volume.

Beyond transportation and geography, Gándara explains that immigrant students experience even more challenges in accessing expanded learning opportunities because of their frequent movement: "Many immigrant parents are much more transient than others, often needing to relocate their families in search of work and affordable housing." Moje adds that some low-income families rely on the extra income from young people working after school and in the summer to make ends meet. These very real challenges—combining the technical and political—must be continually confronted by those developing, implementing, and advocating for expanded learning time.

Measurement issues also raise overlapping challenges. As policies expand the purpose of learning, data-gathering efforts should commensurately capture that expanded understanding of learning. Both NCTL and the Promise Neighborhoods Institute created comprehensive data systems to meet this challenge, as described in their respective chapters. Several other examples from education research, like the Annenberg Institute's Time for Equity framework, provide indicator systems meant to measure a broader range of education inputs and outputs.[20]

Finally, envisioning and using learning time more effectively requires teachers to learn new skills and take on new roles. As Frelow and Berry explain in their discussion of the powerful teaching and learning found within sites implementing expanded learning time efforts, reforming schools exist within resource-scarce public education systems. Yet they need new dollars and policies to "expand learning and redesign school days to give teachers the time to plan together and lead more, as well as to build school-community partnerships." Frelow and Berry continue, "[N]ew compensation systems are also needed for classroom experts to serve in the innovative roles as curriculum developers, assessment experts, and school-community liaisons so critical to powerful learning."

Such resource scarcity arises repeatedly as an issue in providing effective professional development, funding positions and release time, and giving the support required to sustain a program. As Gunderson et al. summarize, "High-quality programs do not happen by chance; it takes intentional policy and resource prioritization."

Lesson 6: There are multiple worthwhile approaches for expanding learning time to increase education equity

Technical dimension. The chapters within this volume outline the details of several expanded learning time models. Frelow and Berry point out some core elements of successful efforts: schools "empower their teachers to have more agency and the opportunity to lead; deploy an adaptive curriculum developed with community-based organizations; and embrace their teaching colleagues as leaders themselves to spread their expertise." The core elements of comprehensiveness, collaboration, coherence, and commitment are similarly outlined in Fehrer and Leos-Urbel's discussion of community schools, and NCTL's seven essential elements provide another useful framework. In the process of expanding time, education leaders have expanded space for their reforms to meet the urgent needs of individual children. They have also built upon the systemic structures of school systems, adding community partnerships, leadership teams, or data-driven decision making. The North Star guiding successful expanded learning time models is comprehensiveness—looking at all major aspects of school transformation.

While these are powerful technical solutions, we again emphasize that the space to implement such reforms did not emerge easily. Reformers could not advance the technical limits of a reform without building political power and challenging normative beliefs about time and learning.

Lesson 7: Building partnerships improves the impact and sustainability of expanded learning time

Inertial, technical, and political dimensions. Successfully designing and implementing an education reform strategy often depends on extending the responsibility for educating our young people to a collective of people and groups, within and outside the school. As explained by Gunderson et al., community-based organizations add capacity and bring a level of established trust to the effort, since the organizations often interact with students and families in out-of-school spaces. Fehrer and Leos-Urbel provide a rich example of this approach in their description of the Oakland community schools initiative:

> In partnership with CBOs or public agencies, OUSD community schools offer a wide range of on-site integrated services and supports far beyond what the school would be able to provide on its own. These services and supports aim to address student barriers to learning and increase the amount of time available for instruction and enrichment. These include primary health care, dental and vision services, mental

health counseling, health insurance enrollment, social services, peer conflict resolution (e.g., restorative justice circles), chronic absence intervention, and other health and behavioral health supports.

McAfee and Pizarek explain that "a portfolio of disparate programs will not create dynamic change." Rather, for lasting, widespread change, Promise Neighborhoods engage the whole community in the project of increasing educational opportunities. This does not mean that each organization or person takes on the exact same role in the Promise Neighborhood effort. Instead, people engaged in each Promise Neighborhood identify their own unique skills, the promise and limit of how they can apply each skill to a unique role, and how their roles can have an impact on the larger system.

As explained throughout the preceding chapters in this book, these partnerships take on a dynamic nature. They require attention, coordination, and constant revision to remain effective over the lifetime of a project.

Lesson 8: Expanded learning time leaders should strategically build upon local, state, and federal opportunities

Political dimension. Because education funding comes from multiple levels of government and because many of the education programs connect with multiple public sectors, it is critical for expanded learning leaders to identify strategic opportunities across these levels and sectors. The benefits of this strategy are illustrated in Davis and Farbman's detailed account of Mass 2020 and NCTL's state and national campaigns to increase funding for expanded learning time. Both the statewide Mass 2020 coalition and the national Time to Succeed Coalition began by bringing together high-profile leaders from the education, government, and business sectors. In Massachusetts, the coalition was able to align state and philanthropic resources toward a common set of goals. At the federal level, the coalition succeeded in making funding available for expanding learning time through the federal School Improvement Grant, the 21st Century Community Learning Center, and the i3 program. By coordinating work simultaneously across several states, education leaders were also able to continue to learn about successful state and local funding sources to support their work.

In addition to securing resources for expanded learning time implementation, it is equally important for school and community leaders to align local, state, and federal efforts so that the whole is more than the sum of its parts. This may include aligning the vision and resources of different initiatives, and developing data-sharing systems and agreements between different systems and even shared messaging to the public about why expanded learning time is important.

Lesson 9: Expanded learning time reforms should build on the strengths of students' families and culture

Normative, inertial, technical, and political dimensions. Strong expanded learning time reforms design learning opportunities in ways that intentionally include parents and value students' culture. For example, Kirshner and Kaplan explain that "community schools expand the focus on learning beyond cognition to consider how the whole body, whole family, and whole community need to be supported as a part of learning and schooling . . . [and] they create potential for linking a culture-as-resource approach to the everyday practices and routines of schools." The authors then explain that this broader focus aligns with research on how learning takes place.

This inclusive approach can take on different forms, but Moje offers a description of what including an understanding of family and culture in expanded learning time may look like:

> Attention to cultural values and practices might require adjusting how projects are assigned, where and when work gets done, and the provision of supports for students to carry out extended tasks. Making cultures, social groups, and homes a part of the instruction also holds power for extending learning beyond the regular school day, as families are invited to be part of youth learning, rather than outsiders to it.

When expanded learning time approaches do not make the shift toward including cultural values and practice, Moje argues, programs are often met with resistance.

Beyond designing programs that include and value a students' culture, expanded learning time programs should also create meaningful roles for parents in design, implementation, and monitoring. In Oakland, for example, Fehrer and Leos-Urbel explain that parents are provided the opportunity to participate in school visioning, are engaged in cycles of inquiry around student data, provide solutions to persistent challenges on campus, and set "priorities for the work ahead." Similarly, McAfee and Pizarek explain that the

Promise Neighborhoods model includes student and families not as the "passive observers of their children's education; they are the utmost authority on their scholars' progress and success."

CONCLUSION

Equity-minded change efforts such as the expanded learning time approaches described in this volume are difficult to initiate. They are even harder to implement with high fidelity to their original social-justice elements. Experience and evidence may guide us toward the technical needs of these reforms, but reform leaders must also confront the inertia, the norms, and the politics that can combine to create enormous pushback. If these latter three dimensions are not deliberately and powerfully addressed, the resulting zone of mediation is very likely to be inhospitable to equity-minded change. But by actively shaping that zone through careful attention to all four dimensions, such change can move forward.

Together, the nine lessons drawn from the chapters in this volume and outlined above provide a comprehensive understanding of the challenges and the potential of pushing the expanded learning time zone of mediation toward equity. While it is not reasonable to expect every model to master every lesson, we hope that these lessons provide guideposts for national and local efforts to close the nation's shameful opportunity gaps.

CHAPTER 13

TIME IN THE STRUGGLE FOR EDUCATION JUSTICE

JEANNIE OAKES

OUR PUBLIC SCHOOLS AND, more broadly, the promise of universal public education are contested terrain in the struggle for equity, justice, and democracy.[1] Alongside fostering individual learning and development, education is a cultural process that prepares, certifies, and socializes members of succeeding generations to become workers, citizens, and community members. As such, education can either expand or constrict the life chances of those from economically disadvantaged and socially marginalized groups. Education also shapes culture. As powerful societal institutions, schools and universities help create, legitimize, reproduce, and transmit knowledge and values that underlie shared views of what is true and good. Accordingly, education helps perpetuate and/or disrupt norms of inequality and injustice, frame social "rules" that bound democratic participation, and shape possibilities for individual and community well-being.

Around the globe, more young people than ever before are attending and completing school, and knowledge is exploding. Yet, alongside these gains, societies remain locked into structures, cultures, and practices that effectively maintain inequality and injustice. Victories in the struggle for social justice remain partial, fragile, and, too often, fleeting.

Nearly everywhere, the structures, cultures, and practices of education reinforce this inequality. The education of marginalized and disadvantaged people lags persistently behind, as do their life chances. These gaps engender much handwringing, but they also allow advantaged families to maintain a comparative life advantage for their own children. The development and influence of knowledge and technologies supporting socially just societies are swamped by the increasing dominance of market ideology in social and political, as well as economic, spheres. Using market metaphors to guide the provision of education and other public goods normalizes the idea that individuals seek to "consume" the best opportunities in a competitive and unequal schooling marketplace, with "bottom-line metrics" (test scores) as proxies for quality. Winners and losers are inevitable and consistently linked to economic and social advantage.

Even so, public education remains a democracy's most hopeful social enterprise for disrupting inequality and injustice. The public expects education to be egalitarian and inclusive. It charges schools and universities with preparing future citizens and community members who will contribute to the common, public good, as well as to pursue their private interests. It supports knowledge building that will advance the collective social and political welfare of the country, as well as promote individual innovation and economic productivity. These tensions between the public and private goals of education create opportunities and spaces for bending the political system and society toward equity, justice, and democracy.

PRINCIPLES AND PRAGMATICS

We find ourselves in a highly contentious education policy environment. After more than a decade of "progressives" pitted against "reformers"—with each side claiming both the moral high ground and more effective strategies for improving schools—we now face threats to public education itself. The Trump administration, for example, favors privatizing mechanisms, such as education savings accounts and school vouchers—funded by tax dollars or through a system of tax credits—that would ultimately direct public dollars to private and religious schools. These market-based "choice" strategies would increasingly place education beyond collective accountability for public values and threaten to further undermine the ability of public schools to provide all students with rigorous, equitable educational opportunities. A Senate vote to repeal the Every Student Succeeds Act and state plan regulation, expected to be signed into law by President Trump, threatens to remove important safeguards for our most vulnerable students.

Despite the turbulence in today's politics, the chapters in this volume remind us that we ought to remain committed to a set of principles and pragmatics that follow from our understanding of education's pivotal position in the struggle for social justice and from their grasp of the contextual realities in which that struggle is waged. Those realities include dominance of market thinking; skewed attention and opportunity for high-income students in the context of increasingly unequal childhoods; continued structural racism and class struggle; inadequate resources for poor schools; and more. Together, they reflect a complex and sometimes contradictory cultural dynamic:

- Education is central to individual life opportunity, and the impact is intergenerational; well-educated adults tend to raise well-educated children with abundant life chances, while less-well-educated parents' children grow up with less education, diminished life expectancy, productivity, earnings, and civic participation. Today, education and life chances are more tightly connected than ever before. Individuals without high-quality schooling face dim prospects for decent work and dignified lives.

- Education also helps societies prosper; they advance or lag in economic growth, social well-being, and political stability based on how many children and which children succeed in school. But healthy societies require that their members learn more than just the basics of literacy and numeracy. Critical thinking, creativity, flexibility, broad knowledge, ethical values, and lifelong learning are also fundamental. Access to quality education matters; going to school is simply not enough.

- Persistent educational inequality reflects more than technical failures. It is sustained by prevailing cultural norms and politics. Dominant beliefs cast disparities as "expected." It seems "normal" for young people from materially and culturally advantaged groups to succeed at higher rates than others. Accordingly, lessening inequality requires new thinking and new politics, as well as technical remedies—that is, new policies and practices.

- Dominant political ideologies limit the range of acceptable government action, including neoliberal ideas of improvement through competition and measurement; the view that spending more won't bring better education; the shift from need- to merit-based scholarships in the reputational arms race among colleges and universities; and more.

- Consequently, education justice can't be approached as an engineering problem to be solved by system insiders, even if they have the technical expertise. Rather, such reform requires insiders to work along outsiders, including those most marginalized by the system. Only then can we make the cultural and political landscape hospitable to the adoption, implementation, and sustainability of structures and practices that push the education system toward equity, justice, and the public good.

These principles can guide efforts to change policies and systems in ways that bring more equitable schooling to marginalized students. They can inform a pragmatic theory of change to guide strategy. That theory argues that equitable change requires powerful "proof points" of scalable alternative policies and practices that address problems of inequality and injustice. It also requires powerful ideas (well-grounded theories and empirical evidence) be infused into public and policy discourse to illuminate and energize the possibility of change. Also essential is the active engagement of powerful people—both advocates and organized members of the communities most disadvantaged by current inequalities. Together, these elements comprise a technical, cultural, and political ecosystem that can drive change.

WHY FOCUS ON TIME IN THE STRUGGLE FOR EDUCATION JUSTICE?

It's nonideological and, in fact, a no-brainer to argue that the traditional school schedule is out of sync with twenty-first-century life (families with adults not available to care for children when school ends in the mid-afternoon) and twenty-first-century work (family-wage jobs requiring far more knowledge, skills, and intellectual flexibility than can be provided in a six-hour, 180-day school year). It's not genius to assert that expanded and better conceived learning time could lessen inequalities. Schools in neighborhoods of concentrated poverty could provide learning opportunities, resources, and relationships more like those enjoyed by students in communities where families routinely provide learning time and enriched opportunities beyond the school day. It's noncontroversial to say that such practices have been inspired both by successful public charter schools with expanded schedules, as well as by regular district schools with strong afterschool programs and wraparound social services.

In the day to day, however, working for expanded learning time as an equity strategy requires understanding and adhering to the admittedly controversial principles outlined above. It requires a multidimensional approach, seeking technical solutions accompanied by normative change and political shifts. It requires adherence to core values of building knowledge, strengthening networks, and engaging the people closest to the problems. No one-size-fits-all-approach will work; each community, coming together, must enact the principles of "more" and "better" time in ways that fit its context. And it must emphasize that time, in itself, is not enough; education leaders must attend to policies and practices that build the other foundations of equitable, high-quality schooling—effective teaching, adequate funding, and meaningful accountability. In short, time provides a clear avenue into the murky world of comprehensive school reform.

Over the past several years, advocates and researchers have mounted a successful national campaign, weaving together a nascent coalition of unusual bedfellows (including civil rights activists, charter school operators, teachers' union leaders, Democrats and Republicans, and more). They have lifted up powerful and diverse examples, such as those highlighted in this volume, that have inspired national and state policy changes, as well as local implementation. What began as an effort to expand the school day and to better cohere the efforts of teachers and afterschool partners around common learning goals has blossomed into more robust community school approaches that connect entire families to the design of more democratic schools. Reaching even further beyond the school bell, Linked Learning and Promise Neighborhoods initiatives take entire neighborhoods, regional employers, and all youth-serving agencies in a common geographic zone as a unit of collection action. In some communities, the work has nurtured innovations such as thin contracts and professional workdays and years through labor-management collaborations that few thought were possible. In others, it began to bridge the acrimonious gulf between afterschool and extended-day communities, building relationships and joint work around the vision they share.

But this is the big lesson: these time reforms matter, even in a world of political vagaries in the external environment and shifting internal preferences. That is because the reforms' focus was not on a particular technical innovation, although many might mistake it for such. Rather, the core focus is deeply principled—to use pragmatically accessible ideas and available tools to drive systemic, policy-driven improvements in the learning resources, opportunities, and relationships provided to young people who suffer most from larger social and economic inequalities. The reformers' surface strategies never wavered from that deeper, principled focus; nor should they in the future. The most essential and toughest work is and will continue to be sustaining policies and practices that reflect these deep and powerful principles through the hard realities of implementing reform in a system and society so wedded to an unequal status quo.

Drawing from the experience of the time reforms over the past decade, including those described in this book, we offer the following recommendations for those who seek to use time as a lever for equity.

Make time reforms "roomy," but preserve the novel but no-brainer idea that more time, used well, is a significant, usually overlooked resource for learning, youth development, and preparation for full participation in adult life. Particularly important here is to make more explicit the connections between expanded and well-conceived learning time and other core elements of high-quality education, including the three other elements of the schooling infrastructure:

- *Time and effective teaching.* A key to improving teaching is increasing the time that teachers have available to participate in collegial, school- and classroom-based professional learning communities where educators work together to perfect the skills required to be effective teachers. US teachers have less time to improve their practice than teachers in countries with higher-performing schools. Accordingly, we should support efforts to improve the quality of teaching in schools by increasing the time available for teachers to work to improve their practice in the context of an expanded and redesigned school day and/or year.
- *Time and equitable funding.* Policies that add time should also provide increased funding for schools serving students with the greatest needs. Although some expanded learning time models are designed to function within the same funding levels as the traditional school calendar, these are largely confined to states that currently provide high levels of funding—for example, New York. Most public traditional and charter schools (e.g., KIPP, Success Academy Harlem, etc.) require additional resources.
- *Time and assessment/accountability.* What is measured and reported publicly is what gets taught and learned. High-quality learning time requires the development of assessments and accountability mechanisms that go beyond students' scores on standardized "bubble" tests in math and language arts, for which all schools are now held accountable. Without that, additional time is likely to devolve into test prep and what many community leaders worry will be more of a bad thing.

Also important is making explicit connections between time reforms and other initiatives that share the larger values and vision of high-quality schooling that provides all students with pathways to meaningful adult lives. In this volume, for example, we have shared efforts to incorporate Linked Learning, Promise Neighborhoods, community schools, and youth organizing groups as instantiations of expanded learning time. In addition, longer school days and years and robust afterschool and summer programming can provide these pathways.

Be clear that time is a means to educational justice, even though it may seek a third way of educational improvement. Now, more than ever, advocates, educators, and researchers must redouble efforts to be loud and clear about a commitment to high-quality, equitable public schools in every neighborhood as the bedrock of a healthy, diverse democracy. Current forces, including efforts to privatize public education and pressures to develop balkanizing school choice systems, pose enormous threats to the one social institution we expect to prepare every young person "on equal terms" to be a citizen as well as a productive worker.

Strategies for asserting those commitments without falling into a trap of simply being against neoliberal and increasingly conservative reforms include the following:

- Infuse into the public sphere an examination of childhood inequality that makes clear how increasing educational inequality (nested in the context of forty years of widening social, economic, and political inequality) is bad for everyone—individually and collectively. Point out how it undermines the promise of the American Dream (see, for example, Robert Putnam's recent work).[2]
- Reaffirm expanded and better conceived learning time as a promising leverage point for dramatically increasing learning opportunities and results for the most vulnerable young people. Do this not because it provides time for "more of the same" test-focused instruction in low-performing schools, but rather because it creates the conditions for more complex, project- and problem-based instruction, personalized learning relationships with caring adults, and engaging learning experiences on and off school campuses. All these factors foster a wide range of positive schooling outcomes.

- Continue to build an ecology for equitable education reform, including compelling new ideas and evidence; effective and scalable proof points.
- Engage in advocacy and organizing for policy change that increases system capacity for improvement.
- Develop a broad set of indicators of good schools and student success that force attention to conditions, processes, and results far beyond narrow conceptions of outcomes.

Forge connections with other social and economic sectors. The huge social justice challenges we face cut across health, jobs, housing, and more, all of which are necessary for creating equitable and full lives for the young people in our nation's schools. As we noted earlier, education is intimately connected to both advancing and curtailing social justice reforms in many spheres. It would be extraordinarily exciting to link the structures, cultures, and practices of education improvement. That being said, we must caution about over-romanticizing the idea of breaking down silos and fostering collaboration. The challenge is to recognize where it makes the most sense programmatically. Collaboration and cross-sector work should not be allowed to swamp the essential task of building the social justice infrastructure of knowledge, leaders, and institutions within fields such as education.

In sum, we must continue to strive to identify and promote those structures, cultures, and practices that lift and expand the life chances of all children and dismantle prevailing beliefs that normalize current achievement gaps. The chapters in this volume remind us that we must remain committed to a set of principles that maintain education's central position in our struggle for social justice. Indeed, we must continue to work to improve and advance our most hopeful social enterprise for disrupting inequality and injustice—public education.

NOTES

INTRODUCTION

1. Orsetta Causa and Åsa Johansson, "Intergenerational social mobility in OECD countries," *OECD* 2010, no. 1 (2011):1–44.
2. See Greg J. Duncan and Richard J. Murnane, *Whither Opportunity? Rising Inequality, Schools, and Children's Life Chances* (New York: Russell Sage Foundation, 2011), 3–26; Robert D. Putnam, *Our Kids: The American Dream in Crisis* (New York: Simon & Schuster, 2012); Sean F. Reardon, "The Widening Academic Achievement Gap Between the Rich and the Poor: New Evidence and Possible Explanations," in *Whither Opportunity?*, ed. Duncan and Murnane, 91–116; Prudence Carter and Kevin G. Welner, *Closing the Opportunity Gap: What America must do to give every child an even chance* (New York: Oxford University Press, 2013).
3. Sean F. Reardon, "The Great Divide: No Rich Child Left Behind," *New York Times*, April 27, 2013, https://opinionator.blogs.nytimes.com/2013/04/27/no-rich-child -left-behind/?_r=0.
4. Ibid.
5. Annie E. Casey, Kid's Count Data Center, http://www.aecf.org/work/kids-count /kids-count-data-center/.
6. Sean F. Reardon tabulations of data from US Census (1970–2000) and American Community Survey (2005–2009). Proportions based on all families in 117 metropolitan areas with at least 500,000 residents in 2007.
7. Population Reference Bureau analysis of data from the US Census Bureau, 2006–2010 to 2010–2014, American Community Survey five-year data.
8. Gary Orfield, John Kucsera, and Genevieve Siegel-Hawley, *E Pluribus . . . Separation: Deepening Double Segregation for More Students* (UCLA: The Civil Rights Project, 2012), http://escholarship.org/uc/item/8g58m2v9.
9. Reardon, "The Widening Academic Achievement Gap."
10. Martha J. Bailey and Susan M. Dynarski, "Inequality in Postsecondary Education," in *Whither Opportunity?*, ed. Duncan and Murnane, 117–32.
11. Sean F. Reardon, Rachel Baker, and Daniel Klasik, *Race, Income, and Enrollment Patterns in Highly Selective Colleges, 1982–2004* (Center for Education Policy Analysis, Stanford University, 2012), http://cepa. stanford. edu/content/race-income -and-enrollmentpatterns-highly-selective-colleges-1982-2004; Bailey and Dynarski, "Inequality in Postsecondary Education"; Philippe Belley and Lance Lochner, "The Changing Role of Family Income and Ability in Determining Educational Achievement," *Journal of Human Capital* 1 (2007), 37–89.

12. Richard J. Coley, and Bruce Baker, *Poverty and Education: Finding the Way Forward* (Princeton, NJ: Educational Testing Service Center for Research on Human Capital and Education, 2013); William Duncombe and John Yinger, "How Much More Does a Disadvantaged Student Cost?," *Economics of Education Review* 24, no. 5 (2005): 513.

13. Bruce D. Baker, Danielle Farrie, and David G. Sciarra, "Mind the Gap; 20 Years of Progress and Retrenchment in School Funding and Achievement Gaps," *ETS Research Report Series* (2016): 1–37; Steven W. Barnett et al., *The State of Preschool 2012: State Preschool Yearbook* (New Brunswick, NJ: National Institute for Early Education Research, 2012).

14. US Department of Education, *For Each and Every Child—A Strategy for Education Equity and Excellence* (Washington, DC: National Commission on Educational Equity and Excellence, 2013), 15.

15. Duncan and Murnane, *Whither Opportunity?*

16. Sabino Kornrich, "Inequalities in Parental Spending on Young Children: 1972 to 2010," *AERA Open* 2 no. 2 (2016).

17. Ibid.

18. Duncan and Murnane, *Whither Opportunity?*, 3–26.

19. Meredith Phillips, "Parenting, Time Use, and Disparities in Academic Outcomes" in *Whither Opportunity?*, ed. Duncan and Murnane, 207–28.

20. "The 6,000-Hour Learning Gap," ExpandEd, http://www.expandedschools.org /policy-documents/6000-hour-learning-gap#sthash.6ZHDXOoj.dpbs.

21. Afterschool Alliance, *America After 3PM: Afterschool Programs in Demand* (Washington, DC: Afterschool Alliance, 2014).

22. Reardon, "The Widening Academic Achievement Gap."

23. Karl L. Alexander, Doris R. Entwisle, and Linda S. Olson, "Lasting Consequences of the Summer Learning Gap," *American Sociological Review* 72, no. 2 (2007): 167–80.

24. Anthony S. Bryk, Penny Bender Sebring, Elaine Allensworth, Stuart Luppescu, and John Q. Easton, *Organizing Schools for Improvement: Lessons from Chicago* (Chicago: University of Chicago Press, 2010), 47–64.

25. See Michael Fullan, *Choosing the Wrong Drivers for Whole System Reform*, Seminar Series Paper No. 204, May 2011 (Centre for Strategic Education, East Melbourne Australia), http://michaelfullan.ca/wp-content/uploads/2016/06/13396088160.pdf.

26. US Department of Education, "For Each and Every Child," 16.

27. National Education Commission on Time and Learning, *Prisoners of Time,* a Report of the National Education Commission on Time and Learning (original 1994 report was republished, with a new forward, by the Education Commission of the States, Washington DC, October 2005), http://files.eric.ed.gov/fulltext/ ED489343.pdf.

28. Ibid. (See report forward by the Education Commission of the States (2005); deeper learning skills include critical thinking skills, interpersonal collaboration skills, communication skills, and intrapersonal mindsets (e.g., academic identities, growth mind-set).

29. Robert Halpern, Paul Heckman, and Reed Larson, *Realizing the Potential of Learning In Middle Adolescence* (West Hills: The Sally and Dick Roberts Coyote Foundation, 2013), http://www.realizinglearning.org/rlwp/.

30. David Hursh, *High-Stakes Testing and the Decline of Teaching and Learning* (Plymouth, UK: Rowan and Littlefield Publishers, 2008); Gail L. Sunderman, James S. Kim, and Gary G. Orfield, eds., *NCLB Meets School Realities: Lessons From the Field* (Thousand Oakes, CA: Corwin Press, 2005); Angela Valenzuela, ed, *Leaving Children Behind: How "Texas-style" Accountability Fails Latino Youth* (Albany, NY: SUNY Press, 2005); Katie White and James E. Rosenbaum, "Inside the Black Box of Accountability: How High-Stakes Accountability Alters School Culture and the Classification and Treatment of Students and Teachers," in *No Child Left Behind and the Reduction of the Achievement Gap: Sociological Perspectives on Federal Educational Policy,* ed. Alan R. Sadovnik et al. (New York: Routledge, 2008), 97–116; George Wood, "A View from the Field: NCLB's Effects on Classrooms and Schools," in *Many Children Left Behind: How the No Child Left Behind Act Is Damaging Our Children and Our Schools,* ed. Deborah Meier et al. (Boston: Beacon Press, 2004), 33–52.

31. Halpern et al., *Realizing the Potential.*

32. See National Research Council, *Education for Life and Work: Developing Transferable Knowledge and Skills in the 21st Century,* Committee on Defining Deeper Learning and 21st Century Skills, ed. J. W. Pellegrino and M. L. Hilton, Board on Testing and Assessment and Board on Science Education, Division of Behavioral and Social Sciences and Education (Washington, DC: National Academies Press, 2012). An online PDF of this report is available from the National Academy Press at: http://www.nap.edu/catalog.php?record_id=13398.

SECTION I: INTRODUCTION

1. *Regions Encouraged to Apply for $250 Million Career Path Trust* (Sacramento, CA: Linked Learning Alliance, 2014), http://linkedlearning.org/regions-encouraged-to-apply-for-250-million-career-pathways-trust/.

CHAPTER 1

1. National Commission on Excellence in Education, *A Nation at Risk: The Imperative for Educational Reform* (Washington, DC: US Department of Education, 1983), 3.

2. In the commission's words, "If the United States is to grasp the larger education ambitions for which it is reaching, we must strike the shackles of time from our schools." National Education Commission on Time and Learning, *Prisoners of Time* (Washington, DC: US Department of Education, 1994), 5. A similar commission established in Massachusetts the following year, subsequent to the commonwealth's own adoption of standards-based education reform, declared much the same: "It has become increasingly obvious that campaigns for higher standards of learning on the one hand and for sufficient time to achieve those standards on the other are wholly interdependent. They stand or fall together. Only a public determined to apply higher standards for all students will support more time and better time. But only more and better time will provide the teaching and learning needed to open the way for students to reach those standards." Massachusetts Commission on Time and Learning, *Unlocking the Power of Time* (Boston: Massachusetts Department of Education, November 1995), 16.

3. Charles Fisher et al., *Teaching and Learning in the Elementary School: A Summary of the Beginning Teacher Evaluation Study* (San Francisco: Far West Lab for Educational Research and Development, 1978); and R. A. Rossmiller, *Resource Utilization in Schools and Classrooms: Final Report* (Program Report 86-7) (Madison: University of Wisconsin Center for Education Research, 1986).

4. Douglas Downey, Paul T. Von Hippel, and Beckett Broh, "Are Schools the Great Equalizer? Cognitive Inequality during the Summer Months and the School Year," *American Sociological Review* 69, no. 5 (October 2004): 613–35; Malcolm Gladwell, summarizing the research, states plainly in his book, *Outliers*, "Schools *work*. The only problem with school, for the kids who aren't achieving, is that there isn't enough of it." See Malcolm Gladwell, *Outliers: The Story of Success* (New York: Little Brown, 2008), 259. For a summary of the research, see David Farbman, *The Case for Improving and Expanding Time in School: A Review of Key Research and Practice* (Boston: National Center on Time & Learning, 2015).

5. Massachusetts 2020, Amicus Curiae Brief in *Hancock v. Driscoll*, Massachusetts Supreme Judicial Court, 2004. With this intellectual framing in place, Mass 2020 then aimed to demonstrate that schools operating with substantially more learning time—typically, a school day of at least 7.5 hours and, in some cases, a school year of at least 10 more days than the standard 180—not only already existed, but that they added significant value for their students and teachers. To that end, in 2005, Mass 2020 authored a study entitled *Time for a Change*, which documented the structures and practices at four higher-performing charter schools and four district schools in New York and Massachusetts. These eight schools featured longer days and years, and researchers focused on unpacking how such expanded time might explain why these schools significantly outperformed neighboring district schools on state tests. See David Farbman and Claire Kaplan, *Time for a Change: The Promise of Extended Time Schools for Promoting Student Achievement* (Boston: Massachusetts 2020, 2005).

6. Some higher-income communities experienced some pushback from parents, as they were already selecting and paying for afterschool programming. Meanwhile, families without the option to pay for supplemental learning were eager to see more enrichment opportunities and extra academic support built into the school program.

7. Additionally, the department also conducted annual school visits and reviews of each school based on goals articulated through so-called "Performance Agreements," which were essentially contracts each participating school made with the state to achieve certain levels of improvement in student achievement and the expansion of both enrichment programming and teacher collaboration time.

8. Amy Checkoway et al., *Evaluation of the Expanded Learning Time Initiative Year Four Integrated Report: 2009–10* (Cambridge, MA: Abt Associates, March 2011).

9. Greg Duncan and Richard Murnane, "The American Dream: Then and Now," in *Whither Opportunity?: Rising Inequality, Schools, and Children's Life Chances*, ed. Greg J. Duncan and Richard J. Murnane (New York: Russell Sage Foundation, 2011), 11.

10. Checkoway et al., *Evaluation*, 45–7.

11. Ibid., 45–60.

12. $3.5 billion was made available through the American Recovery and Reinvestment Act, while $500 million was allocated through the "regular" budget of the US Department of Education.

13. See David Farbman, *Learning Time in America* (Boston: National Center on Time & Learning, 2015).

14. It is important to note that while most of these efforts, like NCTL's work, aimed to capitalize on increased time to enhance educational quality, the real outcomes were decidedly mixed, especially in large-scale efforts such as in Chicago.

CHAPTER 2

1. Paul Reville, "Designing 21st Century Education Systems," *Journal of The National Association of Principals and Deputy Principals* 9 (2015): 35.

2. We define social-emotional learning as "patterns of thought, feelings, and behavior" that develop throughout one's life. E. Garcia, *The Need to Address Noncognitive Skills in the Education Policy Agenda* (Washington, DC: Economic Policy Institute, 2014), 3.

3. "What is Expanded Learning," California Department of Education, http://www.caexpandedlearning.com/.

4. Robert Halpern, "A Different Kind of Child Development Institution: The History of After-School Programs for Low-Income Children," *Teachers College Record* 104, no. 2 (March 2002): 178–211.

5. Terry K. Peterson, ed., *Expanding Minds and Opportunities: Leveraging the Power of Afterschool and Summer Learning for Student Success*, (Washington, DC: Collaborative Communications Group, 2013). This comprehensive overview of research on expanded learning includes studies, reports, and commentaries by more than 100 thought leaders including community leaders, elected officials, educators, researchers, and advocates.

6. Nikki Yamashiro and Jen Rinehart, *America After 3PM: Afterschool Programs in Demand* (Washington, DC: Afterschool Alliance, 2014).

7. Ibid.

8. Ibid.

9. Jeff Davis, *State of the State of Expanded Learning in California 2015–2016* (Sacramento: California Afterschool Network, 2016).

10. *Quality Standards for Expanded Learning in California: Creating and Implementing a Shared Vision of Quality* (Sacramento: California Afterschool Network and California Department of Education, 2014), 19.

11. Ibid.

12. *Student Success Comes Full Circle: Leveraging Expanded Learning Opportunities* (Oakland, CA: Partnership for Children & Youth, 2015).

13. James W. Pellegrino and Margaret L. Hilton, eds., *Education for life and work: Developing transferable knowledge and skills in the 21st century* (summary) (Washington, DC: The National Academies Press, 2012), http://www.nap.edu/openbook.php?record_id=13398&page=1.

14. Robert D. Putnam, *Our Kids: The American Dream in Crisis* (New York: Simon & Schuster, 2015).

15. Joseph A. Durlak, Roger P. Weissberg, and Molly Pachan, "A Meta-Analysis of After-School Programs That Seek to Promote Personal and Social Skills in Children and Adolescents," *American Journal of Community Psychology* no. 45 (2010): 294–309.

16. Temescal & Associates, *The LIAS Learning Principles: In the Words of Field Leaders and Afterschool Youth* (Oakland, CA: Learning in Afterschool, 2016).

17. Jenny Nagaoka et al., *Foundations for Young Adult Success: A Developmental Framework* (Chicago: University of Chicago Consortium on Chicago School Research, 2015).

18. California Employment Development Department, Labor Market Information Division, *After-School Program Survey, Final Report of Results* (Sacramento: California Employment Development Department, 2012).

19. *21st Century Community Learning Centers: Providing Afterschool and Summer Learning Support to Communities Nationwide* (Washington, DC: Afterschool Alliance, 2016).

20. In the 2014–2015 school year, there were 6.2 million students enrolled in California Public Schools, 58.6% received FRPM, and 22.3% were English language learners. Data files are provided by the CDE Data Reporting Office at http://www.cde.ca.gov/ds/sd/sd/filesenr.asp.

21. Internal Survey, Partnership for Children & Youth, 2016.

22. Harvard Family Research Project Evaluation Team, *Partnerships for Learning: Promising Practices in Integrating School and Out-of-School Time Program Supports* (Cambridge, MA: Harvard Family Research Project, 2010).

23. LCFF is grounded in two primary principles: (1) It takes additional resources to educate students from low-income households, English language learners, and foster youth, and (2) Local education decision makers are better equipped to decide how to invest resources to meet student needs and improve student outcomes.

24. Mary Perry and Jessica Gunderson, *Time Well Spent* (Oakland, CA: Partnership for Children & Youth, 2014).

25. "Afterschool in Your State," Afterschool Alliance, http://www.afterschoolalliance.org/policyStateFacts.cfm.

26. Davis, *State of the State of Expanded Learning in California 2015–2016.*

27. "Mayor Lee Announces Expanded Summer Programs to Eliminate Wait Lists for City's Children & Youth" (San Francisco: Office of the Mayor, 2015).

28. Durlak, Weissberg, and Pachan, "A Meta-Analysis of After-School Programs," 302.

29. Jean Baldwin Grossman et al., *The Cost of Quality of Out-of-School Time Programs* (New York: The Wallace Foundation, 2009).

30. "California ASES Funding Doesn't Add Up" (Oakland: Partnership for Children & Youth, 2016).

31. California Education Code. Article 22.5.Section 8484.

32. "2016 ASES Survey Results" (Oakland, CA: Partnership for Children & Youth, 2016).

33. California State Board of Education Meeting, Agenda Item 06, May 11–12, 2016.

34. Jessica Gunderson, "Data Sharing: Federal Rules and Best Practices to Improve Out-of-School Time Programs and Student Outcomes" (Oakland, CA: Partnership for Children & Youth, 2012).

CHAPTER 3

1. Prior research indicates that, in high-poverty classrooms, teachers are three times as likely to report that students have stressors such as hunger or medical and dental issues, than low-poverty classrooms. See John Rogers, Nicole Mirra, Michael Seltzer, and J. Jun, *It's About Time: Learning Time and Educational Opportunity in California High Schools* (Los Angeles: UCLA IDEA, 2014). The community school model addresses many assumptions inherent in the traditional approach to time for learning in schools, namely, that students come to school ready to learn and that

the traditional school day and year are sufficient to achieve desired educational success. See Cheryl M. Kane, *Prisoners of Time: Research. What We Know and What
We Need To Know* (Washington, DC: US Government Printing Office, 1994).

2. This chapter is based on research conducted by the John W. Gardner Center for
Youth and Their Communities at Stanford University (Gardner Center) in partnership with OUSD. Since 2014, OUSD has partnered with the Gardner Center to support OUSD's efforts to assess, enhance, and scale its community schools
work. We began by working with the district to develop a system strategy map to
articulate the district's goals, desired outcomes, and key elements of the community school initiative. Our first year of research tested this theory of action by identifying key programmatic and organizational elements of community schools at
mature sites, as well as initial trends in student outcomes. The second year of our
research collaboration (SY2015–2016) expanded to consider the role of the district
in supporting community school implementation, beginning to understand the
relationship between community school participation and student. In this chapter, we draw from both years of this research, which includes nearly 60 interviews
at nine different community school sites, ranging from relatively well-established,
"mature" community schools to some newer "emerging" community school sites.

3. Joy G. Dryfoos, *Full-service Schools: A Revolution in Health and Social Services for
Children, Youth, and Families* (San Francisco: Jossey-Bass, 1994); Martin J. Blank,
Melaville Atelia, and Shah P. Bela, *Making the Difference: Research and Practice in
Community Schools* (Washington, DC: Coalition for Community Schools, Insti-
tute for Educational Leadership, 2003).

4. Nancy Claiborne and Hal Lawson, "An intervention Framework for Collaboration," *Families in Society: The Journal of Contemporary Social Services* 86, no. 1
(2005): 93–103; Ellen Lubell, *Building Community Schools: A Guide for Action*
(New York: Children's Aid Society, 2011)..

5. Insight Center for Community Economic Development, 2015, based on self-
sufficiency index calculated for Alameda County, http://www.insightcced.org/tools
-metrics/self-sufficiency-standard-tool-for-california/.

6. Alameda County Public Health Department, "Life and Death from Unnatural Causes: Health and social inequity in Alameda County," August 2008, http://
www.acphd.org/media/53628/unnatcs2008.pdf.

7. US Census 2000 SF1, SF3, DP1-DP4, CTPP, Census 2010 DP-1, http://www
.bayareacensus.ca.gov/cities/Oakland.htm; US Census Bureau, American Community Survey 2006–2010, http://www.bayareacensus.ca.gov/cities/Oakland.htm.

8. Charters schools account for about one-quarter of total enrollment, with 12,000
students attending one of 37 district authorized charter schools (Oakland Unified
School District, 2015).

9. California Longitudinal Pupil Achievement Data System (CALPADS), "Enrollment by ethnicity for 2015-16," 2016, http://dq.cde.ca.gov/dataquest/Enrollment
/EthnicEnr.aspx?cChoice=DistEnrEth&cYear=2015-16&cSelect=0161259--Oakland
%20Unified&TheCounty=&cLevel=District&cTopic=Enrollment&myTimeFrame
=S&cType=ALL&cGender=B.

10. Dean E. Murphy, "Dream Ends for Oakland School Chief as State Takes Over,"
New York Times, June 8, 2003, http://www.nytimes.com/2003/06/08/us/dream
-ends-for-oakland-school-chief-as-state-takes-over.html?_r=0.

11. A summary of strategic planning process and taskforce findings can be found at http://www.ousd.org/cms/lib07/CA01001176/Centricity/Domain/6/Strategic _Initiative_and_Taskforce_Overview_10.29.10.pdf.

12. Jill Tucker, "Oakland to Halt School Suspensions for Willful Defiance," *SF Gate*, May 14, 2015, http://www.sfgate.com/bayarea/article/Oakland-to-halt-school -suspensions-for-willful-6262461.php.

13. Before the districtwide initiative, some OUSD schools operated as community schools through other initiatives such as Atlantic Philanthropies Elev8.

14. We would like to acknowledge the Coalition for Community Schools for their foundational thinking in this area. Reuben Jacobson and Martin J. Blank, *A Framework for More and Better Learning through Community School Partnerships* (Washington, DC: Institute for Educational Leadership, 2015), http://www .communityschools.org/betterlearning/.

15. This deep integration often took time to develop. In many cases, some teachers were initially resistant to having partner organizations in their staff meetings. Leadership from the principal was critical in setting the tone that partner organizations belonged and were part of the school.

16. We use the word "parent" to refer to the primary caretaker in a child's life—this could be a grandparent or other relative, an adult neighbor, a foster parent, legal guardian, etc.

17. See description of Academic Parent Teacher Teams at http://www.hfrp.org /publications-resources/browse-our-publications/academic-parent-teacher-teams -reorganizing-parent-teacher-conferences-around-data.

18. Hal Lawson and Katharine Briar-Lawson, *Connecting the Dots: Progress Toward the Integration of School Reform, School-Linked Services, Parent Involvement and Community Schools* (Oxford, OH: Institute for Educational Renewal, 1997).

19. Anthony S. Bryk and Barbara Schneider, "Trust in Schools: A Core Resource for School Reform," *Educational Leadership* 60, no. 6 (2003): 40–5.

20. Coral Mitchell and Larry Sackney, *Profound Improvement: Building Capacity for a Learning Community* (New York: Routledge, 2011).

21. Charles Payne, *So Much Reform, So Little Change: The Persistence of Failure in Urban Schools* (Cambridge, MA: Harvard University Press, 2008).

22. Larry Cuban, "Reforming Again, Again, and Again," *Educational Researcher* 19, no. 1 (1990): 3–13.

23. Indeed, meaningful reform must take into consideration the implementation context, including educational histories, human and organizational capacities, and the quality of relationships of real people and places. See Jennifer A. O'Day and Marshall S. Smith, "Quality and Equality in American Education: Systemic Problems, Systemic Solutions," in *The Dynamics of Opportunity in America* (New York: Springer International Publishing, 2016), 297–358.

24. Anthony S. Bryk, "Organizing Schools for Improvement," *Phi Beta Kappan* 91, no. 7 (2010): 23–30.

CHAPTER 4

1. The After School Alliance, "Expanded learning opportunities," http://www.after schoolalliance.org/Principles%20of%20Expanded%20Learning%20Programs _Jan_2012(2).pdf.

2. US Department of Education, *Results Framework* (Washington, DC: 2016), https://promiseneighborhoods.ed.gov/neighborhoods/promise-neighborhoods-results-framework.

3. Federal Register, 77, no. 77 (Friday, April 20, 2012), https://www.gpo.gov/fdsys/pkg/FR-2012-04-20/pdf/2012-9595.pdf.

4. Anne C. Kubisch, "Structures, Strategies, Actions, and Results for Community Change Efforts," *Voices from the Field III: Lessons and Challenges from Two Decades of Community Change Efforts* (Washington, DC: Aspen Institute, 2010).

5. Rubin Victor and Michael McAfee, "New Ways of Using Data in Federal Place-based Initiatives: Opportunities to Create a Results Framework and to Raise the Visibility of Equity Issues," *What Counts: Harnessing Data for America's Communities*, Federal Reserve Bank of San Francisco and Urban Institute, 2014.

6. A. Wade Boykin and Pedro Noguera, *Creating the Opportunity to Learn: Moving from Research to Practice to Close the Achievement Gap* (Alexandria, VA: Ascd, 2011).

7. Mark Friedman, *Trying Hard Isn't Good Enough* (San Bernardino, CA: FPSI Publishing, 2005).

CHAPTER 5

1. With generous support from the James Irvine Foundation, ConnectEd: The California Center for College and Career launched the California Linked Learning District Initiative in 2008. The initiative included Antioch Unified, Long Beach Unified, Los Angeles Unified, Montebello Unified, Oakland Unified, Pasadena Unified, Porterville Unified, Sacramento Unified, and West Contra Costa Unified. In 2014, when the California legislature made the first of two $250 million investments in career pathways, the approach began spreading to approximately 30 more districts throughout the state. Additionally, Linked Learning initiatives began in other parts of the country—most notably Detroit, MI; Houston, TX; and Rochester, NY.

2. Robert B. Westbrook, *John Dewey and American Democracy* (Ithaca, NY: Cornell University Press, 1991); John Dewey, *The Collected Works of John Dewey, 1882–1953*, ed. Jo Ann Boydston and L. Hickman (Charlottesville, VA: InteLex, 1996).

3. Miya Warner et al., *Taking Stock of the California Linked Learning District Initiative. Sixth-Year Evaluation Report* (Menlo Park, CA: SRI International, 2015).

4. Miya Warner et al., *Taking Stock of the California Linked Learning District Initiative. Seventh-Year Evaluation Report* (Menlo Park, CA: SRI International, 2016).

5. Priscilla M. D. Little, Christopher Wimer, and Heather B. Weiss, *After School Programs in the 21st Century: Their Potential and What it Takes to Achieve It* (Cambridge, MA: Harvard Family Research Project, No. 10, February 2008).

6. Ken Futernick, *A Possible Dream: Retaining California Teachers So All Students Learn* (Sacramento: California State, 2007), www.calstate.edu/teacherquality/documents/possible_dream.pdf.

7. Responding to a wide range of student interests is best accomplished in larger, more economically diverse districts/communities able to offer students a menu of pathways in, say, six to eight different industry sectors. In smaller districts, which often are also more rural, this objective can be difficult to achieve. When options are limited, it is important to define pathways broadly enough to appeal to a wide range of student interests. For example, in a district able to offer only one pathway,

a pathway focused on "engineering and construction technology" is not likely to provide the broader appeal afforded by a pathway in "environmental science and green technology" or "agriculture, ecology, and natural resources."

8. Cohorting students in mathematics can be challenging as at any particular grade level students are often taking different math courses (some ninth graders, for example, may be taking pre-Algebra or Algebra I, while others are taking Geometry or Algebra II). This may be less problematic in schools offering Integrated Mathematics rather than the more traditional curriculum.

9. The seven essential elements are: (1) Student Outcomes-Driven Practice, (2) Equity, Access, and Achievement, (3) Program of Study, (4) Learning and Teaching, (5) Work-Based Learning, (6) Personalized Student Support, and (7) Pathway Leadership and Partnership. *Linked Learning Essential Elements for Pathway Quality*, http://connectedcalifornia.org/ideas_resources/publications.

10. John Kania and Mark Kramer, "Collective Impact," *Stanford Social Innovation Review* (Winter 2011): 36–41.

CHAPTER 6

The authors would like to thank the editors for feedback on prior versions of this chapter.

1. Ellen C. Lagemann, "The Plural Worlds of Educational Research," *History of Education Quarterly* 29 (1989): 185.

2. Ibid., 212.

3. David Berliner, "The Science of Psychology and the Practice of Schooling: The One-Hundred-Year Journey of Educational Psychology from Interest, to Disdain, to Respect for Practice," in *Exploring Applied Psychology: Origins and critical analysis*, ed. Thomas K. Fagan and Gary R. VandenBos (Washington, DC: American Psychological Association, 1993); R. Keith Sawyer, "Introduction: The New Science of Learning," in *Cambridge Handbook of the Learning Sciences*, ed. R. Keith Sawyer (Cambridge, UK: Cambridge University Press, 2006).

4. Sawyer, "Introduction: The New Science of Learning."

5. Daniela K. DiGiacomo, Joshua J. Prudhomme, Hannah R. Jones, Kevin G. Welner, and Ben Kirshner, "Why Theory Matters: An Examination of Contemporary Learning Time Reforms," *Education Policy Analysis Archives* 24 (2016): 44.

6. Jean Lave, "Teaching, as Learning, in Practice," *Mind, Culture, and Activity* 3, no. 3 (1996): 149–64.

7. Kris Gutierrez and Barbara Rogoff, "Cultural Ways of Learning: Individual Traits or Repertoires of Practice," *Educational Researcher* 32, no. 5 (2003): 19–25.

8. Sawyer, "Introduction."

9. National Research Council, *Engaging Schools: Fostering High School Students' Motivation to Learn*, (Washington, DC: The National Academies Press, 2004).

10. We use "nondominant" to refer to people in the United States who are part of racial, ethnic, or cultural groups that experience institutionalized racism or other forms of discrimination (e.g., language discrimination). Carol Lee, *Culture, Literacy, and Learning: Taking Bloom in the Midst of the Whirlwind* (New York: Teachers College Press, 2007); Tara J. Yosso, "Whose Culture has Capital? A Critical Race Theory Discussion of Community Cultural Wealth," *Race Ethnicity and Education* 8, no. 1 (2005).

11. Luis Moll and Julio Cammarota, "Cultivating New Funds of Knowledge Through Research and Practice," *Bringing Literacy Home* (2010): 289; Na'ilah Suad Nasir and Victoria Hand, "From the Court to the Classroom: Opportunities for Engagement, Learning, and Identity in Basketball and Classroom Mathematics," *Journal of the Learning Sciences* 17, no. 2 (2008): 143–79.

12. Kris Gutierrez et al., *Replacing Representation with Imagination: Finding Ingenuity in Everyday Practices* (Berkeley, CA: University of California, 2016).

13. Lave, "Teaching, as Learning"; Na'ilah Suad Nasir and Jamal Cooks, "Becoming a Hurdler: How Learning Settings Afford Identities," *Anthropology and Education* 40, no. 1 (2009): 41.

14. Nasir and Cooks, "Becoming a Hurdler."

15. John Seely Brown, Allan Collins, and Paul Duguid, "Situated Cognition and the Culture of Learning," *Educational Researcher* 18, no. 1 (1989): 32–42.

16. Lee, *Culture, Literacy, and Learning.*

17. National Research Council, *Community Programs to Promote Youth Development* (Washington, DC: National Academies Press, 2002).

18. Na'ilah Suad Nasir, "Everyday Pedagogy: Lessons from Basketball, Track, and Dominoes," *Phi Delta Kappan* 89, no. 7 (2008): 529.

19. Catherine Cooper, *Bridging Multiple Worlds: Cultures, Identities, and Pathways to College* (New York: Oxford University Press, 2011), 208.

20. Norma González, Luis C. Moll, and Cathy Amanti, *Funds of Knowledge* (Mahwah, NJ: Lawrence Erlbaum Associates, 2005).

21. Kristen Pozzoboni and Ben Kirshner, *The Changing Landscape of Youth Work: Theory and Practice for an Evolving Field* (Charlotte, NC: Information Age Press, 2016).

22. Nasir and Cooks, "Becoming a Hurdler."

23. Ibid.

24. Ibid.

25. Ibid.

26. Ibid.

27. Joseph L. Polman, "Trajectories of Participation and Identification in Learning Communities Involving Disciplinary Practices," in *Design Research on Learning and Thinking in Educational Settings: Enhancing Intellectual Growth and Functioning,* ed. D. Yun Dai (New York: Routledge, 2012), 225.

28. John D. Bransford et al., "Foundations and Opportunities for an Interdisciplinary Science of Learning," in *The Cambridge Handbook of the Learning Sciences,* ed. Keith Sawyer (New York: Cambridge University Press, 2006), 19–34.

29. Bransford et al., "Foundations and Opportunities."

30. Ibid., 26.

31. Ibid., 27.

32. Ibid.

33. Ben Kirshner and Kimberly Geil, "'I'm About to Really Bring It!' Access Points between Youth Activists and Adult Community Leaders," *Children, Youth and Environments* 20 (2010): 1–24.

34. Ben Kirshner and Shawn Ginwright, "Youth Organizing as a Developmental Context for African American and Latino Adolescents," *Child Development Perspectives* 6, no. 3 (2012): 288–94.

35. Clayborne Carson, *In Struggle: SNCC and the Black Awakening of the 1960s* (Cambridge, MA: Harvard University Press, 1995); Francisco Arturo Rosales, *Chicano!: The History of the Mexican American Civil Rights Movement* (Houston: Arte Publico Press, 1997).

36. Jesica Fernández, Ben Kirshner, and Deanna Lewis, "Strategies for Systemic Change: Youth Community Organizing to Disrupt the School-To-Prison Nexus," in *Contemporary Youth Activism: Advancing Social Justice in the United States* (Santa Barbara, CA: Praeger, 2016), 93–112.

37. Ben Kirshner, *Youth Activism in an Era of Education Inequality* (New York: New York University Press, 2015); Jerusha Conner, "Youth Organizers as Young Adults: Their Commitments and Contributions," *Journal of Research on Adolescence* 21, no. 4 (2011): 923–42; Seema Shah, *Building Transformative Youth Leadership: Data on the Impacts of Youth Organizing* (New York: Funders Collaborative on Youth Organizing Occasional Paper Series, 2011).

38. Roderick Watts, Ben Kirshner, Rashida Govan, and Jesica Fernandez, *International Youth Organizing: A Report on Key Research Findings* (in press).

39. Ben Kirshner, "Introduction: Youth Activism as a Context for Learning and Development," *American Behavioral Scientist* 51, no. 3 (2007): 367–79.

40. Milbrey McLaughlin, *Community Counts: How Youth Organizations Matter for Youth Development* (Washington, DC: Public Education Network, 2000).

41. Shawn Ginwright and Taj James, "From Assets to Agents of Change: Social Justice, Organizing, and Youth Development," *New Directions for Youth Development* 96 (2002): 27–46.

42. Harry C. Boyte, *Everyday Politics: Reconnecting Citizens and Public Life* (Philadelphia: University of Pennsylvania Press, 2004).

43. Nilda Flores-Gonzales, Matthew Rodríguez, and Michael Rodríguez-Muñiz, "From Hip-Hop to Humanization: Batey Urbano as a Space for Latino Youth Culture and Community Action," in *Beyond Resistance: Youth Activism and Community Change* (London, UK: Routledge, 2006), 175–96.

44. Shawn Ginwright, "Black Youth Activism and the Role of Critical Social Capital in Black Community Organizations," *American Behavioral Scientist* 51, no. 3 (2007): 403–18.

45. Julio Cammarota, "A Social Justice Approach to Achievement: Guiding Latina/o Students toward Educational Attainment with a Challenging, Socially Relevant Curriculum," *Equity and Excellence in Education* 40 (2007): 87–96.

46. Watts et al., *International Youth Organizing*.

47. We drew on volumes such as Jacquelynne Eccles and Jennifer A. Gootman, eds., *Community Programs to Promote Youth Development* (Washington, DC: National Academies Press, 2002); National Research Council and the Institute of Medicine, *Engaging schools: Fostering high school students' motivation to learn* (Washington, DC: The National Academies Press, 2004); Robert K. Sawyer, ed., *Cambridge Handbook of the Learning Sciences* (Cambridge, UK: Cambridge University Press, 2006).

48. Barbara Rogoff, *The Cultural Nature of Human Development* (New York: Oxford University Press, 2003).

49. Kirshner, *Youth Activism*.

50. Kris Gutierrez et al., "Replacing Representation"; Eve Tuck, "Suspending Damage: A Letter to Communities," *Harvard Education Review* 79 (2009): 409–28; Richard R. Valencia, *Dismantling Contemporary Deficit Thinking: Educational Thought and Practice* (New York: Taylor & Francis, 2010).

51. Gloria Ladson-Billings, "From the Achievement Gap to the Education Debt: Understanding Achievement in U.S. Schools," *Educational Researcher* 35, no. 7 (October 1, 2006): 3–12.

52. The Politics of Learning Writing Collective, "Engagements: The Learning Sciences in a New Era of US Nationalism," *Cognition & Instruction*, http://cognitionand instruction.com/engagements-the-learning-sciences-in-a-new-era-of-u-s-nationalism/.

CHAPTER 7

1. David Farbman, *The Case for Improving and Expanding Time in School: A Review of Key Research and Practice* (Boston: National Center on Time and Learning, 2015), http://www.timeandlearning.org/publications/case-improving-and-expanding -time-school.

2. Carolyn Giroux and Elizabeth Birr Moje, "Learning from the Professions: Examining How, Why, and When Engineers Read and Write," *Theory into Practice* (unpublished manuscript).

3. Maria LaRusso, Suzanne Donovan, and Catherine E. Snow, "Implementation Challenges for Tier One and Tier Two School-based Programs for Early Adolescents," *New Directions for Child and Adolescent Development* 154 (2016): 11–30.

4. Claire Kaplan and Roy Chan, *Time Well Spent: Eight Powerful Practices of Successful, Expanded-time Schools* (Boston: National Center on Time & Learning, 2011), www.timeandlearning.org; Portland Public Schools, *Opportunities to Increase the Amount and Quality of Instructional Time* (Portland, OR: Portland Public Schools, 2007); Sally J. Zepeda and R. Stewart Mayers, "An Analysis of Research on Block Scheduling," *Review of Educational Research* 76 (2006): 137–70.

5. Julie E. Learned, "'The Behavior Kids': Examining the Conflation of Youth Reading Difficulty and Behavior Problem Positioning among School Institutional Contexts," *American Educational Research Journal* 53, no. 5 (2016): 1271–309; Jean Anyon, *Ghetto Schooling: A Political Economy of Urban Education Reform* (New York: Teachers College Press, 1997); Julie E. Learned, *Feeling Like I'm Slow Because I'm in This Class: Secondary School Contexts and the Identification and Construction of Struggling Readers* (Ann Arbor: University of Michigan, 2014), http://hdl.handle .net/2027.42/108819.

6. Yael Kidron and Jim Lindsay, *The Effects of Increased Learning Time on Student Academic and Nonacademic Outcomes: Findings from a Meta-analytic Review* (Washington, DC: NCEE, 2014), http://ies.ed.gov/ncee/edlabs.

7. Ibid.

8. Jennifer Davis and David Farbman, "Sparking an Education Movement: Expanding Learning Time to Raise Achievement, Empower Teachers, and Enrich Education," this volume; Kidron and Lindsay, *Effects of Increased Learning Time on Student Academic and Nonacademic Outcomes*; Jennifer McMurrer, Matthew Frizzell, and Nanami Yoshioka, *Expanded Learning Time: A Summary of Findings from Case Studies in Four States* (Washington, DC: Center on Education Policy, 2015);

Charlie Naylor, *Revisiting the Issue of Year-Round Schools* (Vancouver: British Columbia Teachers' Federation, 2012).

9. I use the term "push-out" to change the discourse from one that blames youth for their failure to stay in school (i.e., "drop-out") and instead acknowledges the ways that schools can make it difficult for students to persevere in negative conditions. In other words, poorly structured schools push students out.

10. See also Mary A. Carskadon, Christine Acebo, and Oskar G Jenni, "Regulation of Adolescent Sleep: Implications for Behavior," *Annals of the New York Academy of Sciences* 1021, no. 1 (2004): 276–91; Matthew Kirby, Stefania Maggi, and Amedeo D'Angiulli, "School Start Times and the Sleep-wake Cycle of Adolescents: A Review and Critical Evaluation of Available Evidence," *Educational Researcher* 40, no.2 (2011): 56–61; Kyla Wahlstrom, "School Start Time and Sleepy Teens," *Archives of Pediatrics and Adolescent Medicine* 164 (2010): 676–77.

11. Peter Hinrichs, "When the Bell Tolls: The Effects of School Starting Times on Academic Achievement," *Education Finance and Policy* 6 (2011): 486–507; Kirby et al., "School Start Times and the Sleep-wake Cycle of Adolescents"; R. Au et al., "School Start Times for Adolescents," *Pediatrics* 134, no. 3 (2014): 642–49.

12. Nickki Pearce Dawes and Reed Larson, "How Youth Get Engaged: Grounded-Theory Research on Motivational Development," *Developmental Psychology* 47, no. 1 (2011): 259–69; Joseph A. Durlak, Roger P. Weissberg, and Molly Pachan, "A Meta-Analysis of After-School Programs That Seek to Promote Personal and Social Skills in Children and Adolescents," *American Journal of Community Psychology* 45, nos. 3–4 (2010): 294–309; Kidron and Lindsay, *The Effects of Increased Learning Time on Student Academic and Nonacademic Outcomes*; Elizabeth G. Soslau and Deborah S. Yost, "Urban Service-Learning: An Authentic Teaching Strategy to Deliver a Standards-Driven Curriculum," *Journal of Experiential Education* 30, no. 1 (2007): 36–53.

13. Sarah N. Deschenes et al., *Engaging Older Youth: Program and City-Level Strategies to Support Sustained Participation in Out-of-School Time* (Cambridge, MA: Harvard Family Research Project, 2010); Ben Kirshner, "Guided Participation in Three Youth Activism Organizations: Facilitation Apprenticeship, and Joint Work," *Journal of the Learning Sciences* 17, no. 1 (2008): 60–101.

14. Elizabeth Grassi, Daniel Hanley, and Daniel Liston, "Service Learning: An Innovative Approach for Second Language Learners," *Journal of Experiential Education* 27, no. 1 (2004): 87–110; Evelyn Newman Phillips et al., "A Case Study of Participatory Action Research in a Public New England Middle School: Empowerment, Constraints and Challenges," *American Journal of Community Psychology* 46, nos. 1–2 (2010): 179–94; Marlene Berg, Emil Coman, and Jean J. Schensul, "Youth Action Research for Prevention: A Multi-Level Intervention Designed to Increase Efficacy and Empowerment among Urban Youth," *American Journal of Community Psychology* 43, no. 3–4 (2009): 345–59.

15. Heinz Reinders and James Youniss, "School-Based Required Community Service and Civic Development in Adolescents," *Applied Developmental Science* 10, no. 1 (2006): 2–12.

16. Kidron and Lindsay, *The Effects of Increased Learning Time on Student Academic and Nonacademic Outcomes*.

17. Ibid.

18. Kaplan and Chan, *Time Well Spent*.
19. John Bransford, ed., *How People Learn* (Washington, DC: National Academy Press, 2000); John Bransford and Suzanne Donovan, eds., *How Students Learn: History, Mathematics, and Science in the Classroom* (Washington, DC: The National Academies Press, 2005); Wahlstrom, "School Start Time and Sleepy Teens"; John T. Guthrie, Allan Wigfield, and S. L. Klauda, *Adolescents' Engagement in Academic Literacy* (Sharjah, UAE: Bentham Science Publishers, 2012); Allan Wigfield, Jacquelynne Eccles, and D. Rodriguez, "The Development of Children's Motivation in School Contexts," in *Review of Research in Education*, vol. 23, ed. P. David Pearson and A. Iran-Nejad (Washington, DC: American Educational Research Association, 1998), 73–118.
20. David Farbman, *The Case for Improving and Expanding Time in School: A Review of Key Research and Practice* (Boston: National Center on Time & Learning, 2015), http://www.timeandlearning.org/publications/case-improving-and-expanding -time-school.
21. Larry Cuban, "Persistent Instruction: Another Look at Constancy in the Classroom," *Phi Delta Kappan* 68, no. 1 (1986): 7–11; Amy Arbreton, *Engaging Older Youth: Program and City-Level Strategies to Support Sustained Participation in Out-of-School Time* (Cambridge, MA: Harvard Family Research Project, 2010); Theodore R. Sizer, *Horace's Compromise: The Dilemma of The American High School*, 4th ed. (New York: Houghton Mifflin, 2004).
22. Jacquelynne S. Eccles and Carol Midgley, "Stage/Environment Fit: Developmentally Appropriate Classrooms for Early Adolescents," in *Research on Motivation in Education*, vol. 3, ed. Carol Ames (New York: Academic Press, 1989), 139–85; Jacquelynne S. Eccles et al., "Negative Effects of Traditional Middle Schools on Students' Motivation," *Elementary School Journal* 93 (1993): 553–74.
23. Bransford and Donovan, *How Students Learn;*. Elizabeth Birr Moje and Jennifer Speyer, "Reading Challenging Texts in High School: How Teachers Can Scaffold and Build Close Reading for Real Purposes in the Subject Areas," in *Best Practices in Adolescent Literacy Instruction*, 2nd ed., ed. Kathleen Hinchman and Heather Sheridan-Thomas (New York: Guilford, 2014), 207–31; Sam S. Wineburg, *Historical Thinking and Other Unnatural Acts: Charting the Future of Teaching the Past* (Philadelphia: Temple University Press, 2001).
24. Todd L. Ely and Paul Teske, *School Transportation in Colorado: Implications for Expanded Learning Time*, a report for Mile High Connects (Center for Education Policy Analysis, University of Colorado, Denver, 2014), http://milehighconnects .org/wp-content/uploads/2014/12/Transportation-Extended-Learning-Time -Report-2014-sm.pdf; Paul Ong and Elena Ong, "Spatial Inequality and Gaps in Expanded Learning Time Opportunities," this volume.
25. Elizabeth Birr Moje et al., "Working Toward Third Space in Content Area Literacy: An Examination of Everyday Funds of Knowledge and Discourse," *Reading Research Quarterly* 39, no.1 (2004): 38–70, doi:10.1598/rrq.39.1.4.
26. Angela Valenzuela, *Subtractive Schooling: U.S.–Mexican Youth and the Politics of Caring* (Albany: State University of New York Press, 1999).
27. Shirley Brice Heath, *Ways with Words: Language, Life, and Work in Communities and Classrooms* (Cambridge, UK: Cambridge University Press, 1983); Luis C. Moll and John Greenberg, "Creating Zones of Possibilities: Combining Social Contexts

for Instruction," in *Vygotsky and Education*, ed. Luis C. Moll (New York: Cambridge University Press, 1990), 319–48.

28. Bransford, *How People Learn*.

29. Bransford and Donovan, *How Students Learn*; Ronald W. Marx et al., "Inquiry-based Science in the Middle Grades: Assessment of Learning in Urban Systemic Reform," *Journal of Research in Science Teaching* 41 (2004): 1063–80; Robert B. Bain, "Rounding Up Unusual Suspects: Facing the Authority Hidden in the History Classroom," *Teachers College Record* 108, no. 10 (2006): 2080–114; Joseph Krajcik et al., "Inquiry in Project-Based Science Classrooms: Initial Attempts by Middle School Students," *Journal of the Learning Sciences* 7 (1998): 313–50.

30. David Fortus et al., "Design-Based Science and Student Learning," *Journal of Research In Science Teaching* 41, no.10 (2004): 1081–110, doi:10.1002/tea.20040.

31. Robert B. Bain, "AP World History Habits of Mind: Reflecting on World History's Unique Challenge to Students' Thinking," in *Teacher's Guide: AP World History*, ed. J. Arno (Princeton, NJ: College Entrance Examination Board, 2000): 237–43; Robert B. Bain, "'They Thought The World Was Flat?' HPL Principles in Teaching High School History," in *How Students Learn,* ed. John Bransford and Suzanne Donovan (Washington, DC: National Academies Press, 2005): 179–214.

32. Reed Stevens et al., "Becoming an Engineer: Toward a Three-Dimensional View of Engineering Learning," *Journal of Engineering Education* (2008): 355–68; Reed Stevens and Rogers Hall, "Disciplined Perception: Learning to See in Technoscience," in *Talking Mathematics in School Studies of Teaching and Learning*, ed. Magdalene Lampert and Merrie Blunk (Cambridge, UK: Cambridge University Press, 1998), 107–50; see Giroux and Moje, "Learning from the Professions."

33. Gary Hoachlander, Tameka McGlawn, and Brad Stam, "Linked Learning: Making the Best of Time for All Students," this volume.

34. Bain, "Rounding Up Unusual Suspects"; Moje and Speyer, "Reading Challenging Texts"; Sam Wineburg, "Teaching the Mind Good Habits," *The Chronicle of Higher Education* (2003): B20.

35. Elizabeth Birr Moje et al., "Maestro, What is 'Quality'?: Language, Literacy, and Discourse in Project-Based Science," *Journal of Research In Science Teaching* 38, no. 4 (2001): 469–96.

36. See also Zepeda and Mayers, "An Analysis of Research on Block Scheduling"; Hoachlander et al., "Linked Learning."

37. See www.edutopia.org/stw-expanded-learning-time

38. It should be noted that although their schedule maintains an early start (7:43 a.m.) and end (2:40 p.m.) time, which runs counter to the best research on adolescent brain development, core academic courses do not start until 9:05 a.m. and end at 1:35 p.m. It is also worth noting that lunch sits squarely in the middle of the day for all students (between 11:30 a.m. and 12 p.m.), rather than the distribution of lunch from any time between 10:00 a.m. and 2:30 p.m. that students in many middle and high school settings across the country experience. (Imagine starting the day at 7:30 a.m.—or earlier, given transit requirements—but not eating until 2:00 p.m.)

39. Farbman, *The Case for Improving and Expanding Time in School*; Kidron and Lindsay, *The Effects of Increased Learning Time on Student Academic and Nonacademic Outcomes*.

40. See LaRusso et al., "Implementation Challenges for Tier One and Tier Two School-based Programs for Early Adolescents"; Portland Public Schools, *Opportunities to Increase the Amount and Quality of Instructional Time*.

41. Fred Frelow and Barnett Barry, "More and Better Learning Time: Strategies for Improving Teaching," this volume.

42. Davis and Farhman, "Sparking an Education Movement."

43. Ely and Teske, *School Transportation in Colorado*.

44. Ward Goodenough, *Culture, Language, and Society*, 2nd ed. (Menlo Park, CA: Benjamin/Cummings Publishing Co., 1981).

45. See Elena Silva, *On the Clock: Rethinking the Way Schools Use Time* (Washington, DC: Education Sector, 2007).

46. Michael McAfee and Jessica Pizarek, "Promise Neighborhoods: Expanding Opportunities to Learn and Succeed from Cradle through Career," this volume.

CHAPTER 8

1. Fred Genesee et al., *Educating English Learners: A Synthesis of Research Evidence* (Cambridge, UK: Cambridge University Press, 2006).

2. Childtrends, "Immigrant Children. Databank. Appendix 2—Of Children Younger than 18, Number and Percentage Who Are First- or Second-Generation Immigrants, and Percentage of First- and Second-Generation Immigrants with Selected Characteristics: Selected Years, 1994–2014," Child Trends Databank, http://www.childtrends.org/wp-content/uploads/2012/07/110_appendix2.pdf.

3. Ariel Ruiz Soto, Sarah Hooker, and Jeanne Batalova, *Top Languages Spoken by English Language Learners Nationally and by State* (Washington, DC: Migration Policy Institute, 2015).

4. Childtrends, "Immigrant Children. Databank."

5. Sarah Pierce, *Unaccompanied Child Migrants in U.S. Communities, Immigration Courts, and Schools* (Washington, DC: Migration Policy Institute, 2015); Randy Capps, Michael Fix, and Julie Murray, *The New Demography of America's Schools: Immigration and the No Child Left Behind Act* (Washington, DC: The Urban Institute, 2005).

6. "Phi Delta Kappan Poll of Public Attitudes toward Public Education," *Phi Delta Kappan* 98 (Bloomington, IN: September 2016), http://pdkpoll2015.pdkintl.org/wp-content/uploads/2016/08/pdkpoll48_2016.pdf.

7. Mark Hugo Lopez, *Latinos and Education: Explaining the Attainment Gap* (Washington, DC: PEW Research Center, 2009), http://www.pewhispanic.org/2009/10/07/latinos-and-education-explaining-the-attainment-gap/; John Goodlad, *A Place Called School* (New York: McGraw-Hill, 1984).

8. Carola Suárez-Orozco, Marcelo M. Suárez-Orozco, and Irina Todorova, *Learning a New Land: Immigrant Children in America* (Cambridge, MA: Harvard University Press, 2008); Albert Bandura, "Recycling misconceptions of perceived self-efficacy," *Cognitive Therapy and Research* 8 (1984): 231–55.

9. Ilana Umansky, "Leveled and Exclusionary Tracking: English Learners' Access to Academic Content in Middle School," *American Education Research Journal* 53 (2016): 1792–1833.

10. Ibid.; Rebecca M. Callahan, "Tracking and high school English learners: Limiting opportunity to learn," *American Educational Research Journal* 42 no. 2 (2005): 305–28.

11. Francesca López, Elizabeth McEneaney, and Martina Nieswandt, "Language Instruction Educational Programs and Academic Achievement of Latino English Learners: Considerations for States with Changing Demographics," *American Journal of Education* (2015): 417–50.

12. Patricia Gándara et al., "English Learners in California Schools: Unequal Resources, Unequal Outcomes," *Educational Policy Analysis Archives* 11, no. 3 (2003): 1–56; Lopez et al., "Language Instruction Educational Programs."

13. Russell Rumberger, Patricia Gándara, and Barbara Merino, "Where California's English Learners Attend School and Why It Matters," *University of California Linguistic Minority Research Institute Newsletter* 15, no. 2 (Winter 2006): 1–3.

14. Author's analysis of data supplied by California Department of Education, 2014.

15. Dafney Dabach, "Teachers as a context for Immigrant Youth. Adaptations in Sheltered and Mainstream Classrooms" (unpublished diss., University of California, Berkeley, 2010).

16. Jorge Ruiz de Velasco, and Michael Fix, "Overlooked & Underserved: Immigrant Students in US Secondary Schools" (Washington, DC: Urban Institute, 2000).

17. Ilana Umansky and Sean Reardon, "Reclassification Patterns Among Latino English Learner Students in Bilingual, Dual Immersion, and English Immersion Classrooms," *American Education Research Journal* 51 (2014): 879–912; Rachel A. Valentino and Sean R. Reardon, "Effectiveness of Four Instructional Programs Designed to Serve English Learners," *Educational Evaluation and Policy Analysis* 37 (2015): 612–37.

18. Rachel Slama, "Investigating Whether and When English Learners Are Reclassified Into Mainstream Classrooms in the United States," *American Educational Research Journal* 51 (2014): 220–52.

19. Kenji Hakuta, Yuko Goto Butler, and Daria Witt, *How Long Does It Take English Learners to Attain Proficiency?* (Santa Barbara, CA: Linguistic Minority Research Institute, 2000).

20. David Murphey, Lina Guzmán, and Alicia Torres, *America's Hispanic Children: Gaining Ground, Looking Forward* (Childtrends Hispanic Institute, 2014), http://www.childtrends.org/wp-content/uploads/2014/06/Child-Trends_HI_Slides_FINAL_20141.pdf.

21. Sean F. Reardon and Claudia Galindo, "The Hispanic-White Achievement Gap in Math and Reading in the Elementary Grades," *American Educational Research Journal* 46 (2009): 853–91, http://aer.sagepub.com/content/46/3/853.full.

22. Barbara Heyns, *Summer Learning and the Effects of Schooling* (Cambridge, MA: Academic Press, 1978); Harris Cooper et al., "The Effects of Summer Vacation on Achievement Test Scores: A Narrative and Meta-Analytic Review," *Review of Educational Research* 66, no. 3 (1996): 227–68; Karl L. Alexander, Doris R. Entwisle, and Linda S. Olson, "Summer Learning and its Implications: Insights from the Beginning School Study," *New Directions for Youth Development* (2007): 11–32.

23. Robert K. Ream, *Uprooting Children. Mobility, Social Capital, and Mexican American Underachievement* (New York: LBF Publishers, 2005).

24. Ibid.

25. Suárez-Orozco et al., *Learning a New Land.*

26. David Farbman, *The Case for Improving and Expanding Time in School: A Review of Key Research and Practice* (Washington, DC: National Center for Time and

Learning, 2015), http://files.eric.ed.gov/fulltext/ED561994.pdf; Yael Kidron and Jim Lindsay, "The Effects of Increased Learning Time on Student Academic and Non-Academic Outcomes: A Meta-Analytic Review," (Washington, DC: American Institutes for Research), https://ies.ed.gov/ncee/edlabs/regions/appalachia/pdf /REL_2014015.pdf; Will Dobbie and Roland G. Fryer Jr., "Getting Beneath the Veil of Effective Schools: Evidence from New York City" (working paper, National Bureau of Economic Research, Cambridge, MA, 2011).

27. Deborah Short and Shannon Fitzsimmons, *Double the Work: Challenges and Solutions to Acquiring Language and Academic Literacy for Adolescent English Language Learners* (Washington, DC: Alliance for Excellent Education, 2007).

28. Laurie Olsen, "Reparable Harm Fulfilling the Unkept Promise of Educational Opportunity for California's Long Term English Learners" (Long Beach, CA: Californians Together, 2010).

29. Aida Walqui and Leo van Lier, *Scaffolding the Academic Success of Adolescent English Language Learners: A Pedagogy of Promise* (San Francisco: WestEd, 2010).

30. Ibid.

31. Sherylls Valladares and Manica Ramos, *Children of Latino Immigrants and Out-of-School Time Programs* (Washington, DC: Childtrends, 2011), 1–6, http://www .childtrends.org/wp-content/uploads/2011/12/Child_Trends-2011_12_01_RB _ImmigrantsOSTProg.pdf.

32. Patricia Gándara and Judy Fish, "Year-Round Schooling as an Avenue to Major Structural Reform," *Educational Evaluation and Policy Analysis* 16 (1994): 67–85.

33. Walqui and van Lier, *Scaffolding the Academic Success of Adolescent English Language Learners.*

34. Patricia Gándara, Julie Maxwell-Jolly, and Anne Driscoll, *Listening to Teachers of English Learners* (Santa Cruz, CA: Center for the Future of Teaching and Learning, 2005), http://files.eric.ed.gov/fulltext/ED491701.pdf; Lucrecia Santibañez and Patricia Gándara, "Teachers of English Language Learners in Secondary Schools: Gaps in Preparation and Support" (unpublished paper, LAUSD survey of teachers of English learners, University of California, Los Angeles, 2016). Paper is available from the authors.

35. Anthony Bryk et al., *Learning to Improve: How America's Schools Can Get Better at Getting Better* (Cambridge, MA: Harvard Education Press, 2015).

36. Jennifer McCombs et al., *Making Summer Count* (Santa Monica, CA: The RAND Corp., 2011), http://www.wallacefoundation.org/knowledge-center/Documents /Making-Summer-Count-How-Summer-Programs-Can-Boost-Childrens -Learning.pdf.

37. Julie Maxwell-Jolly, "English Learners and Out of School Time Programs: The Potential of OST Programs to Foster EL Success," *After School Matters* 14 (2011): 1–12, http://www.niost.org/pdf/afterschoolmatters/ASM_Fall2011.pdf.

38. Ibid.

39. McCombs et al., *Making Summer Count.*

40. Min Zhou and Susan Kim, "Community Forces, Social Capital, and Educational Achievement: The Case of Supplementary Education in the Chinese and Korean Immigrant Communities," *Harvard Educational Review* 76, no. 1 (2006): 1–29, http://dx.doi.org/10.17763/haer.76.1.u08t548554882477.

41. Ibid., 1–29.

42. Patricia Gándara, "Multiple Pathways for Immigrant and English Learner Students," in *Multiple Pathways: High School Reform that Promises to Prepare All Students for College, Career, and Civic Participation*, ed. Marisa Saunders et al. (Cambridge, MA: Harvard Education Press, 2008).

43. Rebecca Callahan and Patricia Gándara, "On Nobody's Agenda: Improving English Language Learners' Access to Higher Education," in *Immigrant and English-Language Learners: Strategies for Success*, ed. Michael Sadowski (Cambridge, MA: Harvard Education Press, 2004), 107–27.

44. Norm Gold and Julie Maxwell-Jolly, "The high schools English Learners need," University of California Linguistic Minority Research Institute (2006).

45. Donald Hernandez, Nancy Denton, and Suzanne Macartney, "School-Age Children in Immigrant Families: Challenges and Opportunities for America's Schools," *Teachers College Record* 111 (2009): 616–58.

46. Luis Moll et al., "Funds of Knowledge for Teaching: Using A Qualitative Approach to Connect Homes and Classrooms," *Theory Into Practice* 31 (1992):132–41.

47. Norma González and Luis Moll, "Cruzando el Puente: Building Bridges to Funds of Knowledge," *Educational Policy* 16 (2002): 623–41.

48. Janet Chrispeels, Margarita González, and Brenda Arellano, "Evaluation of the Effectiveness of the Parent Institute for Quality Education in Los Angeles Unified School District" (Santa Barbara, CA: University of California, Santa Barbara, 2004), http://bridgingworlds.org/P-20/ChrispeelsPIQEevaluation.pdf.

49. Laurel Sipes and Jorge Ruiz de Velasco, *Expanding learning opportunities for youth and their families in the Mission Promise Neighborhood: An Interim Assessment* (Stanford, CA: John W. Gardner Center for Youth and Their Communities, 2017).

50. Daniela DiGiacomo et al., "Why Theory Matters: An Examination of Contemporary Learning Time Reforms," *Education Policy Analysis Archives* 24, no. 44 (2016), http://files.eric.ed.gov/fulltext/EJ1100163.pdf.

51. Joseph Durlak, Roger P. Weissberg, and Molly Pachan, "A Meta-analysis of After-school Programs that Seek to Promote Personal and Social Skills in Children and Adolescents," *American Journal of Community Psychology* 45, no. 3–4 (2010): 294–309.

52. Zhou and Kim, "Community Forces, Social Capital, and Educational Achievement," 1–29; Alejandro Portes and Min Zhou, "The New Second Generation: Segmented Assimilation and Its Variants," *Annals of the American Society of Political and Social Science* 530 (1993): 74–96.

CHAPTER 9

1. John Rogers, Kavitha Mediratta, and Seema Shah, "Building Power, Learning Democracy: Youth Organizing as a Site of Civic Development," *Review of Research in Education* 36, no. 1 (2012): 43–66.

2. Joel Westheimer and Joseph Kahne, "What Kind of Citizen? The Politics of Educating for Democracy," *American Educational Research Journal* 41 no. 2 (2004): 237–69.

3. Mancur Olson, *Logic of Collective Action: Public Goods and the Theory of Groups* (Cambridge, MA: Harvard University Press, 1965).

4. Rogers et al., "Building Power," 43–66.

5. Ibid.

6. Alexie Torres-Fleming, Pilar Valdes, and Supriya Pillai, *2010 Youth Organizing Field Scan* (Brooklyn, NY: Funder's Collaborative on Youth Organizing, 2010).

7. Ben Kirshner, "Guided participation in three youth activism organizations: Facilitation, apprenticeship, and joint work," *Journal of the Learning Sciences* 17 (2008): 61–101.

8. Rogers et al., "Building Power," 43–66.

9. Irene Bloemraad and Veronica Terriquez, "Cultures of Engagement: The Organizational Foundations of Advancing Health in Immigrant and Low-Income Communities of Color," *Social Science & Medicine* 165 (2016): 214–22.

10. Westheimer and Kahne, "What Kind of Citizen?," 237–69; Veronica Terriquez, "Training Young Activists: Grassroots Organizing and Youths' Civic and Political Trajectories," *Sociological Perspectives* 58, no. 2 (2015): 223–42.

11. Veronica Terriquez, "Youth Organizing and the Promise of Education Justice" (presentation at the Grantmakers for Education, Denver, 2016).

12. Roderick J. Watts and Constance Flanagan, "Pushing the Envelope on Youth Civic Engagement: A Developmental and Liberation Psychology Perspective," *Journal of Community Psychology* 35, no. 6 (2007): 779–92.

13. Shawn Ginwright and Julio Cammarota, "Youth Activism in the Urban Community: Learning Critical Civic Praxis within Community Organizations," *International Journal of Qualitative Studies in Education* 20, no. 6 (2007): 693–710; Bloemradd and Terriquez, "Cultures of Engagement," 214–22.

14. Rogers et al., "Building Power," 43–66; Terriquez, "Training Young Activists," 223–42.

15. John Rogers, Ernest Morrell, and Noel Enyedy, "Studying the Struggle: Contexts for Learning and Identity Development for Urban Youth," *American Behavioral Scientist* 51, no. 3 (2007): 419–43.

16. Rogers et al., "Building Power," 43–66; Watts and Flanagan, "Pushing the Envelope," 779–92; Shawn Ginwright and Taj James, "From Assets to Agents of Change: Social Justice, Organizing, and Youth Development," in *Youth Participation: Improving Institutions and Communities*, ed. Ben Kirshner, Jennifer O'Donoghue, and Milbrey McLaughlin (San Francisco: Jossey-Bass, 2002), 27–46.

17. Shawn Ginwright and Julio Cammarota, "Youth Activism in the Urban Community: Learning Critical Civic Praxis within Community Organizations," *International Journal of Qualitative Studies in Education* 20, no. 6 (2007).

18. John Rogers and Ernest Morrell, "A Force to Be Reckoned With: The Campaign For College Access in Los Angeles," in *Public Engagement For Public Education: Joining Forces To Revitalize Democracy and Equalize Schools*, ed. Marion Orr and John Rogers (Palo Alto, CA: Stanford University Press, 2010), 227–49.

19. This research was supported by The California Endowment, Bill and Melinda Gates Foundation, the Spencer Foundation, Atlantic Philanthropies, and the Charles Stewart Mott Foundation.

20. Our survey response rate was 91%.

21. For more information on the CHIS, visit http://healthpolicy.ucla.edu/chis/Pages /default.aspx.

22. All groups had engaged their members in youth organizing for at least a decade. Four of the groups are based in the greater San Francisco Bay Area: Asian Youth Promoting Advocacy and Leadership (AYPAL), Youth Making A Change (Y-MAC)

of Coleman Youth Advocates, Youth Together, and Youth United for Community Action (YUCA). Three are located in Los Angeles: Coalition for Humane Rights of Los Angeles' (CHIRLA) Wise Up!, the Community Coalition's South Central Youth Empowered thru Action (SCYEA), and InnerCity Struggle. The final group, Californians For Justice (CFJ), is a statewide network with youth organizing sites in Fresno, Long Beach, Oakland, and San Jose.

23. Veronica Terriquez and Abdiel Lopez, *BHC Youth Program Inventory Survey: Key Findings* (Los Angeles: USC Program for Environmental and Regional Equity, 2016).

24. Eight percent of survey respondents did not report how long they had been involved in their organizations. These students were grouped with the "newer" members.

25. Response rates for YO alumni and the general population were 78% and 56%, respectively.

26. Individuals who completed their intended degrees are counted among those who attended either community college and four-year universities.

27. John Rogers et al., *Free Fall: Educational Opportunities in 2011* (Los Angeles: UCLA Institute for Democracy, Education, and Access, 2011).

28. Hugh McIntosh and James Youniss, "Toward a Political Theory of Political Socialization of Youth," in *Handbook of Research on Civic Engagement in Youth*, eds. Lonnie R. Sherrod, Judith Torney-Purta, and Constance A. Flanagan (New York: Wiley, 2010): 23–41.

29. Daniel McFarland and Reuben J. Thomas, "Bowling Young: How Youth Voluntary Associations Influence Adult Political Participation," *American Sociological Review* 71, no. 3 (2006): 401–25.

30. Veronica Terriquez, John Rogers, and May Lin, *Youth Voice in School Finance: The Building Healthy Communities Initiative and Young People's Involvement in Shaping Local Control Accountability Plans* (Los Angeles: USC Program for Environmental and Regional Equity and UCLA IDEA, 2016).

CHAPTER 10

1. The authors wish to acknowledge the Haynes Foundation for a grant to the "Widening Divide Revisited" project, which supported some of the analyses reported in this chapter. They also wish to express their gratitude to the staff of UCLA's Center for Neighborhood Knowledge for their assistance in assembling data and preparing maps: Chhandara Pech, Alycia Cheng, Jenny Chhea, and Silvia Gonzalez.

2. Information on data sources and analytical methods is available upon request from the authors.

3. Paul M. Ong and Jordan Rickles, "The Continued Nexus between School and Residential Segregation," in *Symposium, Rekindling the Spirit of* Brown v. Board of Education, *African-American Law and Policy Report* 6:178–93; *Asian Law Journal* 11:260-275; *Berkeley La Raza Law Journal* 15:51-66; *Berkeley Women's Law Journal* 19:379-394; *California Law Review*, 2004.

4. Meredith P. Richards, "The Gerrymandering of School Attendance Zones and the Segregation of Public Schools: A Geospatial Analysis," *American Educational Research Journal* 51, no. 6 (December 1, 2014): 1119–57, doi:10.3102/0002831214553652.

5. Gary Orfield and Erica Frankenberg, "Increasingly Segregated and Unequal Schools as Courts Reverse Policy," *Educational Administration Quarterly* 50, no. 5

(2014): 718–34; Jeannie Oakes, *Multiplying Inequalities: The Effects of Race, Social Class, and Tracking on Opportunities to Learn Mathematics and Science* (Santa Monica, CA: Rand Corp, 1990); F. Chris Curran, *Income-Based Disparities in Early Elementary School Science Achievement*, http://fchriscurran.com/wp-content/uploads/2016/01/ECLS-SES-Gaps-1_1_16-_-Working-Paper-Draft.pdf.

6. Jordan Rickles and Paul Ong, "The Integrating (And Segregating) Effect of Charter, Magnet, and Traditional Elementary Schools: The Case of Five California Metropolitan Areas," *Journal of California Politics and Policy* 9, no. 1 (June 2005):16–38; Nicholas Jacobs, "Understanding School Choice Location as a Determinant of Charter School Racial, Economic, and Linguistic Segregation," *Education and Urban Society* 45, no. 4 (2013): 459–82.

7. Based on estimates from the Pubic Policy Institute of California, about a twelfth of LA's population is undocumented, http://www.ppic.org/main/publication_show.asp?i=818.

8. Rosalie Ray, Paul Ong, and Silvia Jimenez, "Impacts of the Widening Divide: Los Angeles at the Forefront of the Rent Burden Crisis" (working paper #8, UCLA Ziman Center, University of California, Los Angeles, 2014); Paul Ong, Rosalie Ray, and Silvia Jimenez, "Impacts of the Widening Divide—Why is LA's Homeownership Rate So Low?" (working paper #13, UCLA Ziman Center, University of California, Los Angeles, 2015).

9. While 11% of the nation's workers travel 40 or more minutes, 14% of those in the region do. The travel burden is particularly heavy for those using public transportation. While the typical drive-alone worker commutes less than a half hour, the typical transit rider spends more than three-quarters of an hour traveling to work.

10. Paul Ong, Chhandara Pech, Jenny Chhea, and C. Aujean Lee, "Race, Ethnicity, and Income Segregation in Los Angeles" (working paper #8, UCLA Ziman Center, University of California, Los Angeles, 2016).

11. The US Census Bureau reports zip-code-level data as five-year averages from the American Community Survey.

12. Ibid.

13. Each category contains about a quarter of the zip codes in Los Angeles County. The following poverty rates (the percent of persons under the Federal Poverty Level) are used to define the dividing lines between neighborhood categories: 8.9%, 14.9%, and 22.6%.

14. English language learners (ELLs) are those students who are learning English and typically require specialized or modified instruction. Their status is measured by their degree of limited English proficiency (LEP).

15. We use API results because they are readily available, but it should be noted that the test scores are a narrow and imperfect measure of students' learning and progress.

16. Christie Blazer, "A Review of the Research on Magnet Schools, Information Capsule, vol. 1105," Research Services, Miami-Dade County Public Schools, 2012, http://eric.ed.gov/?id=ED536516; Valerie E. Lee, Douglas D. Ready, and Kevin G. Welner, *Educational Equity and School Structure: School Size, School Overcrowding and Alternative Organizational Structures* (UCLA Institute for Democracy, Education & Access, 2002), https://escholarship.org/us/item/2zx2b0w5,pdf.

17. Monica Iannessa, interview by Elena Ong, Los Angeles, August 9 and 12, 2016.
18. Noreen C. McDonald, "Critical Factors for Active Transportation to School among Low-Income and Minority Students," *American Journal of Preventive Medicine* 34, no. 4 (April 2008): 341–44, doi:10.1016/j.amepre.2008.01.004.
19. Regino Chavez, interview by Elena Ong, Los Angeles, August 9, 2016.
20. Unfortunately, the authors do not have consistent and complete data on public safety for the whole region, but analysis of data from a 2011 report by the Advancement Project ("Community Safety Scorecard City of Los Angeles, 2011") shows that poorer zip code areas are consistently ranked among the areas with the highest crime rates, gang activities, and violence.
21. Many of these are not tutoring programs, and many are supervised recreational programs and other forms of childcare; Basmat Parsad and Laurie Lewis, *After-School Programs in Public Elementary Schools: First Look*, NCES 2009-043 (National Center for Education Statistics, 2009), http://eric.ed.gov/?id=ED504193.
22. Elizabeth R. Reisner et al., *Charting the Benefits of High-Quality After-School Program Experiences: Evidence from New Research on Improving After-School Opportunities for Disadvantaged Youth*, Policy Studies Associates, Inc., 2007, http://eric.ed.gov/?id=ED498791; Deborah Lowe Vandell, "Afterschool program quality and student outcomes: Reflections on positive key findings on learning and development from recent research," *Expanding and Opportunities* (2013): 10.
23. While all students can visit during school hours, systematic differences in attendance and participation occur outside of school-sponsored field trips, which affect the course of the achievement gap.
24. James S. Catterall, *The Arts and Achievement in At-Risk Youth: Findings from Four Longitudinal Studies* (Research Report# 55, National Endowment for the Arts, 2012), http://eric.ed.gov/?id=ED530822; Larry E. Suter, "Visiting Science Museums During Middle and High School: A Longitudinal Analysis of Student Performance in Science," *Science Education* 98, no. 5 (September 2014): 815–39, doi:10.1002/sce.21116.
25. Catterall, *The Arts and Achievement in At-Risk Youth*.
26. Douglas Houston and Paul Ong, "Arts Accessibility to Major Museums and Cultural/Ethnic Institutions in Los Angeles; Can School Tours Overcome Neighborhood Disparities?," *Environment and Planning A* 45 (2013): 728–48. Cultural barrier refers the lack of non-Western, nonwhite experiences, artifacts, and history, or to negative depictions of non-Western and nonwhite people.
27. Pam Martinez, interview by Elena Ong, Denver, August 16, 2016.
28. Robin Manzer, interview by Elena Ong, Los Angeles, August 9, 2016.
29. Katya Bozzi, interview by Elena Ong Los Angeles, August 17, 2016.
30. Dee Ann Rivera, interview by Elena Ong, Los Angeles, August 9, 2016.
31. Ibid.
32. Dee Ann Rivera, interview.
33. Regino Chavez, interview.
34. Pam Martinez, interview.
35. Ibid.
36. Dee Ann Rivera, interview; Monica Iannessa, interview.
37. Robin Manzer, interview.
38. Monica Iannessa, interview.

39. Pam Magee, interview by Elena Ong Los Angeles, August 9, 2016; Monica Iannessa, interview.

40. Dee Ann Rivera, interview.

41. Monica Iannessa, interview.

CHAPTER 11

1. James Baldwin, "A Talk to Teachers," in *City Kids, City Schools: More Reports from the Front Row*, ed. William Ayers et al. (New York: The New Press, 2008), xiv.

2. Zakia Redd et al., "Expanded Time for Learning Both Inside and Outside the Classroom: A Review of the Evidence Base," *Child Trends*, 2012, www.childtrends.org/Files/Child_Trends-2012_08_16_RB_TimeForLearning.pdf.

3. John F. Pane et al., "Continued Progress: Promising Evidence on Personalized Learning," RAND Corporation, 2015, http://k12education.gatesfoundation.org/wp-content/uploads/2015/11/Gates-ContinuedProgress-Nov13.pdf.

4. Robert Halpern, Paul Heckmen, and Reed Larson, *Realizing the Potential of Learning in Middle Adolescence*, Sally and Dick Roberts Coyote Foundation and William T. Grant Foundation, 2013, http://www.howyouthlearn.org/pdf/Realizing%20the%20Poential%20of%20Learning%20in%20Middle%20Adolescence.pdf.

5. John Dewey, *Democracy and Education* (New York: MacMillan, 1916).

6. David Tyack and Larry Cuban, *Tinkering Toward Utopia. A Century of Public School Reform* (Cambridge, MA: Harvard University Press, 1995).

7. "Youth Unemployment Soars in Past Decade," *Annie E. Casey Foundation* (blog), December 3, 2012, http://www.aecf.org/blog/youth-unemployment-soars-in-past-decade/.

8. Motoko Rich, "As Graduation Rates Rise, Experts Fear Diplomas Come Up Short," *New York Times*, December 26, 2015, http://www.nytimes.com/2015/12/27/us/as-graduation-rates-rise-experts-fear-standards-have-fallen.html?_r=0.

9. "What Matters Now: A New Compact for Teaching and Learning," National Commission on Teaching & America's Future, 2016, 4, http://nctaf.org/wp-content/uploads/2016/08/NCTAF_What-Matters-Now_A-Call-to-Action.pdf.

10. Ibid.

11. Wayne Au and Melissa Bollow Tempel, *Pencils down: Rethinking high stakes testing and accountability in public schools* (Milwaukee: Rethinking Schools, 2012).

12. Carola Suárez-Orozco, Marcelo Suárez-Orozco, and Robert Teranishi, "Disrupting Narratives Of Social Exclusion For Immigrant Children And Youth," *UCLA Ed&IS* (Fall 2016): 30–7, https://issuu.com/uclaedis/docs/ucla_ed_is_magazine_fall_2016.

13. Carola Suárez-Orozco, Marcelo Suárez-Orozco, and Robert Teranishi, "Pathways to Opportunities: Promising Practices for Immigrant Children, Youth & Their Families," Institute for Immigration, Globalization, & Education, 2016, http://ige.gseis.ucla.edu/PromisingPracticesWhitePaper4.25.16/.

14. Ibid.

15. Jacqueline Ancess and Bethany Rogers, "Social Emotional Learning and Social Justice Learning at El Puente Academy for Peace and Justice," Stanford Center for Opportunity Policy in Education, 2015, 14, https://edpolicy.stanford.edu/sites/default/files/publications/scope-pub-elpuente-case-report.pdf.

16. Tom Dewar and Sharon Ramirez, "El Puente Academy for Peace and Justice: A Case Study of Building Social Capital" (Minneapolis: Rainbow Research, 1994).

17. Ancess and Rogers, "Social Emotional Learning."
18. Gene I. Maeroff, *Altered Destinies: Making Life Better for Schoolchildren in Need* (New York: St. Martin's Press, 1999).
19. Maria Brenes in discussion with Fred Frelow, October 20, 2016.
20. "Winning Change for Eastside Schools," InnerCity Struggle, http://innercity struggle.org/section/view/new_schools.
21. Susan Frey, "LA Groups Model of Community Engagement," *EdSource*, November 16, 2014, https://edsource.org/2014/l-a-groups-model-community-engagement /69669.
22. California Department of Education, Data Reporting Office, http://data1.cde.ca .gov/dataquest/; see also Jonathan P. Raymond, "Making Their Voices Heard," *Medium*, June 7, 2016, https://medium.com/keeping-children-first/making-their-voices-heard-290152b7da1c.
23. "Detroit: Ruin and Renewal," *New York Times*, March 10, 2015, http://www.nytimes .com/interactive/2014/07/06/us/detroit-the-path-to-recovery-from-bankruptcy .html?_r=0.
24. Joel Kurth and Christine MacDonald, "Volume of abandoned homes 'absolutely terrifying,'" *Detroit News*, May 14, 2015, http://www.detroitnews.com/story/news /special-reports/2015/05/14/detroit-abandoned-homes-volume-terrifying/27237787/.
25. "Game Changer: Linked Learning Detroit," ConnectEd, May 2016, http:// connectedcalifornia.org/direct/files/linked%20learn-DetroitFINAL.pdf.
26. Ibid.
27. John Hattie, "What Works Best in Education: The Politics of Collaborative Expertise," *Open Ideas at Pearson*, 2015, https://www.pearson.com/content/dam /corporate/global/pearson-dot-com/files/hattie/150526_ExpertiseWEB_V1.pdf.
28. Dylan Wiliam, "The Formative Evaluation of Teaching Performance," Centre for Strategic Education, 2014, http://www.dylanwiliam.org/Dylan_Wiliams_website /DW_publications_files/The%20formative%20evaluation%20of%20teaching %20performance%20(CSE%202014)%20secure.pdf.
29. Jennifer York-Barr and Karen Duke, "What Do We Know About Teacher Leadership? Findings From Two Decades of Scholarship," *Review of Educational Research* 74, no. 3 (2004): 255–316.
30. William R. Penuel et al., "Using Social Network Analysis to Study How Collegial Interactions Can Augment Teacher Learning from External Professional Development," *American Journal of Education* 119, no. 1 (2012): 103–36, doi: 10.1086/667756.
31. Andy Hargreaves and Michael Fullan, *Professional Capital: Transforming Teaching in Every School* (New York: Teachers College Press; Toronto: Ontario Principals' Council, 2012).
32. Barnett Berry, "The five secrets that help this high-poverty school succeed," Center for Teaching Quality, February 22, 2016, http://www.teachingquality.org/content /blogs/barnett-berry/five-secrets-help-high-poverty-school-succeed.
33. Ibid.
34. For more information on teacher-powered schools, see https://www.teacher powered.org/.
35. Berry, "The five secrets that help this high-poverty school succeed."
36. Ibid.

37. To access the toolkit, see https://www.scoe.net/castandards/Documents/state _guidance_professional_learning_funds.pdf.

38. National Center on Time & Learning, "Time for Teachers: Leveraging Expanded Time to Strengthen Instruction and Empower Teachers," http://www.timeand learning.org/sites/default/files/resources/timeforteachers.pdf.

39. "PDK Poll of the Public's Attitude Toward Public Schools," PDK International, 2016, http://pdkpoll2015.pdkintl.org.

40. Ibid.

41. The Illinois Update, "Chicagoans Willing to Pay More Taxes for Improved Services, Poll Finds," 2016, https://illinoisupdate.com/2016/08/25/chicagoans-willing -to-pay-more-taxes-for-improved-services-poll-finds/.

CHAPTER 12

1. Jeannie Oakes, Kevin Welner, Susan Yonezawa, and Ricky Lee Allen, "Norms and Politics of Equity-Minded Change: Researching the "Zone of Mediation," in *International Handbook of Educational Change*, ed. Michael Fullan (Norwell: Kluwer Academic Publishers, 1998), 952–75.

2. Linda Darling-Hammond, *Flat World and Education* (New York: Teachers College Press, 2014); Robert Putnam, *Our Kids: The American Dream in Crisis* (New York: Simon & Schuster Paperbacks, 2016).

3. Prudence Carter and Kevin Welner, *Closing the Opportunity Gap: What America Must Do to Give Every Child an Even Chance* (New York: Oxford University Press, 2013).

4. Gloria Ladson-Billings, "Lack of Achievement or Loss of Opportunity?," in ibid., 11–22.

5. Louise Lamphere, "The Shaping of Diversity," in *Structuring Diversity: Ethnographic Perspectives on the New Immigration*, ed. Louise Lamphere (Chicago: University of Chicago Press, 1992), 1–34.

6. Kevin Welner, *Legal Rights, Local Wrongs: When Community Control Collides with Educational Equity* (Albany, NY: SUNY Press, 2001), 8.

7. Ibid.

8. Michelle Renée, "Knowledge, Power, and Education Justice: How Social Movement Organizations Use Research to Influence Education Policy" (PhD diss., University of California Los Angeles, 2006).

9. Jeannie Oakes and John Rogers, *Learning Power: Organizing for Education Justice* (New York: Teachers College Press, 2006).

10. Rachel Moran, "Brown's Legacy: The Evolution of Educational Equity," *University of Pittsburgh Law Review* 66 no. 1 (2004): 155–79.

11. Welner, *Legal Rights, Local Wrongs.*

12. Renée, "Knowledge, Power, and Education Justice."

13. Welner, *Legal Rights, Local Wrongs.*

14. Welner, *Legal Rights, Local Wrongs*, 93.

15. "ConnectEd California," http://www.connectedcalifornia.org/.

16. Patrick McQuillan, *Educational Opportunity in an Urban American High School: A Cultural Analysis* (Albany: SUNY Press, 1998).

17. Miya Warner et al., *Taking Stock of the California Linked Learning District Initiative. Seventh-Year Evaluation Report* (Menlo Park, CA: SRI International, 2016).

18. Daniela DiGiacomo, Joshua J. Prudhomme, Hannah R. Jones, Kevin G. Welner, and Ben Kirshner, "Why Theory Matters: An Examination of Contemporary Learning Time Reforms," *Education Policy Analysis Archives* 24 (2016): 44.
19. John Rogers, Nicole Mirra, Michael Seltzer, and J. Jun, *It's About Time: Learning Time and Educational Opportunity in California High Schools* (Los Angeles: IDEA, University of California Los Angeles, 2014).
20. Jaime Del Razo, Marisa Saunders, Michelle Renée, Ruth López, and Kerri Ullucci, *Leveraging Time for School Equity: Indicators for the More and Better Learning Initiative* (Providence: Annenberg Institute for School Reform, Brown University, 2014).

CHAPTER 13

1. Some of the ideas in this chapter appeared earlier in Jeannie Oakes, "Research in the Ongoing Struggle for Educational Equity: An Agenda for the Future," *Opening the Doors for Opportunity for All: Setting a Research Agenda for the Future* (Washington, DC: American Institutes of Research, 2015).
2. Robert D. Putnam, *Our Kids: The American Dream in Crisis* (New York: Simon and Schuster, 2016).

ABOUT THE EDITORS

MARISA SAUNDERS is a principal associate for research and policy at the Annenberg Institute for School Reform (ASIR) at Brown University. Before joining AISR, Marisa was a senior research associate at UCLA's Institute for Democracy, Education, and Access (IDEA). She is co-editor (with Jeannie Oakes) of *Beyond Tracking: Multiple Pathways to College, Career, and Civic Participation*, published by Harvard Education Press. Marisa is a graduate of the University of California, San Diego, and holds an MA in Latin American studies from Stanford University, and an EdD from the Harvard University Graduate School of Education.

JORGE RUIZ DE VELASCO is associate director for policy and community partnerships at the John W. Gardner Center for Youth and Their Communities at Stanford University. Before his Stanford appointment, he served terms as a program officer for educational opportunity and scholarship at the Ford Foundation and as a senior program officer at both the James Irvine Foundation and the William and Flora Hewlett Foundation. Jorge also served as a senior research associate at The Urban Institute and as a lawyer for the US Department of Education's Office for Civil Rights. He is a graduate of Harvard College and the University of California, Berkeley, School of Law. Subsequently, he earned an MA in education administration and policy analysis and a PhD in political science, both from Stanford University.

JEANNIE OAKES is a senior fellow at the Learning Policy Institute, a member of the National Academy of Education, past president of the American Educational Research Association, and former director of educational opportunity and scholarship at the Ford Foundation. Jeannie is also Presidential Professor Emeritus in Educational Equity at the University of California, Los Angeles (UCLA); and founder of UCLA's Institute for Democracy, Education and Access (IDEA), and Center X; as well as former director of the University of California's All Campus Consortium on Research for Diversity (ACCORD).

ABOUT THE CONTRIBUTORS

BARNETT BERRY is founder and CEO of the Center for Teaching Quality (CTQ), which was founded in 1998 to support equitable and excellent public education for all students driven by the bold ideas and best practices of their teachers. He is a former high school social studies teacher, think tank analyst (RAND Corporation), senior state education agency leader (South Carolina), and university professor (University of South Carolina). He also directed the state partnership network for the National Commission on Teaching and America's Future. He earned a BA in sociology at University of Carolina, an MA in education at the University of South Carolina, and subsequently a PhD in educational administration and policy research at the University of North Carolina-Chapel Hill.

KATIE BRACKENRIDGE is the vice president for programs at the Partnership for Children and Youth in Oakland, California. She develops and oversees the partnership's initiatives to expand and improve afterschool, summer, and community school programs and systems. Her work includes Expanded Learning 360°/365, which supports school districts in strengthening and aligning their social-emotional learning strategies across the school day, in afterschool, and throughout the summer. Through these initiatives, Katie develops and promotes local, state, and federal policies to support improved programming at ground level. As co-chair of the California Afterschool Network's Quality Committee, she works with the California Department of Education (CDE) to provide advice about CDE's role in improving the quality of expanded learning programs.

JENNIFER DAVIS is senior associate for national policy and partnerships at the Education Redesign Lab at the Harvard Graduate School of Education. Before her appointment, Jennifer was cofounder of the National Center on

Time and Learning (NCTL)—initially known as Massachusetts 2020—an organization dedicated to expanding learning time to narrow achievement and opportunity gaps for children in high-poverty schools. NCTL's work is now embedded within the Education Redesign Lab. Jennifer's previous positions include US Department of Education deputy assistant secretary and special assistant to Secretary of Education Richard W. Riley in the Clinton administration. She also served as executive director of Boston mayor Tom Menino's afterschool learning initiative. Early in her career, Jennifer worked for the National Governors Association and Communities in Schools. Jennifer holds a BA from Connecticut College, an MPP from the Claremont Graduate University, and served as a Coro Fellow in Public Affairs in St. Louis.

DAVID FARBMAN has written extensively about school and district efforts to expand time and to optimize time use in schools and in the classroom. Most recently, David served as a senior researcher at the National Center on Time and Learning (NCTL), where he worked on NCTL's policy and communications teams. Before his work with NCTL, he held policy and research positions at Recruiting New Teachers, Inc.; Achieve, Inc.; and Jobs for the Future. He has also served as an advisor on educational and other policy issues to gubernatorial candidates in Massachusetts. David earned his BA from Brandeis University and an MA and PhD in American history from Brown University.

KENDRA FEHRER is a qualitative research associate at the John W. Gardner Center for Youth and their Communities at Stanford University. Before joining the Gardner Center, she conducted ethnographic research on citizen engagement, with the support of the National Science Foundation and the Social Science Research Council. She holds a BA and MA in international development and social change from Clark University, and an MA and PhD in anthropology from Brown University.

FRED FRELOW is a national expert on organizational and professional development strategies for improving the quality of teaching in secondary schools that serve low-income, minority, and immigrant children. Most recently, Fred was appointed interim president and CEO of the Southern Education Foundation in Atlanta. In early 2017, he completed a term as senior program officer for youth opportunity and learning at the Ford Foundation. Fred has also served as director of national affairs and associate director of urban initiatives for the National Commission on Teaching and America's Future at Teachers College, Columbia University; director of curriculum for the Nyack, New York, public schools; and director of the US Department of Education's Magnet School Assistance Program at Louis Armstrong Middle School in Queens, New York. He has an EdD in educational administration and policy analysis from Teachers College, Columbia University, and an MA in education and policy analysis from Boston University.

PATRICIA GÁNDARA is professor of education at the University of California, Los Angeles (UCLA), Graduate School of Education and Information Studies. Her professional interests in graduate teaching include education policy/education reform, social context of learning, learning and assessment, and educational equity/bilingual and multicultural education. She has been a bilingual school psychologist and a social scientist with the RAND Corporation. In addition, she has directed education research in the California legislature, and has also served as commissioner for postsecondary education for the State of California. For nine years, she was associate director of the Linguistic Minority Research Institute, and she is currently the co-director of the Civil Rights Project/Proyecto Derechos Civiles at UCLA. Patricia was president of the Sociology of Education Association in 1995. In addition to teaching and leading research at UCLA, she is an alumna, having received both her BA (sociology and English literature) and PhD (education psychology) from UCLA.

JESSICA GUNDERSON is the senior director of policy and communications at the Partnership for Children and Youth (PCY). Before joining PCY, Jessica worked as a senior planner at the Vera Institute of Justice in New York City. Jessica has also served as a staff member in the office of then California State Assembly Majority Leader Karen Bass. Her work for the legislature focused on child-welfare and social-service issues, including staffing the California State Assembly Select Committee on Foster Care. Jessica received her MPA in nonprofit management from the Robert F. Wagner School of Public Service at New York University.

GARY HOACHLANDER is president of ConnectEd: The California Center for College and Career. He has consulted extensively for the US Department of Education, state departments of education, local school districts, foundations, and a variety of other clients. He earned his BA at Princeton University and holds both MA and PhD degrees from the Department of City and Regional Planning at the University of California, Berkeley.

REBECCA G. KAPLAN is a PhD candidate in education in the Department of Learning Sciences and Human Development at the University of Colorado, Boulder. A former middle and high school English teacher, she currently teaches for the INVST Community Leadership program and engages in justice-oriented youth participatory action research projects. She works with researchers and teachers to design project-based curriculum for high school students. Her interests include teacher learning, anti-oppressive pedagogy, queering literacy, and participatory action research.

BEN KIRSHNER is associate professor of learning sciences and human development in the School of Education at the University of Colorado, Boulder, and faculty director of CU Engage: Center for Community-Based Learning and Research. He serves as advisor for the MacArthur Foundation's Connected Learning Research Network. His 2015 book, *Youth Activism in an Era of Education Inequality*, received the social policy award for best authored book from the Society of Research on Adolescence. He received his PhD in education at Stanford University.

JACOB LEOS-URBEL is associate director for youth data strategies at the John W. Gardner Center for Youth and their Communities at Stanford University. Before joining the Gardner Center, he was an assistant professor of public policy at Claremont Graduate University and has also worked as the director of policy research and analysis at The After-School Corporation (TASC). He holds a BA in sociology from Oberlin College, an MPA from Princeton University, and a PhD in public administration from New York University.

MICHAEL MCAFEE is the president of PolicyLink where he leads the executive and program teams in strategic planning, policy development, policy campaign strategy, capacity building, and programmatic design and implementation at the local, state, and national levels. Before joining PolicyLink, he served as senior community planning and development representative in the Chicago Regional Office of the US Department of Housing and Urban

Development (HUD). He is also an Annie E. Casey Foundation Children and Family Fellow, Aspen Institute Ideas Scholar, and Leap of Reason Ambassador. He served in the United States Army, completed Harvard University's Executive Program in Public Management, and earned his doctor of education in human and organizational learning from the George Washington University.

TAMEKA L. MCGLAWN is the director of equity and impact for ConnectEd: The California Center for College and Career. Earlier in her career, she served as the instructional dean of students at Construction Technology Academy at the Kearny High Educational Complex. She is a proud graduate of both the California State University, San Diego, Community-Based Block Multicultural & Social Justice Master's Program, and the Rossier School of Education at the University of Southern California, where she earned her doctorate in educational leadership.

ELIZABETH BIRR MOJE is the dean of the School of Education, the George Herbert Mead Collegiate Professor of Education, and an Arthur F. Thurnau Professor in the School of Education at the University of Michigan. She is also a faculty associate in the Institute for Social Research and in the Latino/a Studies program. Elizabeth is a member of the National Academy of Education, where she chairs the Professional Development Committee. She serves as a vice president of the American Educational Research Association representing research on the social contexts of education (Division G) and as the chair of the William T. Grant Foundation Scholar Award Selection Committee.

ELENA ONG is director of public policy and public affairs at Ong & Associates, an elected member of the American Public Health Association's Executive Board, founding president and CEO of the Asian & Pacific Islander Caucus for Public Health, and past first vice chair of the California Commission for Women. She received a BSN from the University of California, San Francisco, an MS in health policy and management from the Harvard School of Public Health, and was a Coro Executive Fellow.

PAUL ONG is a professor at the University of California, Los Angeles (UCLA) School of Public Policy. He also holds appointments in Asian American Studies and in the Institute of the Environment and Sustainability. He received an MA in urban planning from the University of Washington and a PhD in economics from the University of California, Berkeley. He currently directs the Center for Neighborhood Knowledge, and his research focuses on urban spatial inequality.

JENNIFER PECK is the president and CEO of the Partnership for Children and Youth (PCY) in Oakland, California, a statewide organization that supports community school development, afterschool, and summer partnerships through training, assessment, planning, policy, and advocacy. Before joining PCY, she spent eight years as an appointee of President Bill Clinton at the US Department of Education, where she supported implementation of numerous initiatives including student loan reform, School-to-Work, and 21st Century Community Learning Centers. She has a BA in sociology and women's studies from Colgate University.

JESSICA PIZAREK is the program coordinator at PolicyLink. Before she joined PolicyLink, her professional and academic work focused on the development of social policy and community engagement efforts to support the educational outcomes of young children. She earned a BA in social welfare from the University of California, Berkeley, and an MA in education policy and social analysis from Teachers College, Columbia University.

JOHN ROGERS is a professor at UCLA's Graduate School of Education and Information Studies and director of UCLA's Institute for Democracy, Education, and Access (IDEA). He also serves as the faculty director of Center X, which houses UCLA's Teacher Education Program, Principal Leadership Program, and professional development initiatives. He received his PhD in education from Stanford University and his BA in public policy and African American studies from Princeton University.

BRAD STAM is the vice president and chief operating officer of ConnectEd: The California Center for College and Career, supporting organizational development and business development. Before coming to ConnectEd, he served as chief academic officer for Oakland Unified School District, leading dramatic academic improvement at the elementary and middle grades, and initiating a systemic Linked Learning approach to high school reform.

He received his AB at Harvard University and his MA in teaching at Columbia University.

VERONICA TERRIQUEZ is an associate professor of sociology at the University of California, Santa Cruz. She is the principal investigator of the California Young Adult Study and the Youth Leadership and Health Study. She earned her BA in sociology at Harvard University, an MA in education at the University of California, Berkeley, and subsequently a PhD in sociology from the University of California, Los Angeles.

MICHELLE RENÉE VALLADARES is associate director of the National Education Policy Center at the University of Colorado, Boulder. She leads and partners in a series of projects that aim to increase educational opportunities for all students in our nation's education systems. She serves on the advisory board of the Family Leadership Design Collaborative and is a member of AERA's Exemplary Contributions to Practice Engaged Research Award Committee. Before joining the National Education Policy Center, Michelle was associate director and assistant clinical professor at Brown University's Annenberg Institute for School Reform (AISR). Michelle has a PhD in education from the University of California, Los Angeles.

KEVIN WELNER is a professor at the University of Colorado, Boulder, School of Education, where he serves as director of the National Education Policy Center and specializes in educational policy and law. Welner's research examines the use and misuse of research in policy making, explores the intersection between education rights litigation and educational opportunity scholarship, and considers issues of tracking and detracking, small-school reform, tuition-tax-credit vouchers, and the change process associated with equity-minded reform efforts. He earned his BS in biological sciences at University of California, Santa Barbara; a JD from University of California, Los Angeles (UCLA); and subsequently a PhD in educational policy at UCLA.

INDEX